Pelican Book A1017

WORK · VOLUME 2

Ronald Fraser was born in Hamburg, where his father was in business, in 1930. Educated in England and in the U.S.A., he spent five years as a foreign correspondent in Europe, subsequently working in the U.S.A. as a journalist. He has published a novel, and is now on the editorial board of *New Left Review*, where he has edited the series of work articles, twenty of which were published in *Work*, Volume One (1968).

WORK

VOLUME 2

TWENTY PERSONAL ACCOUNTS

Edited by Ronald Fraser
With a concluding essay by
Alvin Gouldner

PENGUIN BOOKS
in association with NEW LEFT REVIEW

Penguin Books Ltd, Harmondsworth,
Middlesex, England
Penguin Books Inc., 7110 Ambassador Road,
Baltimore, Maryland 21207, U.S.A.
Penguin Books Australia Ltd, Ringwood,
Victoria, Australia

First published in *New Left Review*
This collection published by Penguin Books 1969

Made and printed in Great Britain by
Cox & Wyman Ltd, London, Reading and Fakenham
Set in Monotype Baskerville

Contents

Introduction	Ronald Fraser	7
The Toolmaker	Jack Pomlet	21
A Miner's Life	Chris Evans	41
Steelman	Patrick McGeown	56
On the Trawlers	Peter Martin	70
The Machine-Minder	Mike Taylor	87
The Convenor	Phillip Higgs	109
The Subby Bricklayer	Max Gagg	130
The Architect	Christopher Gotch	147
The Town Planner	Jon Rodes	165
Managing Science	R. Andemann	178
Child-Care Officer	Norma Vince	195
The Schoolteacher	S. G. Turvey	215
The Secretary	Catherine Dracup	228
Methodist Minister	Douglas Wollen	240
The Actor	Ronan O'Casey	257
The Stockbroker	William Hopper	272
Factory Money	Edward Sutcliffe	287
The Forelady	Alice Brown	298
Member of Parliament	Stan Newens	311
Negotiating at the Top	Robert Bonnar	330
The Unemployed Self	Alvin Gouldner	346

Introduction

This book, written by twenty men and women as personal accounts of their jobs, is both a sequel to, and explores a range of experience uncovered by its predecessor *Work*: trawlerman, toolmaker, miner, forelady, town planner, convenor, to name only a few. The proportion of working-class contributors has been purposely increased in this second volume as a response not only to statistical reality (the manual working class forms just under 70 per cent of the population), but to a need to understand experiences which, for obvious reasons, too often remain unarticulated. For the rest the purpose of these as of the earlier essays, is to discover through their own words what people really think and feel about their work, how it shapes their lives and experience of the world, their aspirations and assumptions – in short, its intimate meaning to them as individuals.

Work, as has often been noted, is not only the way each of us makes a living; it is one of the principal ways in which we 'make' the society we live in and which in turn 'makes' us; work – the human activity of mastering and transforming the given – is (or should be) therefore one of the principal ways in which we make ourselves. If this relationship is obscured, it is because an existing social system – capitalist in this case – confronts us with an apparently readymade and opaque organization of the means and end product of work, in which participation is necessary but over whose purpose the majority has little or no control. In their individual ways, most of these essays reflect the problems and assumptions common to the organization and purpose of work in this society, not least the question of money. This theme, though by no means the only one, recurs with varying intensity throughout almost all the articles. The frequency of its mention, as the reader will note, is in direct proportion to its lack; the less a person earns the more frequently money or its shortage is invoked. This is true not only of working-class writers – understandably, since most workers have less of it – but also of those professionals whose income is relatively small or precarious. At the top of the scale, however, mention of money becomes suddenly muted, becomes something else: possibilities, freedom, absence of lack – and its mention is inhibited by 'social convention' which draws a discreet veil of 'good taste' (and self-interest) over quantifying the exact cash measure of these privileges. Almost everywhere else such conventions are pointless: money is of self-evident importance, a primary concern. It is a lack which even in those cases where 'good money' is earned, as in the trawlerman's case, is filled only at the expense of long hours and of great physical and mental strain. Money, we seem to be hearing, is what work is about. Given the system's rationale, which makes money the purpose of work, we might well expect to hear nothing else. Or are we only hearing what we expect? Let us listen first to a worker who claims that his sole purpose is to make as much of it as he can.

Max Gagg, a bricklayer, will quit any job if offered a 'bigger penny' elsewhere; his determination to make it has led him to become self-employed, to go on the 'lump'. Neither union nor management command his respect. He is out for what he can make, despite the risks: the loss of rights to unemployment pay, workmen's compensation, the opportunity of a secure job with promotion prospects. At the same time, he stresses, there are non-monetary advantages to going it alone: he feels himself freer, can control his own work pace, is no longer a subordinate in a chain of command. He sums it up by saying that rather than working *for* the general foreman, he feels he is working *with* him. This element of controlling his work pattern is important to him, but as he retraces the events which have led him to his present situation, we see that he is contrasting his money-oriented present with something else: when he was young he thought himself fortunate to be a bricklayer. 'I found the job itself pleasurable and I felt I was performing a social service.' This was most evident when he was working on houses, especially working-class housing in the post-war slum clearance. But today? 'I feel no sense of being socially useful . . . nor can I get any pleasure from building those architectural monstrosities we call office blocks and homes.' Disillusionment has come, he reflects, because of the way employers in particular, and society in general, treat him as a bricklayer – 'a means to an end, an expendable item to be discarded like an old boot, when no longer required'. In this situation his only purpose is to sell his skill to the highest bidder; money has become his single purpose, but in a sense it has also become a substitute for purpose. Put another way, in viewing money as the only purpose, he confirms the system's rationale which reduces everything to money. The sense of a different, though not always explicit, purpose is suggested by Gagg even where money is seen as the main goal of work. In capitalist society, which expresses needs and their satisfaction in money terms, it is not always easy to make explicit needs that cannot be expressed in these terms. Is this to say that the need for money must be understood simply as such, that it is both need and its satisfaction in one? No, says Edward Sutcliffe, a factory worker, who takes the argument a step forward: 'a man's pay is a status symbol as well as a means of existence; "not getting the rate for the job" is a blow to a man's pride as well as his pocket.'

This is an important amplification. Lack of money, where money is the socially validated measure of all human activity and worth, is a derogation of a person's possibilities, a *human* lack. It is the impossibility of possessing those things by which his condition as man is recognized, it is a denial of freedom, or rather of the equation, money equals freedom. Over and above the biological, needs are social in origin, and as such relative. A man who has less is less of a man in a class society where a 'man' is defined by the possibilities wealth offers, where the dominant values are those of the dominant class. His loss is of 'status' and consequently stature, he experiences a human lack which is also (in as far as the possession of *things* has become the criterion or symbol of a man's worth) a lack of the human. But the question of money cannot be left at this level, since status symbols are but another way in which present-day capitalist society expresses need in money terms; a consumer society where status appears related to what a person possesses rather than to what he or she does, where a hierarchy based on possessions is supposed to supplant the less welcome reality of class division and its basis in capitalism. Status, as used here, is obviously a bid to express something more fundamental, something specific about the nature of class, rather than the nature of the symbols by which it is currently evaluated. To understand this the question must be returned to the condition of work.

'We didn't create these conditions,' Sutcliffe succinctly remarks at one point, 'they "happened" to us.' While he is speaking here not of factory life in general but of specific improvements in his own plant, the awareness is of something quite basic: the job in no sense 'belongs' to the worker any more than the product which results from his work; both belong to, and are controlled by, the enterprise which buys his labour. In his factory, improvements in working conditions are not even controlled by those they affect most: management may again become autocratic, new management take over, new forms of pay (or restraint) enforced. A relatively weak and unorganized work force will not be able to counteract such managerial decisions; a highly organized and strong shop will to varying degrees. But the basic situation is the same for both. Control, in capitalist society where the means of production are privately owned, is the private prerogative of the owners or their representatives. Labour is bought for its ability to work, not for its ability to decide what shall be produced, in what conditions or how. In factory and office a command structure exists to see to it that the decisions are executed. Not surprisingly, any challenge to this power of decision is seen as a threat to the rationale of the system, a rationale that exists in the production of profit. Democratic choice is not found in the work place. The one thing that the system appears to offer in its place – though not without struggle – is money. The system's justification, it is also its surrogate: for loss of freedom, in exchange for the status of tools, the compensation is money, money with which 'freedom' can be purchased elsewhere, outside the work place. Private consumption, 'status', personal choice (regulated as they are by the unequal distribution of income *and* by the criterion of profitability in what is produced) compensate outside for a situation of powerlessness inside – a situation rejected and combated by militant trade unionists in the knowledge precisely that it is fundamental to the capitalist system. Is it not recognition of this that leads Sutcliffe to write: 'Most of the workers are not driven by an urge to get as much for their labour as possible. In part they are seeking those things that make them human – a certain dignity, a measure of equality, and above all, their self-respect.' Is it not these needs, so largely denied, that underlie all that has so far been said and which no amount of money can either express or satisfy?

A one-sided view? Certainly, since these needs arise from a specific class situation which is basic to the capitalist organization of work. But not entirely, by any means. For what does the man at the other end of the scale, a man with a salary in the surtax bracket, have to say? 'Most modern managers,' writes William Hopper, a stockbroker, 'are concerned with more than their own salary; it is necessary for them to earn their self-respect in terms of feeling they serve a useful function.' The emphasis is similar, the choice of word to resume the deepest-felt need the same. In this context, perhaps, the word 'self-respect' is misleadingly ordinary; it might better be rendered here as 'respect for the self'. In this sense it goes beyond self-regard and becomes a collective need for each to accord to the other, and to recognize in the other, the possibility of fulfilling individual potential, of realizing the self's capabilities. Regardless of function, most professionals would probably agree: to a far greater extent than a factory worker, say, they can exercise freedom over their work environment, understand and identify with its purpose, feel themselves human. The fact that they receive higher rewards is not without point since, as we have said, self-respect, personal validation, is also a function of money.

Nor is it irrelevant that society validates their work and accords it an importance with which they can identify, a point to which we shall return. But despite these very considerable differences in situation, the needs experienced in work express themselves similarly at both ends of the scale and yet receive, in a class society, a quite different resonance depending on their point of origin. To return: money, status, self-respect – the terms most often used – are clearly needs, but they are also a bid to express a yet more fundamental need that underpins them. Trade unions exist precisely to advance the workers' claim to these three, as is made clear, and the reason explained, in one of the most eloquent expositions to be found in these essays. Jack Pomlet, a toolmaker, writes:

For me the union was never the purely economic institution concerned only with getting larger earnings that the middle-classes naïvely believe it to be. Certainly, the union was the organization which we looked to in the struggle to increase wages, but it was by no means its only function, and perhaps not even its prime function. For me the union was 'us' and 'ours'. It stood between us and the power of the foreman and under-managers to direct us at will. It was the collective instrument by which we asserted our right partly to control our daily destiny. The union stood between us and that concept of slavery and degradation called 'managerial prerogative'. We never really believed that the union could do any more than hold the ring on the question of wage levels. If the union had really possessed that 'dangerous power' to 'blackmail' employers into paying high wages, so avidly believed by the middle classes, why then has the proportion of national income going to wage earners remained basically unchanged for more than a century? . . . At the bottom of the instinct for trade unionism lies the instinct of the worker to be a fully integrated creative being, finding his salvation through work . . . . The union assists him in the struggle to assert his personality over these forces which threaten to disintegrate his wholeness.

Industrial workers (and, one might add, many other types of workers) perform fragmented tasks under conditions they can only marginally control, Pomlet points out. Through his reflections on the meaning of union we understand the significance of status, money and self-respect which others have used. They are the terms which express a basic need for control – control over the process and purpose of work and by extension over society which shapes that work. In this need are resumed, and finally made explicit, the terms in which it is usually expressed.

The struggle to extend this control and the need that it contains is most clearly articulated by Phillip Higgs, the convenor. Running a firm, he stresses, is not a matter of a few brilliant minds at the top, but a total process in which the workers play the vital role. There is a contradiction here, he says. On the one hand owners, or their managers, determine what shall be produced and how and control the work process in the interests of profit. On the other, actual production is in the hands and skill of the workers, who frequently can execute more efficiently than management can plan because they *know* the job, but who do not control the process to which they are essential. Active in the functioning of the process, labour's given role is passive in determining how that process works. This contradiction is but part of a larger one: requiring labour – skills, energy, activity – for their enterprises, the owners of capital buy this human energy in the market as they buy the other necessities of production. Cooperative and social, this labour serves to create new capital which is appropriated by the minority controlling the means of production. Capital's role is made to seem active (though shareholders in fact are generally passive); labour's role passive (though workers are active). More explicitly, capitalism characterizes labour as an active-passivity – active in the production of what is required, passive in deciding why or for whom it is required. Production exists for the product, not for the producer, who is divorced from the product while being vital to its production. This reduction of human activity to a single function – to produce whatever the enterprise determines for its own ends – this alienation, is but another aspect of the exploitation of one class by another that is more usually seen in straight money terms.

This contradiction, in the convenor's experience, is felt on the shop floor. The worker there is well aware that the greater part of responsibility for production rests on the shop floor. That his essential part in the process should be reflected in a desire to increase control over the work environment generally, in a desire to express and satisfy human needs as against the inert requirements of capital, should come as no surprise.

Earnings – and here the question of money is placed in perspective – are one of the components in the tactical struggle for control, but by no means the only one, writes the convenor. (Control, with its aim of limiting the scope of management's unilateral disposition of prerogative, is not – and should not be confused with – participation, which is an attempt to involve workers in the system's rationale, to involve them in their own exploitation. A critical insight into the low-level functioning of participation is provided by a manager himself in this book.) High earnings won through struggle are tangible proof of the shop floor's importance in the productive process, proof that one important area of work is accessible to concerted struggle. In itself money is both a real need and a deflection of other needs, a means whereby the responsibility and decision amputated at the work place is 'restored' to the worker in the 'freedom' of non-work.

'How much do you pay to bore a man to death?' someone is overheard by Mike Taylor, the machine-minder, asking at the employment exchange. A question that has resonance in these essays, for the reader will note that the degree of personal interest in the job – and thus the possibility of fulfilling the self's potential – varies with what is produced and the skill required to produce it (as it varies in inverse proportion, one might say, with the frequency with which money is mentioned). Two aspects need distinguishing here. The first is the intrinsic nature of the work itself, its variety, its relatively fragmented or total nature, its difficulties and the skill required to overcome them: in short, the work process. Here, as the steelman Patrick McGeown shows, even a fundamentally hard and repetitious job never lacks interest because each pot of steel is different, requires all his skill to make perfect. He compares himself to a sea captain bringing his ship in after a stormy passage – the long voyage that 'allowed me and my kind to exercise our skills and so to feel at home with our jobs'. His knowledge of the properties of the raw materials he works with, his skill in combining and controlling them, are essential to the difficult process of making steel. (Is it purely accidental that in this essay McGeown never mentions money?) But skill is more than knowledge and ability expressed as technical capability; it is also, and principally, *control* over a certain area of the technological environment. By his knowledge of the machines and the tools, the skilled worker is able to use them rather than to be used by them. He is not so liable to be dominated by the immediate tasks that the work process requires, irrespective of the fact that the total productive process is outside his control. But the uses to which the final product are put are also important. Steel, to return to this example, is more than a ladle of boiling metal flowing from a furnace: it has multiple uses, is one of the principal components of industrial societies; to be involved in its making is already to be involved in a vital social activity. Here we touch on the second, though by no means secondary, aspect: the purpose of work, the aim for which it is done.

Like all human action, work is always done *for* something, for an end beyond itself. This end or purpose gives meaning to what is done since it is the reason directing why it is done; what is produced cannot be divorced from why it is produced, for the why conditions the what (and, incidentally, the how). Made to use, steel contains this potential use (or uses) in itself as one of its properties. But to say that it, or any product, has a use is to say that it must be useful to the society for which it is destined. Its use, and consequently its meaning, depend on that society. At this level, to be engaged in making steel may well be more meaningful individually than to be mining coal in a coalfield condemned by the society's priorities to a slow death, more significant to be making jet engines than chemical toilets. If this is so, it is because society validates one job more than another, and this validation comes to the worker (as it does to the professional) as a reflection of the significance of his work. Of similar importance is the fact that this validation, an aspect of the society's priorities, is often – though by no means always – reflected in employment security, which studies have shown to be a significant aspect of work satisfaction. But these points, however important, only touch the surface. For the purpose of production in capitalist society is first and foremost the production of profit and only secondarily the production of use-value. Anything will be produced that will sell at a profit. From this outlook, one product is as good as the next if the rate of return on capital derived is the same. Its use-value is a matter of relative indifference, though capitalist ideology obscures this by maintaining that what can be profitably sold must *per se* be of use. (Needs, being social, can be manipulated to this end.)

But it is not a matter of indifference. For when the useful character of a product is abstracted from it, the useful character of the labour that goes into making it also disappears. An intrinsic value – use – is reduced to an extrinsic value – profitability. But it is the intrinsic value that work is directly concerned in creating, it is this value that gives purpose to work. The purpose, by the transformation of the material environment through human skill, of creating a wealth of use-value for man, a human activity creating a human world. Expropriating not only the surplus which labour creates, capitalism appropriates the meaning of work for its own purpose. A double exploitation for a single end. . . .

This exploitation will be more or less clear, experienced more or less sharply, depending on the type and extent of the work, its fragmented or total nature, the degree of skill required, the possibility or impossibility of identifying its use-value. What is produced is as important as how it is produced; control over their work process *and* over their work product is what a great number of contributors to this book are talking about when they refer to human dignity and self-respect. We return here to the bricklayer's point: there is a difference between working on housing to replace slums and working on apartment blocks for the rich or speculative office blocks – and the difference is not purely objective but subjective, is lived as a qualitative difference in the purpose of work. Social in origin, work receives its full meaning when it is conceived and fulfilled as social in purpose. This is both the argument for and the purpose of socialism; it alone, in a developed country, can satisfy this need by resolving the capitalist contradiction between work that is inherently social and that yet remains controlled for private and sectional ends. This contradiction, as we have seen, is not something abstract, but a lived experience for many. Lack of control is powerlessness, and powerlessness, as evinced in these articles, is not confined to shop floor and office, but extends through a wide range of work situations, even to positions where power is publicly thought to reside. Robert Bonnar, as a top union negotiator, and Stan Newens, a member of parliament, give ample testimony: the closer one comes to its apparently public source, the more the locus of power seems to withdraw. Who has control? No one? we are left asking. Surely not. For the logic of capitalism is such that society is controlled by the requirements of capital itself – an anonymous power whose controlling positions are occupied by men who must attend to its logic or make way for others better able to do so. Control of society for ends other than these is thus not simply a personal but a social need. In resolving capitalism's basic contradiction, socialism inaugurates social control of society, proposes human goals for society in place of capital's aims, and restores the unemployed, amputated part of responsibility and decision to the self, without which the individual cannot develop.

The 'unemployed self', brilliantly delineated in Professor Alvin Gouldner's concluding essay, is that part of each of us that this society excludes because it does not serve the system's functional needs. Author of *Wildcat Strike* and *Patterns of Industrial Bureaucracy*, Professor Gouldner's theme is the development of a new form of capitalist oppression – the oppression of uselessness – and the social and political crisis attendant on this. We invited Professor Gouldner, well known in this country as a leading American sociologist, to contribute this essay on the developing nature and relations of work from his position in the most affluent capitalist country, where new forms of contradictions are becoming increasingly manifest.

Two-thirds of the contributors to this book are writing for publication for the first time. Naturally, the way in which people see and think of themselves in their job influences the way they approach the task of writing. Some, like Higgs, are directly concerned with an objective condition, allowing their personal feelings to be expressed through their awareness of this condition; others, like McGeown, tend to the reverse, leaving the objective condition to emerge from more detailed personal narration. A third form, exemplified by Jack Pomlet, successfully combines both techniques, so that the condition is shown in its relation to personal feelings and feelings to the objective condition. Since the form chosen is itself an expression of the individual, since it is the individual himself we want to hear, no attempt has been made to impose a stereotyped format on these contributions.

On the contrary, the purpose of these two books has been to elicit deliberately subjective responses to the experience of work, to evoke the quality of this experience. It has been asked why, in originating these personal accounts, *New Left Review* did not use a tape-recorder to record the experiences of the 'less articulate', as the critics have put it. The choice not to do so was quite deliberate: we did not want to introduce an outsider, an interviewer with a set series of questions to whom the subjects would necessarily have to react and perhaps furnish an equally set series of answers. This is not to deny the validity of an extensive method of sociological inquiry, but only to say that we preferred an equally valid intensive method in which a limited number of individuals speak for themselves. It was, incidentally, a far harder task for the contributors to confront themselves alone on paper than to face an interviewer.

With this intensive method it has obviously been impossible to cover, in the forty-odd essays that *New Left Review* has collected, more than a fraction of the jobs that an increasingly complex society requires. The reader will rapidly make his own list of those missing; for our part we regret, among others, the shopworker, the corporation executive, the process worker and the immigrant who, for reasons of time, were unable to write. (Another significant absence, and this in the essays themselves, is mention of leisure and how this is shaped by the experience and condition of work. This lack suggests a gulf between work and non-work that is in itself suggestive of the qualitative experience of most work situations.)

Finally, while it is no accident that *New Left Review* should concern itself with these aspects of work, this is not to say that all the contributors share our views or would agree with the inferences drawn from their essays. But in a sense the significance of these books lies not in any particular view, but in a common agreement to engage with the task of opening discussion about an experience that is common to all.

RONALD FRASER
New Left Review, 7 Carlisle Street,
London W1

The Toolmaker

To be taken abruptly from school at fifteen and thrust into a mammoth factory is a second weaning. Leaving a secondary-school system which offers little more than a taste of the fruits of intellectual civilization before being thrust into the relative barbarity of the industrial system ensures that personal development inevitably depends on the occupation and the social culture of the workplace. Fortunately, some industrial workplaces do provide environments where full and humane personalities can develop.

I was just fifteen when I left secondary modern school to start an apprenticeship in a heavy engineering factory. The vividness of the transfer left an indelible imprint. One day I was a boy among boys – and girls – the next I was a boy among men. The school had been small and within it I had established my identity and pattern of relationships. The factory was immense and strange. Within its one square mile, perimetered by high wire and company police, twenty-two thousand men, women, boys and girls spent a considerable part of their conscious lives. The noises of the school had been the human sounds of endless chatter and the movement of bodies: the sense of space was confined to classrooms and playing fields. The crescendo of the factory was mechanical: the cacophony of machines and of the disintegrating brotherhood of metal molecules was only punctured by the irrepressible screech of the buzzer regulating the working existence of so many people. As the notes of the buzzer descended the decibel ladder the sounds of the mechanical world were replaced by those of the workers intermingling, uncontrolled for a short interval by work discipline.

Because in many ways its demands were similar to those of school, where periods of classroom were punctuated by play periods, I fell relatively easily into the pattern of factory discipline. But I never fully accustomed myself to the fundamentally alien world of machines and patterns of production not involving intimate human participation.

This huge plant which was to be my daily horizon of experience, and within which much of my personality was formed, employed eleven hundred apprentices. Such a large number had created the need for a special administrative department dealing with all aspects of apprentice training and welfare. And it was into the hands of this department that I fell on my first day of work. We – that year's crop of chosen fifteen-year-olds – were assembled in a small hall at 7.30 a.m. Drawn almost exclusively from working-class families we huddled together, half expecting that our first working day would, after all, begin like school with the managing director reading prayers. Instead, the head of the apprentice training scheme introduced us to the religion of factory discipline: we were now men, he told us, and we must work hard and diligently not only for the good of the firm, but also for the good of our own souls. Our satisfaction in life would come from acquiring the status of modern craftsmen; we were the fortunate few who would escape the 'dead end' jobs and the ignoble fate of the labourer. And with this message locked in our hearts we were assigned to different parts of the plant.

I was instructed to report to the foreman of a small workshop which produced components out of which electrical instruments were constructed. My future place of work lay on the far side of the plant, in that part which dated back to the firm's origins in the late nineteenth century. To reach it I had to pass through sights as alien to my past boyhood experiences as the moon's landscape will appear to the first men to tread it. On every piece of open ground lay metal shapes; some mere bars and sheets straight from the steelworks; others gigantic welded constructs covered in a deep brown rust. Besides these objects in the open spaces of the plant were small huts reminiscent of building site 'cabins'. Then I entered the great main workshops. Each chamber, or 'aisle' as they were called, was about one hundred and fifty feet across and anything between five hundred and seven hundred yards long. Several of these great vulcan halls lay parallel to each other. Within them the huge steam turbines which drove the equally massive electrical generators were built. Overhead rolled the girdered cranes capable of carrying weights of more than two hundred tons. As I made my bewildered way through this strange place one passed over my head. At once I understood the instinct which makes small creatures freeze as the bird of prey encircles overhead. My startled attitude to the crane's passage amused the men at work upon the turbine shells. One glance revealed my newness and a series of catcalls followed my passage down the 'aisle'. Mostly the shouts were good-natured advice to get out of the plant while I had the youth to do so. Such advice never even penetrated my outer consciousness, for how could anybody abhor this great masculine domain with its endless overtones of power and violence? During my short journey through that place of steel and power my memories of school and all it stood for were largely erased. It must have been an experience similar to that of young country boys recruited from the old English shires, and then thrust into the trenches of the Somme.

Coming out at the far end of the 'aisle' I was directed to a cotton-mill type building and told to see the foreman on the fourth floor. Climbing up the perforated steel stairs with my dinner sandwiches in my hand, I wondered what form of authority the foreman would turn out to be. I soon found out. He sat behind a long, burdened trestle table clad in a starched white dust coat. In front of him were rows of small machines and benches attended by about one hundred men and women: the men wore khaki dust coats and the women green ones. I surveyed the scene disappointedly; it was like having been taken past Armageddon and put to work in the cookhouse. Calling a chargehand over the foreman warned me 'not to lark about with the girls', and 'to keep my nose clean' and he would give me a 'good report'. The chargehand was a patient, worn-looking man of middle age. He took me to a small machine with a rotating abrasive belt, and indicated a box containing small brass plates. He said each had to be polished by pressing them against the belt.

He demonstrated how to start and stop the machine and how to polish the plates, and with a word of warning about keeping fingers out of the 'works' he left me.

As soon as he had gone the workers near me extended the unforgettable claustrophobic comradeship of the factory. It is a friendship generated of common experience, common income and common worktasks. Out of this shared pattern of experience grows a common culture of the workplace. And like other cultures it can never be fully understood by the outsider. For no matter how hard the would-be swimmer seeks to understand the experiences of the people in the pool, he can only ever grasp the quintessence of the water by jumping. The same applies to any circumscribed culture. On that first morning at work I began to learn all the expected patterns of response, all the rewards and sanctions, just as an infant learns its native tongue. I quickly learned the harsh language of aggressive friendship; the need to identify myself with the workgroup in opposition to all forms of authority from the chargehand up. Nothing must be allowed to threaten the cohesion of the workers, for only through this 'sticking together' could we solve the problems facing us. It was the instinct upon which all formal trade unionism is based.

The workshop I had been sent to was an unskilled one. The work was routine and performed mainly by women and unskilled youths, with some elderly men. Within a few days I had decided that compared with the rest of the plant it was a very dull place. The work was not very demanding and to a boy with an alert eye authority held little danger. I soon learnt to chat to the 'girls', as they sat at their small drilling machines, with that masculine aggressiveness which is the basis of a respectable Andy Capp relationship with the opposite sex. But above all I learnt the art of evading work and of being able to slip out and wander about the factory. The very size of the place made it an explorer's delight. And so long as I didn't attempt to enter places where my presence would be questioned, I was free to explore. These daily excursions soon made me dissatisfied with the 'shop' I worked in. It was so obviously unimportant, and contained none of the fascinating machinery of the larger shops where boiler-suited men and not green-coated women dominated.

One day about a month after starting work, and when the sheer boredom of polishing small pieces of brass had sent me out on my daily foray, I found myself in a small shop where men sat at work before large benches covered in hand-tools. None of the usual heavy machinery was present; the men did not wear boilersuits but instead were clad in clean brown dust coats. I soon understood that these men shaped and fashioned things with their hands much as a carpenter does. With youthful lack of inhibition, I leaned against a tubular rail and watched them. But not for long; the foreman had walked up behind me: 'What are you doing, kid?' he demanded. 'Just watching,' I replied, to which I quickly added, 'it looks a difficult job,' knowing that foremen, as other mortals, are not averse to flattery. The rest was relatively easy, for I had touched upon his pride of being a craftsman. He not only allowed me to watch but even explained some of the mysteries of the work to me. He told me the place was called a 'toolroom' and that the men were toolmakers. They were among the most highly skilled men in the manual engineering trades. Their task was to produce the tools and 'jigs' which enable the mass-production of components by semi-skilled and unskilled labour.

A few days later I was back to ask this foreman if I could be apprenticed as a toolmaker under his supervision. He said yes, if I first obtained the permission of the apprentice training officer. This was done and I found myself on a bench under the watchful eye of an experienced toolmaker. Under his guidance I was to be trained in the mysteries of craftsmanship. He obtained a number of handtools for me from the toolroom stores, and advised me to begin to buy some of the measuring tools which formed part of the personal equipment of each toolmaker. The brown dust coat was also essential, and that evening I proudly requested that my mother get one in the market.

The toolroom was a very different place from the unskilled

'shop' I had first been sent to on starting work. It contained about forty men, all of whom had served apprenticeships. There were only four apprentices, of whom I was the youngest. The atmosphere, while still being informally friendly, had a faint air of professionalism about it. Right from my first day there, it was made clear to me that toolmakers were craftsmen, and as such inherently superior to all the other workers except for a few other small and highly skilled trades. The ethos which has been graphically described as the 'aristocracy of labour' was very present. At the centre of this ethos lay a strict adherence to very high standards of workmanship. The demands of the work were technical, rather than the accomplishment of the semi-artistic tasks which are usually associated with handcrafts like carpentry, stone masonry and engraving. The chief demand of the job was the attainment of linear accuracy to one-thousandth of an inch. The blending of lines and curves using the coordination of hand and eye as in carving wood or stone were scarcely ever needed. But the attainment of constant dimensional exactitude and symmetry was very important. This meant that firm command over the use of many types of measuring instruments constituted the essential skill required of the toolmaker. He was a master of precision tools rather than the embodiment of a personal skill. He was, therefore, more of a technician than an artist-craftsman in the William Morris sense.

The toolmaker lies at the base of the mass-production technique. It is his task to produce from exact drawings a 'tool' which will enable the unskilled worker with the use of a machine to produce large numbers of components or finished objects. In a car factory, for example, the toolmaker will fashion a two-piece tool or 'die' which will produce as many exactly similar components from sheet steel as are needed. A 'punch' is made out of extremely hard steel to the exact size and shape of the product required. Then a 'die' is made, which is in effect a hole in a hard piece of steel which is the exact shape of the punch. When the two parts are fitted in a power press and brought together under great force, then any sheet steel between the punch and die will be pierced by them, and an exact shape cut. Thus millions of exact components for a watch, or whole car body shells can be produced.

The importance of the toolmakers' existence in the scheme of things was explained to me by many of the men I worked with. It was obviously a source of much ego-contentment and status. Each man made a complete tool, jig or punch and die by himself. While he might have to make tools based on similar principles, no two were ever the same. And since each man made the tool assigned to him by himself, with perhaps the assistance of an apprentice, he was able to lavish much self-satisfying effort upon it. Some tools which took more than a month to complete became objects of self-identification-tion for the toolmaker.

My first task was to assist the toolmaker I worked with, and in return he instructed me in the use of all the complex and often delicate measuring instruments. The man I worked with was middle aged and the son of a retired foreman from the same plant. He was held in great respect by the men, not only because of his considerable skill but also for his knowledge of many diverse subjects. Owing to his possession of a studied articulateness he was the tool-room shop steward. For the best part of three years I worked under his influence. As time went by I matured from assisting him to producing complete tools of a simpler nature by myself, with just a little judicious guidance from him. Later the ability to produce, largely by myself, a rather complex tool which then passed the inspector's experienced eye, gave me a feeling of satisfaction which subsequent achievements could not rival. And at the same time my personality underwent a change which reflected this satisfaction in creating something. It gave me the instinct for creative work, and the realization that in work alone can personal fulfilment be found. The craftsman is not *socially* superior because he can perform a given task which others cannot, he is *personally* superior because within his work he can find himself. The tragedy of most industrial occupations is their inability to afford satisfaction at this personal level.

The work in the toolroom was one of the very few places in that massive factory where no payments by results systems applied. The men were paid a standard bonus rate which was supposed to keep their wages above the best-paid bonus workers. This absence of time-measured output working was in striking contrast to the large machine shop which lay next to the toolroom. This shop was made up of capstan lathes operated by union-classified semi-skilled workers on regressive bonus systems of payment. The majority worked extremely hard in order to achieve maximum earnings. Tension pervaded the atmosphere as insidiously as the smell of the cooling oil used in the lathes. The relationship was not the comparatively congenial one between the craftsman and his work; but one of worker and machine, working as fast as the man was capable of in order to maximize the 'cash nexus'. Every now and again the tension would surface in a row over the price set by the 'rate-fixer' for the bonus paid for so much hourly output. The row usually took the form of a conflict between the man concerned and the shop steward, and the rate-fixer supported by the foreman. Sometimes even physical violence against the rate-fixer might be threatened, or the shop steward might call a temporary stoppage; but more usually a long bitter harangue over the rate-fixer's price would ensue.

By comparison the life of the toolroom was harmonious and peaceful. Neither was there any love lost between the two shops. The differences in status and 'cultures' of the two shops would no doubt have been undetectable to the outsider; but just like the Indian caste system, the shades and nuances were living, vivid realities to the participants. Both shops formed separate social units or 'in-groups', and little real contact was ever made, which beyond all doubt was due to the separate influences developed by the very different types of work and methods of payment. It provided an excellent example of a division within a social class.

My daily life throughout the four years I spent as an apprentice toolmaker followed an orderly pattern of existence. Each morning, winter and summer, my mother got me out of bed at 6 a.m., prepared breakfast and cut my sandwiches. By 6.45 I was on my bike and ready for the six-mile cycle journey I made each day to work. My father, a bricklayer, stayed in bed a little longer, as he worked locally. My two working sisters rose much later, as they held local office jobs; the youngest in the family, boy and girl twins, were still at school. The six miles had to be pedalled away before the 7.30 buzzer blew and another working day began. On arriving at work I would lock my cycle away in one of the racks which contained literally hundreds of machines, and run to 'clock on' before the buzzer blew. To be late was not only to risk a reprimand, but also involved the loss of half an hour's pay.

Once at the bench work would slowly begin, and just to help it on its way the foreman would take a walk round the toolroom. At 9.30 the labourer would push a large trolley slowly down the central gangway and we would place our brew cans on it. When he returned with the steaming trolley work would break off for about ten minutes and conversation begin. Then on until the dinner buzzer went at noon for the three-quarter-hour break. Then on again until 5 p.m., when the rush to 'clock-off' and get out before the crowd would begin as soon as the buzzer's lilt broke the air. As the evening buzzer sounded the factory police at the four exits would open the gates, and out would stream a human tide of over twenty thousand people. This daily pattern would repeat itself five days a week; fifty weeks a year; year in year out. It was a pattern of working existence as repetitive and predictable as the life of the peasant following the seasons through the fields. A surprising number of men had spent their entire working lives within the confines of that gigantic plant, from leaving school to receiving their retirement watches. God knows why watches, for why should an old pensioned-off worker desire to carry about with him an incessant reminder of the tragedy of passing time, with its evocative recall of long-passed hopes and the empty years which lie ahead? In my eyes the sight of some of the old toolmakers with fifty years of company service behind them was a horrible portent of the future. Would I know no more of the great world and the infinite complexity of the varied civilizations it housed than the confines of this fenced industrial concentration camp? Would the world and history pass me by, and leave me an old grey man carrying his toolbox home, clutching to his heart a ticking demon? These fears led me to that now rapidly dwindling breed: the self-educated working man.

The work environment of the toolmaker is, compared to that of men operating machines against the clock, quite conducive to reflection and conversation. The men I worked with were, for the most part, only interested in their personal lives, and in their particular working-class subculture which ranged from football to beer drinking, with a smattering of pigeon fancying and aggressive sexuality. They were not for the most part, thank God, made up of that mixture of piety and self-help which the Victorian middle classes so admired in the 'superior artisan'. But quite a few had managed to steer a middle course between the excessively physical and the excessively Calvinistic aspects of working-class culture. And one such workmate, widely read and with considerable practical experience in workers' organization, undertook my political education. He was about fifty years old, the son of an Irish docker and one of a very large family. He had left school during the First World War and managed to obtain a skilled apprenticeship, despite his background, because of the munitions boom. During the long inter-war period he had suffered long spells of unemployment, and *Love on the Dole* was very much the story of his life. While a still very young man he had abandoned an ancestral faith in Rome, for a burning faith in socialism. For him, socialism was a religion far removed from the economic rationale of the Fabians.

Under his guidance I began to read my way through his personal library. I cut my teeth on a battered copy of Robert Blatchford's *Merry England*, before grinding my way painfully through Engels' *Condition of the Working-Class in England*. And under the pretence of consulting him about a tool I was making, we would discuss what I had read. Years later I understood how unfortunate the undergraduate is in trying to learn politics in a university. He will never savour a real educational experience such as I enjoyed.

Not only did I receive a wonderful introduction to the world of books, but my 'mentor' also persuaded me to join the union as a junior member. Not that I needed much persuasion, for I had long been fascinated by the huddled dinner-break meetings at which my benchmate, the shop steward, would make slightly pompous speeches. For me the union was never the purely economic institution concerned only with getting larger earnings that the middle-classes naïvely believe it to be. Certainly, the union was the organization which we looked to in the struggle to increase wages, but it was by no means its only function, and perhaps not even its prime function. For me the union was 'us' and 'ours'. It stood between us and the power of the foreman and under-managers to direct us at will. It was the collective instrument by which we asserted our right partly to control our daily destiny. The union stood between us and that concept of slavery and degradation called 'managerial prerogative'. We never really believed that the union could do any more than hold the ring on the question of wage levels. If the union had really possessed that 'dangerous power' to 'blackmail' employers into paying high wages, so avidly believed by the middle classes, why then has the proportion of national income going to wage earners remained basically unchanged for more than a century? Indeed, one of the first political truths to hit me was the impotency of the trade union movement to change fundamentally the lot of the working class. For a change in 'the system' the movement would have to rely upon its child: the Labour Party. And every parent knows how difficult it is to fashion children in their own image.

The satisfaction membership of the union gave me cannot be separated from the satisfaction given me by membership of the workgroup. At the bottom of the instinct for trade unionism lies the instinct of the worker to be a fully integrated creative being, finding his salvation through work. Unfortunately, the normal lot of the industrial worker is a very unsatisfactory work experience of performing a fragmented task under conditions he can only marginally control. The union assists him in the struggle to assert his personality over these forces which threaten to disintegrate his wholeness. Fortunately, being an apprentice craftsman, I was saved from the type of work which so quickly destroys the creative personalities of so many industrial workers. My work was satisfying to a surprisingly high degree, and this was reinforced by the 'intellectual' discussions I was able to have with my 'tutor' without authority being able to detect them. A further factor which enabled me to reach out to that personal fulfilment denied to so many in that cavern of a factory was the making of 'foreigners'.

A 'foreigner' was the name given to things made by the toolmaker for himself and then smuggled out of the factory. The majority of 'foreigners' were domestic objects such as brass letterboxes, fire pokers, ornamental candlesticks and other house and garden adornments. Some were very ambitious, such as large petrol engine repairs for cars and motorbikes, or even complete bench lathes. All these things were made in the firm's time and out of their materials, and then taken home. It was, strictly speaking, criminal; and if the gate police detected a man removing his 'foreigner' they would have him sacked and charged with theft. But due to the amazingly ingenious methods of beating the gate police, the detection rate was very low.

Some of the 'foreigners' made were beautiful examples of craftsmanship, and care and effort was lavished upon them such as was never bestowed upon the firm's work. One man made exquisite brass Spanish galleons with burnished copper sails. Another made a working model of a racing car engine and then dismantled it and took it home piece by piece. Some people might have regarded all this as dishonest and even morally wrong, but not a single worker I met in those long years of apprenticeship considered it to be other than his birthright. It was their just compensation for the wage slavery they had to endure, and a life and work not of their making. Through the production of 'foreigners' we found personal satisfaction in work: personal work, not alienated task performance.

Throughout the years of my apprenticeship I had attended night school in order to obtain the technical qualifications necessary to train as a draughtsman. To become a draughtsman was the only path of promotion open to a young toolmaker. And shortly after my nineteenth birthday, I left the toolroom for the 'jig and tool drawing office'.

I have never experienced a more painful social dislocation. During the four years spent 'on the bench' I had forged close emotional ties with my workmates. The fact that very few men joined or left the toolroom made the workgroup a cohesive unit with strong personal attachments. When I let it be known that I was leaving for the drawing office I became the centre of much good-natured banter. The usual comments were, 'going up in the world, eh?' 'leaving us for that toffee-nosed lot' and 'bet you don't talk to us when you join the staff'. Here I was, going to an office only a few hundred feet away to join a group of men who had, like the toolmakers, left school at thirteen or fourteen, but to judge by the comments it would seem I was leaving for another country to join their upper class! The truth is that the rate of what sociologists call social and occupational mobility was still very low, even within the confines of a single factory.

My new job was in no real sense a break with my trade as a toolmaker, but instead of constructing the tools and jigs from blueprints, it was to be my job to design the tools and make the drawings. My family thought it a great promotion, and my mother said I should have to go to work in my best suit and save up for a new one. Of course, I should have to wear a clean white shirt: full well I later realized the reality behind the term 'white-collar worker'. On my first day in the drawing office I was able to stay in bed a full hour later as the 'shops' started an hour before the offices. What luxury!

The drawing office was as different a place from the toolroom as it had been from the first shop I had been sent to on starting work. On the few occasions I had had to visit the drawing office when in the toolroom, my impression had been one of quietness, and an air of gentlemanliness, bordering on the posh. Yet the great majority of the draughtsmen had in fact once been toolmakers, who had studied a technical course at night school to qualify for draughtsmanship. But there was an air of sobriety about them as they stood before their drawing-boards clad almost to a man in dark suits. Gone was the ribald repartee that marked the beginning of another day in the toolroom. It was almost as if some ghost had whispered to each man on being promoted to the drawing office: 'Draughtsmen are gentlemen and members of the company staff, and toolmakers are workmen and only paid by the hour.' To the external observer the status differences might have been difficult to detect, but to the factory worker they were as obvious as the nose on his face.

On arriving in the office the chief draughtsman, like the toolroom foreman before him, placed me under the tutelage of a competent draughtsman. But instead of the pally atmosphere of a shared workbench, I was placed before a large drawing-board covered by a challenging sheet of virgin white paper. I had to learn how to design a tool which would allow unskilled labour to produce thousands of exactly similar articles. This design had then to be converted from a rough sketch to a precision blueprint, so that the toolmaker could follow a plan when making the tool out of steel. The job, therefore, required more 'brain work' and far less hand skill than toolmaking.

Once I had grown accustomed to my new atmosphere, I found the actual design stage of my work an absorbing and fascinating process. Sometimes hours would pass as I sketched away at my pad before beginning the less interesting job of drawing the actual blueprint. But much of this absorption was an attempt to conceal from myself a feeling of isolation. Gone was the camaraderie of the shop floor; gone was the undercurrent of political intrigue; gone was the heat of the dinner-time steward's meetings; gone was the sensual feeling of shaping metal beneath the hands. Instead, there I stood in my Sunday best and white collar, pencil in hand, taking my tea-break from a teacup instead of a good honest brew-can. All this was the price of being thrust into an occupation which might allow my passage into the lower echelons of the 'great English middle-classes'. But wasn't I really just a young working man clad in his once-best suit instead of an overall?

My drawing-board was near a large window, and as the drawing office was on a fourth floor, I was able to gaze out on an industrial landscape, which at one and the same time could appear pulse-quickeningly attractive and hideously repellent. And just as the toolroom had contained many men whose whole lives had been spent in the company's service, so did the drawing office, but even more so. Gazing at these company 'warriors' and out of the window at the serried rows of tall chimneys, factory blocks and street housing stretching into the grey horizon of the ship canal, I would be filled with an irrational despair. Irrational, because had I not managed to get my foot on to the ladder of job promotion, security and relative future prosperity, yet still felt cheated and empty of real experience? Did I suffer from a dissatisfied personality; would the other side of the hill always look greener? Or was there something basically and profoundly dissatisfying about working in a large industrial plant? I didn't know.

Fortunately these workaday blues did not occur too frequently because of the pressure of learning the job and my growing involvement in the draughtsmen's union. Like most other people, and even organizations, the pressure of immediate circumstances pushed long-term problems and dissatisfactions back into the semi-conscious areas of my mind. Though it might well be that, in my case, the everyday activities I involved myself in were an attempt to solve by sublimation the deep and fundamental doubts I had about the whole direction of my life.

Many academic studies have been made of the involvement, or lack of it, by workers in their trade unions, but few have asked the question why some men spend so much effort and time in trade-union work, at heavy cost to their personal and family lives and the job promotion they often forego as a result. My personal experience suggests that the satisfaction found by some men in trade-union involvement offsets all these other pastimes and advantages. The union was 'ours', 'mine', it embodied a number of ethical goals which it shared with other working-class organizations. And these common points of direction made me and other trade-union activists feel part of a 'movement' which sought the short-term aim of adjusting pay, hours and working conditions; and the long-term aim of reorganizing society according to the theoretical objectives of socialism. The task of ameliorating working conditions was the objective which occupied almost all our energies, and the achievement of socialism was left to the political wing of the movement. Only the communists integrated the two aims, and for this reason they were very difficult to work with, as the procedural agreements which are invariably incorporated into factory-level deals over concrete industrial changes are, to me, incompatible with a desire to turn industrial unrest to political advantage. In my view a formal industrial relations system and spontaneous industrial militancy do not go together.

The draughtsmen's union was always something of a mystery to me. The drawing office I worked in, and the majority of those in the rest of the factory, were staffed by men drawn largely from the working class; but from the viewpoint of my background and experience they were middle class. For a start they were not manual workers, and they did not go to work in working clothes. They were not paid by the hour and did not lose money if they arrived late for work. They enjoyed longer holidays, a shorter working week, good overtime rates, and they were not subjected to real factory discipline. Their working life was very different from that of the toolmakers I had just left, and this was reflected in their social life.

In the toolroom all the men over twenty-one received a flat pay rate common to all, and as they received a bonus rate equal to the factory average – but without working for it – their gross earnings were also identical. Only different rates of income tax caused wage variations. Thus, regarding earnings, the toolmakers presented a common challenge to management. On the other hand draughtsmen over twenty-five received different rates of pay according to technical qualifications, age, length of service and ability. These differences could amount to almost five pounds a week between the lowest and highest paid senior draughtsman. And unlike the toolmakers, a young draughtsman on finishing his apprenticeship at twenty-one did not go on the minimum rate, he reached it by increments up to the age of twenty-five.

A further divisive element among draughtsmen was the existence of section leaders. Roughly one in ten of the draughtsmen was a section leader. They were paid an extra rate as they coordinated projects requiring a number of men, usually between eight and ten, to work in concert. The assistant chief draughtsman would keep each section leader supplied with work and pass or veto certain technical decisions. The chief draughtsman operated at a much higher organizational level, as he made the broad technical decisions on how a job or project should be tackled. He then left the detailed design and drawing to be distributed by his assistant, who would ensure that the section leaders and their teams executed it. Thus in almost every way the organization of work, the authority hierarchy and the system of payment was far more complex in the drawing office than in the toolroom. Yet the draughtsmen's union was infinitely more militant and committed to left-wing politics than the toolmakers' union. And the same applied to the draughtsmen's factory negotiating body. Obviously, some of the differences in attitudes and methods between the two workplaces can be explained by the very different union structures and methods of bargaining, but other factors also played their part.

To begin with most draughtsmen were the sons of skilled industrial workers, and a surprising number had fathers working in, or retired from, positions of shop-floor authority such as foremen and chargehands. Nearly all had served some years, mostly as apprentices, on the 'bench' and a majority had some kind of technical qualification. They were very strongly influenced by self-help ideals and saw in their union an excellent instrument for exploiting the chronic post-1945 shortage of trained draughtsmen. Trade unionism was something with which they had had family experience stretching back in some cases several generations. Thus the draughtsmen had fashioned a union, which in terms of the concrete economic gains it made for its members could not be bettered throughout the long history of trade unionism. Yet what puzzled me was the obviously more middle-class, individually orientated attitude to work and social life displayed by the draughtsmen compared to the toolmakers I had just left. This, it must be stressed, is only my personal experience in one large factory. It might be different in other factory drawing offices and toolrooms in other parts of the country, though I doubt it.

The longer I spent in the drawing office and the more time I spent as a representative of junior draughtsmen, the more I came to realize that the union's left-wing leadership was strangely at variance with its predominantly right-wing membership. At first I thought it could be explained by the usual fact that those willing to do union work and forego promotion were the politically conscious and militant who, quite naturally, rose by virtue of service to positions of leadership. But this I decided was a superficial analysis, as it did not explain why the right-wing and socially conservative membership, which was not apathetic to union policy, supported this type of leadership. And the more I thought about it, the more I felt that the paradox could be explained in terms of the union's policy of high militancy on questions of pay and hours. For the leadership it expressed part of their vigorous opposition to 'the system'; to the membership it expressed a higher income and a middle-class way of life: a mind-disturbing paradox for an evolving socialist. My union experience did not at all fit my political belief that politics was about class confrontations, rather it made me realize that the status and income graduations created *within* the working class by technological advancement constituted a formidable barrier to the creation of an homogeneous labour movement. Only within such an explanation could the paradox of low militancy among the lower paid and high militancy among the higher paid within 'my' factory be understood.

These thoughts, when coinciding with my blue moments of gazing out of the high window beside my drawing-board, filled me with a desire to get out of the factory completely. I needed to escape for a period while I still could. To be a good designer and draughtsman involved with my union was not enough. Neither could I find sufficient compensation in the desperately hedonistic leisure-time activities which I pursued with my friends. No, my escape must be practical for I knew that it could only be temporary. What I needed were new experiences, new horizons, and contact with a variety of people with different backgrounds and occupations, to give me some insight into the many types of human experience. A kaleidoscope of condensed experiences would prepare me psychologically for the return to the industrial world I had known since leaving school. It would also help me to arrive at some basic personal commitments concerning the type of socialist society I could help work towards through the institutions of the British Labour Movement.

JACK POMLET

THE AUTHOR

I was born in Manchester in 1936, and lived there until moving to the south, as a married man with one child, twenty-six years later. My father, a lifelong socialist, worked then, and still does, as a bricklayer. By modern standards we were quite a large family: three girls and two boys.

Leaving secondary school at fifteen, I was four years on the 'bench' as an apprentice toolmaker before becoming a trainee draughtsman. Then came two years in the army as a radio technician. After demob I spent two rotten years as a draughtsman working for several firms, during which time I read a great deal, particularly studies of industrial societies. Spurred on by this reading, I took a job as a research assistant and interviewer with a university sociological research team studying a coal and cotton town in South Lancashire. After two absorbing years I went to Ruskin College, Oxford, to study politics, economics, socoilogy and, I hoped, socialism. I am now doing research work in trade unionism and industrial relations.

A Miner's Life

Seven Sisters – a small Welsh mining village situated in the centre of a once beautiful valley, surrounded by mountains now polluted with dust, grime and the ever increasing tips of rubbish from the coal mines . . .

The owner of the colliery was the owner of the land, the majority of the houses, and the public house, and he had also built the church. He owned the reservoir that supplied the village water and the power plant that supplied the electricity. He was a member of the district council.

One could safely say that he owned the people's souls as well. Anyone not born in the village was classed a foreigner, notwithstanding that many of these so-called foreigners had lived in the village for more than fifty years. During the early days the parish council always consisted of the local colliery manager as chairman and the local colliery officials as councillors.

This was the world I grew up in between the wars.

When I left school at fourteen to look for work I felt rather privileged to have obtained employment at the local colliery. Going to work with my father on that first morning, wearing my first long trousers and a red scarf round my neck, I felt a thrill. With the safety lamp I had collected from the lamp-room I walked to the pit head. The cage came to the surface, the banksman opened the gates and told the first eight men to enter the cage. I was number eight.

'Put that boy in the middle,' he ordered. 'We don't want him to fall out on his first day.' Obediently I moved into the centre, and the cage started to descend slowly. All of a sudden I thought the bottom had fallen out. The men roared with laughter as I picked myself up. The darkness was so intense I couldn't see my hand in front of me. When we got to the bottom, old Bill Adams, the man I'd been assigned to work with, took hold of my hand. 'We will have to sit down for a minute or two, boy bach, to get used to the dark,' he told me.

The roadway became more visible at last. It was quite wide, with several narrow roadways leading away from the pit, and the sides and roof were well supported with strong timber. 'Let's get along to see the fireman then,' Bill said. I followed him along one of the roadways; we hadn't gone far before some men walking behind us started shouting, 'You there in front, put that bloody light out.' Bill turned and said, 'It's you they are shouting at, you haven't put a shade at the back of your lamp.' He took it from me and fixed a small piece of cardboard round one side of the glass, explaining that one of the worst things to a miner underground was the glare of the light from a lamp. The majority of miners suffered from nystagmus, a disease of the optic nerve caused by working in poor light.

It seemed to me as if we had been walking for hours before we finally reached our working place. It was called Adams level, it being the practice to name the place after the man who worked there. Bill handed me a shovel which must have weighed a ton, and we went on to the coalface. The seam was about a yard thick and the total width Bill had to work was about thirteen yards. Bill, one of the old type of miner, crawled up to the top end of the face and started cutting the coal away from the bottom of the seam with a razor-sharp pick. He worked quietly, picking the coal away all along the face until he reached the bottom end. With a splitting noise and a loud report the whole coalface suddenly seemed to collapse. Bill was skilled in his trade and knew every trick. 'Feeling fit, boy bach?' he said, and without waiting for a reply told me to hang up my lamp and fetch the curling box. I looked at him without understanding. 'What's the matter with you, boy, are you blind? – that's the curling box by there.' He threw a piece of coal against an iron scoop-shaped box with handles on both sides. I lifted it. 'That's it, now start scraping the coal into it and then put it into the tram – the coal I mean, not the box.' I began scraping the coal into the box with my hands, but the coal was so sharp it cut my fingers. When the box was full I tried to lift it; it was so heavy I couldn't tip it into the tram. I tried several times, but there was more coal falling on top of me than ever got into the tram.

Seeing it was impossible, Bill shouted to throw the bloody thing away and use the shovel. 'But for God's sake watch the roadway for a light coming, if you are caught using the shovel to fill the tram we will both have our cards.'

After filling two more trams, Bill said it was time to have food. We went back along the roadway to where we had hung our coats and sat down in the dirt. There was no water to wash my hands so I tried to hold my bread and cheese with a piece of newspaper. I had more paper in my mouth than bread, so I gave up that idea and wiped my hands on my shirt. Birds need a bit of grit to live, I thought, so a little won't hurt me. A horse pulling an empty tram came by and dropped its manure which smelt terribly, but we continued to eat. 'Come on,' Bill said, getting to his feet, 'we have a lot more work to do before you go home to see mammy.'

One Saturday Bill failed to turn up. The seven o'clock hooter had blown, so the fireman sent me to work with another collier, Thomas Thomas, commonly called Twm Twm. Now Twm Twm had a bad habit of sitting down all morning telling stories, some of them not too clean, and starting work only after food time. This Saturday it was past three o'clock in the afternoon and everyone else had gone home a half-hour before when, marking our last tram of coal, I accidentally knocked over my oil lamp and the light went out. Twm started to shout, calling me all the names he could lay his tongue to, and saying we couldn't work with only one light. I collected the tools together and put them on the tool-bar; as Twm snapped the lock on the bar he hit his lamp and before he could get hold of it that light went out as well. 'Such bloody luck,' he screamed, 'some bastard's watching us today.' We had to feel about for our clothes, then with one hand on the iron rail of the roadway we made our way back towards the pit bottom. Twm was only about a yard in front of me but I couldn't even see the shape of his body, it was darker than the darkest night. As we stumbled the mile of roadway, my hand scraped through horse manure and my feet were soaked in pools of water. Though they were cut and bleeding I didn't dare take my hands off the rail, for this was the only guide back to safety. All of a sudden Twm let out a loud yelp. 'What the hell is here?' Our way forward had been blocked by a fall of rock.

'It's all your bloody fault,' he shouted. I kept quiet, knowing he must be as scared as I was. Then he started to shout for help. I didn't believe that even Twm thought anyone would hear him, for every sane person was at home by now enjoying themselves. He went on shouting all the same. We were about giving up hope when we saw a light shining over the fall. Old Arthur Powell, the afternoon pumpsman on his way down to attend to one of the pumps at the far end of the district, had heard Twm's voice. With the light we could see that the fall wasn't as big as we had first thought, although it was big enough, about five feet high and covering the roadway's whole width. You can imagine our relief at being found. Twm never worked late after that.

I'd been working about three months and getting used to the job when a special meeting was convened by the union to discuss the question of coming out on strike. I didn't know a great deal of what was involved, and to be honest I wasn't deeply interested. I didn't go to the meeting but was told later that there had been a unanimous decision in support of the strike.

Monday night, 3 May 1926, was the start of the great General Strike.

As though made to order, the weather was perfect and the sun shone all day and nearly every day. A soup kitchen was started at the local reading room which apart from providing us with one square meal a day gave us something to look forward to. What a welcome sound the cook's voice became as he shouted 'come and get it' long before you got near the hall. There wasn't a great variety, but what we had was good. Sometimes it was pea soup, then it would be sausage and mash. You always knew when it was pea soup day: you could see everyone marching towards the reading room with a basin in his hands.

For the first week or two the strike wasn't too bad. To me, a boy, it was one big holiday and I still had money in my pocket. My father made me do an hour or two a day in the garden because, he said, I'd only get stiff if I didn't do anything. But as the weeks grew into months life became harder; the one thing in our favour was that everyone else was in the same boat. Since there were no buses and the railwaymen were also on strike, we started to organize our own entertainment. Every Saturday the strike social committee held a sports meeting or carnival. For one of these a crowd of young men shaved all the hair off their heads, blackened their faces and bodies, made skirts out of reeds from the river and formed a Zulu jazz band to compete in the carnival. The idea caught on and soon jazz bands became a regular feature. Another common sight was groups of men sitting on the pavements outside their homes playing cards for matches. If we gained nothing else out of the strike, we developed a strong community spirit. Our common poverty made us feel equal and interdependent.

But at the end of the eight long months when we finally returned to work many found they had no work to return to. The men at the Seven Sisters colliery were rather fortunate to have work three and sometimes four shifts a week. By agreement between the colliery owner and the local union, the colliery hooter would be blown at seven o'clock in the evening if there was no work the next day.

Although we were fortunate to have any work at all, our living standards were far from satisfactory. Every week my mother would send me to the butcher's for sixpennyworth of meat scraps and a bone for the dog – though we had no dog. My mother would boil the bone to make stock for a stew that would last us the whole week. The scrap meat would be our Sunday joint.

When I started again after the strike, I was told to report for work at the Big Vein district, which was where only the most skilled miners worked. No one could claim to be fully trained until he had worked the Big Vein. The seam of coal there averaged nine feet thick, and the number of timber supports was colossal. I felt rather nervous. I was young to start working in this district because, although I had started work eleven months before, I had only actually been employed about three. I had no choice but to accept, for if I didn't it meant losing my job and starving.

The conditions were deplorable. The heat was so intense that everyone worked stripped to the waist and a few only wore short pants, knee pads and boots. Often the cheese in my food tin melted. Black beetles swarmed everywhere, and when you shone your light into any dark corner it seemed as if the whole earth was moving. The fireman in charge told me to report to David Thomas, a collier who worked in the main drivage. This didn't look in any way like the Big Vein; the timber supports that formed the roadway were all broken and squeezed out of shape, and in many places I had to bend as I walked under them. But when I arrived at the coalface I understood why it was called the Big Vein: the seam of coal at this point was over ten feet thick. Dai was a member of the lodge committee and a good and honest man. I worked hard and learned fast under his skilled instruction. He paid me well, ten shillings a week over my standard rate, which was equal to a third of my normal weekly wage.

One day I was busy helping Dai erect a pair of double timber supports when the fireman came rushing up to us shouting, 'Come quick, Bob Williams is trapped back on the main tunnel.' We dropped our tools and followed him back to the site of the accident. We saw Bob wedged between the side of the tunnel and an empty tram. The tunnel there was low and narrow, and in trying to squeeze past the empty tram Bob had dislodged some of the broken timber supports which held back the loose rock on the side of the tunnel. The whole rock side had caved in, pinning Bob to the tram. His oil safety lamp hanging on his belt was between his body and the tram. Due to the intense heat of the lamp it had started to burn into his body. The sounds of his screams went through me. 'Wyn llosci, wyn llosci' ('I'm burning, I'm burning'), he kept screaming. He was only about four feet away from us but we stood there helpless. We tried to move some of the timber but the rock kept sliding down, so we started to erect new timber supports and move the rock piece by piece.

We had been working only twenty minutes when his screams stopped. We shouted to him, 'Bob, Bob boy, are you all right?' There was no reply; life had been burnt out of his poor body.

It took us two hours before we finally freed his body. The air was full of the stench of burnt flesh, the lamp had burnt a hole into his stomach. I felt sick and dropped to the ground, the sweat pouring out of my body. Then I started to cry like a baby. I couldn't help myself. Dai came and put his arms round my shoulders. 'Have a good cry. This is something you will have to live with. This is the price of coal.'

I worked with Dai for several years; I enjoyed listening to his opinions of what the miner's working conditions would be like in the not too distant future, a future he himself wasn't going to see. One afternoon, walking out of the district, he stopped and sat down by a manhole in the side of the roadway. He could hardly breathe. I asked what was wrong and between gasps of air he told me quietly, 'You go on, my old chest is none too good.' I didn't want to leave him but he insisted and I went. I had noticed that he had lost a considerable amount of weight lately; he wasn't an old man, he was only about fifty. Though he certainly didn't look fit enough, he was back at work again the next morning. But then came the morning when he didn't turn up, and I was told to continue working the place on my own. He never came back; soon afterwards I learnt that he had died.

There was a big inquiry after his death. An amendment to the Various Industries (Silicosis) Act of 1928, which meant that you had to have proof of the existence of silica rock in the workplace before compensation could be claimed, had come into force a month before his death in 1931. Several strangers visited the place looking for silica, but they failed to find any; the claim for death benefit under the scheme was turned down and Dai's widow didn't receive a penny.

As trade gradually improved, work became more regular and output at the colliery increased, but wages remained the same. Many of the older men didn't receive the minimum wage and nor did they bother to claim it; the fear of losing their jobs still lurked in the back of their minds. It was during this period that the local miners' lodge affiliated to the National Council of Labour Colleges. Classes were held every Sunday and had been going for about two years when we decided as students that it was time to start putting our newly acquired understanding into practice. A few of us were nominated to stand for the lodge committee, and I was elected as workmen's examiner.

My first inspection was in the Big Vein district. I started to condemn unsafe conditions and breaches of the Coal Mines Act as soon as I entered the main drivage, one part of which was so low that holes had been cut into the floor between the sleepers to allow the ponies to walk on to the inner part of the district. When we eventually reached the last place in the district where the heat was unbearable, we saw an oil safety lamp hanging on a timber support. No one was in sight, but we could hear someone working in the coalface. I asked the manager whose place it was, and he replied that it was Joe Williams'. Then he shouted, 'Joe, come out of there at once.' There was a sound of shuffling feet and tools being thrown down. Joe came towards us feeling his way with one hand on the iron rail. 'What the hell are you working in the dark for?' the manager asked him.

'Trying to cut a bloody hole through to get some fresh air into the damn place,' was Joe's reply.

With the increase in trade and regular work, men began to agitate for better working conditions and higher wages, and I found myself getting more and more involved in union work. During this period the method used in the coalfield generally to gain concessions from the owners was the 'stay-in' strike, although we never adopted it. We had only one owner to contend with, while all the surrounding collieries were owned by combines. Knowing that we lived in a dog-eat-dog society, we were well aware that these combines would close in on the owner of our colliery if they had the least chance.

Whenever we contemplated putting forward a demand – and in the unbearable working conditions we did so frequently – we would first of all check the newspapers to see if the owner had a ship in dock waiting for coal and then, but only then, put forward our case. If our application was turned down we would call a meeting of the men and recommend a 'lightning strike'; we had so many that they became a permanent feature of our pay tickets. We secured many improvements both in conditions and wages: new return airways were driven into the district to give better ventilation, steel arch supports were installed in place of the old timber, and electric light was put in at the bottom of the pit shaft. A new surface agreement was signed granting a shift extra per week for all men employed in the coal circuit, and a shilling a day extra for all men in the screening plant until the dust was eliminated from the screens. The colliery prospered. Over a thousand men were employed there, the output was the highest ever, and the conditions and wages were second to none.

Then came the Second World War and with it the inevitable changes in the village's social life. Being exempt from war service, the mines were graced with the presence of many of the local business and so-called professional people. Our lodge formed a village vigilance committee to deal with the food question, and played our part in the newly proposed pit production committee, to which I was elected as one of the co-chairmen. In 1942, after the Czechoslovak village of Lidice was burnt to the ground by the Nazis, Seven Sisters was chosen as the site on which to make a film of the atrocity, and many local people were called on to play parts. At one pit-head scene the director, the late Humphrey Jennings, asked me to stand on a barrel and say something to the crowd. I climbed up and said a few words about the stand we should take against the German invader, ending with: 'Comrades, I move we strike.' Then one of the men from the crowd shouted, 'I second the motion.' It turned out to be a colliery official who had never been on strike in his life.

1 January 1947 – the realization of the dream of every progressive-thinking miner in the country, the dream shared by the miners of our colliery. We stood on the colliery surface on that cold morning, watching the raising of the NCB banner declaring the new ownership. Standing alongside the colliery manager on a small platform, Will Thomas addressed the crowd: 'Comrades, pioneers of the socialist and trade union movement fought for nationalization, they fought in the knowledge that it would be the first step in the direction of socialism.'

To many this was true, but there were some who held a different view; to them nationalization of the coal-mines was an essential step to preserving the industry in the interests of the private enterprise system. In itself nationalization was not a guarantee of a step forward towards socialism – it would depend largely on who controlled the state machinery and in whose interest it would be used.

The miners' union had put forward a charter which, among other things, called for a five-day week, two weeks' holiday with pay, miners' sick benefit, pensions, free pithead baths at every colliery. Had the charter been fully implemented at the time of nationalization, or had the NCB shown their willingness to operate it fully, the miners would have been satisfied that the board was taking the right direction. As it was, much of it was ignored. Although a week's paid holiday was granted, it took nearly twenty years before the second week was given; miners' sick pay did not start until 1958, and then no payment was made for the first week of sickness. And some of the improvements were already enjoyed by men at our colliery: the five-day week, which was introduced four months later, had been worked by the afternoon and night shifts for many years – though the fact that miners all over the country would now share these conditions was a step forward. Free pithead baths were gladly accepted as a sign of progress, though again this was an amenity we had enjoyed ten years before nationalization; while the ambulance service provided by the new National Health scheme meant a loss of service to us: we already had two ambulances with full-time drivers at our call day and night and for only threepence each per week contribution. Concessionary house coal was a particularly sore point. Previously we got thirteen tons a year; now we got only eight. Gradually all the local concessions that had been gained as the result of years of hard struggle faded away.

The year after nationalization I was elected as the union lodge compensation secretary, and one of my first tasks was to deal with the compulsory retirement of the over-seventies. The board gave each of them a certificate thanking them for their years of loyal service; after that no one took any further interest in them and they were left to rot. Many died within a year.

This new form of ownership demanded new thinking on the part of the workmen. No longer could we use one owner against the other. The strike weapon was no longer so effective. A single colliery unit could no longer effectively take action on its own. Each question was now dealt with by the coalfield as a whole.

As the result of a national mechanization programme, the 'plough' was introduced into the colliery. This was a combination of coal-cutter and conveyor which stretched the whole length of the coalface, 150 yards. To give some idea of the size of this machine, each cutter knife weighed 26 lb. and there were 15 such knives. With every run through the coalface the cutter sliced away 6 inches of coal 3 feet high over 150 yards in about 6 minutes. In other words, it produced and conveyed out of the coalface about 12 tons of coal every 6 minutes and reduced the number of men needed to half.

And year after year, as the output of coal increased, the

market dropped owing to the lack of a national fuel policy. Soon, after the Coal Board invited Lord Fleck to advise them on industrial organization, the pit closures began. These meant uprooting men from one pit and transferring them to another pit or another kind of job. Inevitably, men in the older age-groups and the disabled found themselves out of work. The closures were grouped into four categories: those due to exhaustion of workable reserves; those due to the merging of the coal reserves into bigger units; those deemed necessary for the concentration of production and manpower into more productive units; and those due to economic reasons. No mention was made of the social consequences of closures.

On 1 January 1960 an agreement on the compulsory retirement of miners over sixty-five was introduced. To soften the blow a lump sum of £200 was paid by the Coal Board to each of the retired men. Evan Jones was waiting for me outside the colliery office. As soon as he saw me coming he started shouting, 'Such a bloody committee. After working fifty years in that hole this is what I get.' He waved a piece of paper in my face.

'Let me have a look.' I knew what it was all about – a letter from the Board explaining the redundancy payment Evan was entitled to. 'How would you like to be thrown on the scrap heap?' he asked. 'I wouldn't like it at all,' I replied, 'but let us look at your position.' And then I explained that at present for a full week's work he took home £7 12s. 6d. out of which he paid rent of £1 6s. leaving him with £6 6s. 6d. When he retired, he would be entitled to £4 retirement pension for him and his wife, £1 from the Mineworkers' pension and a rent allowance from the National Assistance Board of 16s. 6d., so he was only losing 10s. a week and a week of hard dirty work. Besides, he would have £200 as a small nest egg to draw from as and when he wanted. 'Daro, I didn't look at it like that,' Evan said with relief.

By now a crowd of miners had gathered round. 'It looks like you're in favour of pushing the old men on the road,' one of the younger men in the crowd said to me. 'No,' I said, 'but

I do believe that a miner who has given fifty years of his life to the industry should retire young enough with an adequate income to enable him to enjoy his retirement.'

In the latter part of 1961 the board informed our executive council that certain pits would have to close the following year. Four of the valley's six collieries were included in this list. The effect on members was demoralizing. Mass meetings, exceptionally well attended, were held, at which it was decided that while the men employed in the threatened pits would be asked to do everything in their power to maintain the colliery in production – even to the extent of surrendering their hard-earned practices and customs – the union would examine all aspects of planning and production to see what improvements could be effected.

Towards the end of the year the first colliery was closed and the men were transferred to neighbouring collieries, where even the disabled were fitted up with satisfactory jobs.

The following year colliery number two was closed. Not all were found employment, especially the older men and the disabled. The union even went round the neighbouring collieries to ask the over-sixties to retire to make room for younger men.

This insecurity caused the young men to leave the industry; and the drift away not only threatened the uneconomic pits but the profitable ones as well. March seemed to be the month for closures and true to form colliery number three closed in that month the following year. Transfers to other collieries got more difficult and men now no longer thought of alternative employment, but how much redundancy pay they were entitled to.

Each Friday we now open our pay packet, not to check the money but to see if it contains our notice to quit. It didn't come as such a great shock to me when I opened my packet this week and took out a single sheet of paper.

Dear Sir,

Because of reorganization, I am sorry to have to tell you that your present job at this colliery will come to an end on March 17th, 1967.

Unfortunately, the National Coal Board are unable to keep you in their employment by offering you another job and regretfully they have no alternative in the circumstances but to give you notice that your contract of employment with the Board will come to an end in four weeks' time on the 17th March, 1967.

The Board wish you all the best for the future and thank you very much for your past service.

CHRIS EVANS

THE AUTHOR

I was born in August 1911, during a period of great unrest and depression in the mining valleys of South Wales. Two months after I was born my parents, who owned a grocer's and a fish and chip saloon, were forced by the depression to sell their property and move to a small mining village in west Wales.

I enjoyed my school days so much that when I left elementary school at the age of fourteen I was presented with a silver medal and a drawing set by the educational authorities. I started work in January 1926; in May I was involved in the General Strike that lasted eight long months. I married in 1932; as a result I was entitled, though not yet twenty-one, to claim the full adult rate of wages of £2 12s. under the Lord Porter award. This proved too great an expense to the colliers, so I was promoted by the colliery manager to the grade of collier and given a place to work on my own. In 1934 I was elected local workmen's examiner and representative on the local trades and labour council. I refused to accept the constitution of the Labour Party, however, claiming that I had the right to represent my union on all matters dealt with by the council that involved the interests of trade unions. I was finally expelled. This was the beginning of the end of this council, which was soon disbanded and a local Labour Party ward formed.

In 1938 I was elected member of the local miners' union committee, and subsequently served as vice-chairman and chairman. During the war I was also chairman of the pit production committee. Until 1953, when payment based on the ton of coal was done away with, I was miners' checkweigher at the local colliery.

Vice-Chairman of the local historic society and author of the Social and Industrial History of Seven Sisters, *I am also treasurer of the Rowen Factory for Peace, a factory owned by, and worked for, its employees.*

I have four sons and two daughters. Not one of my sons is a coal-miner.

Steelman

These days I don't work at all. I quit four years ago after making steel on open-hearth furnaces for forty-eight years. From 1915 to 1963.

During that period there were two world wars which I never fought in, I was too busy making shell steel for those who did, and a trade depression which lasted about fifteen years, in my case from 1921 to 1936. In those depressive years I still made steel, but intermittently, my peak periods being stretches of three consecutive working weeks followed by one idle week. This way we shared the work so as to save redundancy. The steel melters called it 'working round'.

In slacker periods my quota of work and idleness was week about. The furnacemen had a name for this too. It was 'Off agin, on agin, gone agin, Flanagin'. The mythical Flanagin being an Irish rail ganger whose style, when reporting replaced rails, was laconic.

The first steel furnaces I ever saw, but never worked on, were in the West of Scotland where I was born. They were the cold-metal, hand-charging sort and they catered for strong men only, very strong men. About one steelworker in every ten could stand up to them successfully, which was one reason why the furnacemen were looked up to in the world of heavy industry. That they got the biggest pay packets was another reason.

They also had the biggest thirsts and that too was a prideful possession in that part of the world.

But the chief reason for the high standing was the daily exercise of a skill that seemed almost mystical to outsiders. Those who were near it but didn't understand it, told those who had never seen a steel furnace. So a legend grew up about the steel melters.

They charged their furnaces by hand, 35 tons or so of solid steel scrap, cold iron and lime stone, and they controlled the flame that played on it, and in the end came steel. At that time, in the early years of the present century, every pot of steel was an act of creation. It was something derived from the absorbed attention of dedicated men. So dedicated, so absorbed, that often they overlooked the misery and the hardship of their lives. They had been given a chance to create, and that made up for plenty.

The whole district and for miles beyond it was a hotbed of steel works, iron puddling works and coal mines. It was a place given over to the worship of strength and durability. Indeed it needed strength to look at it, and durability to live in it. The steel furnacemen, the iron puddlers and the coal miners were mostly men of few words, which they repeated eternally about steelmaking, iron puddling and coal mining. They were so proud of their occupations that they never shut up. It was a simple age, and the masters hoped to keep it that way. In fact they thought that the workers had already advanced too far.

I thought myself that the miners came out last of the three trades. They were a good third but still behind the others, for they didn't produce anything, they took something out that had been there a long long time. But still they were proud. Has anyone ever thought that there's such a man as a proud coal miner? Well, there is, and he has a right to be so.

The iron puddlers, since they were the first in the metal game, thought that their trade was the tops, and they had a case too. There was skill and skill aplenty in the way they puddled those balls of semi-molten iron, and served them up to the bar mills and the forges, to be finalized into wrought iron.

It was a fact too that they had the most exhausting job in the whole wide world. No one denied it, but there were two schools of thought on the matter. There were the puddlers themselves who were proud of it, and the other workers who thought them damn fools for doing it. And that was rich coming from miners or steel furnacemen.

But in my mind, and my father's mind, and with no doubt about it, the steelmen were in the top trade of them all.

My father was an Irishman from Co. Armagh who had

stumbled on the melting shop for just another spell of harsh work, and had found a trade. It took him twenty years to become a leading hand, a first-hand steel melter, and wasn't he proud of it, he surely was at home with his job. He brought the job home with him too, all the weariness, the anxiety and the satisfaction. My mother watched always, concerned about his condition at the end of each shift and to assuage him by all the means in her power. She knew that he was proud to be a steelman, and because he was proud then she was proud too.

It was her pleasure to feed me well, for she wanted me to grow up with strength to sell to the steelmasters for money. She could see no other way of life but hard manual labour for me.

I sought other ideas; I'd seen the exhaustion, and the sweat-drenched shirts my father came home with, and I wondered if there was any escape. I didn't fancy above all that fourteen-hours' stretch he did every second week when on night work.

These thoughts I kept to myself, for I had puzzled her once or twice by talking about books, and by reciting some verses I had written. She feared I might grow up an oddity, someone who didn't regard strength and the will to expend it as the most important things in life.

There had been a chance, of course, that I might grow up lacking the strength to work on steel furnaces, but each year that chance diminished. If only I'd kept off her good Scotch broth and her Irish griddle cakes, then I might have been a pale lank poet and too weak physically to prop up a lead pencil. But I never did, in fact I always asked for second helpings, and that was treading for sure the broad road that led to the damnation of the steel furnaces . . .

But not, thank heavens, to the cold-metal, hand-charging ones in the West of Scotland. Instead I emigrated across the border to England, to civilization, where I found the furnaces machine-charged and the cold iron replaced by hot liquid iron from the firm's own blast furnaces. I was in a modern integrated steel works where the eight-hour shift was in vogue, and that first day I liked very much what I saw there.

I'd no sooner stepped on a furnace than the melters concentrated on it in communal fashion, and I knew enough to realize that the steel would soon be tapped from it. The heavy hammers, two of them, were rising and falling in unison as they smashed the long iron bar up the taphole. Then the men who had wielded them stepped back as the metal sparkled from the furnace into the ladle waiting below.

There was drama in it, in the flowing steel, and in the noise, and in the blast furnaces away to the right where the hot iron was filling in the sand beds. Drama too in the nearby rolling mill where the strips of steel became longer and longer and faded slowly from a white glow to a dull red. Drama even in the tanned sweating melters, who I saw were at peace with themselves in the midst of all the confusion, and I liked that.

My job that day, and for many a day after, was furnace labouring. Chargewheeling we called it. I was the man who wheeled the charge to the furnace and although it was constant it was far from killing. Not like those furnaces in the West of Scotland, and besides I only had an eight-hour shift.

That eight-hour shift was humanity's breakthrough on steel-melting shops. A man could do his job like a man and walk off like a man, and still have energy left for his own devices. Like the machines it speeded up production but who cared about that, the speed-up made the place more exciting than ever.

I don't think that I was more than a week in that place before I knew that I would never leave steel. There was a something about it that was almost hereditary. It had thrilled my father under far harsher conditions, and although it still was nobody's paradise, it thrilled me. There were things that I hated, and the night work was one of them, but nothing drove me away.

All the years I was at it I never got used to night shifts, each succeeding one seemed more trying than the previous one, each one was a little lifetime on its own. The compensations came every morning as I walked down the melting shop on the way for home. I had a delightful feeling of liberty and relief, and I experienced it more when, on the main street, I strolled at my ease, past the silent hurrying day workers. I was a man of leisure, while they were the sleepy slaves.

Shift work, I always thought, was a lonely thing and a sort of sheltered existence. It was a silent coming and going, we slept while the rest of the world worked and we worked while the rest of the world slept. What social life we had was on the early morning weeks when our evenings were free. It always seemed ten chances against one that one would be on the wrong turn when anything exciting was happening. It was so enclosing that one could be aware of a day worker friend and yet not see him for months. I knew two men who met delightedly after thirty years' lapse. They were astonished to know that they had each worked on the steel works for more than twenty-five years and that they lived within a mile of each other.

I knew plenty of men on the furnaces who longed to be away from them and who went off in the end, but I never met anyone who hated the job. Some left reluctantly for health reasons; some left relievedly through incompatibility with a foreman, and some left because steel was getting into their blood. They wanted a working life with less limitations and they went off before they were hooked.

There were some whose talents would have paid off far more in other walks, but they stayed on contentedly. Those were the fellows I loved to meet and I think I was one with them. We talked intelligently on many subjects, but there on the melting shop steel was our first love. Yet few of us bothered about the technology of the craft – and it was a craft then – the few who did were usually devilish bores, men to be avoided, forever galumphing about something they had only half digested.

We were practical men, we gazed in our furnaces through our blue-glassed spectacles and we made sure the flame was doing its work and not threatening to burn the metal out around our feet. Sometimes we were too late, and then all hell was let loose as the white-hot liquid tore through the furnace bath burning all before it like a forest fire. My heavens, there was nothing lovely about steelmaking then, especially when the sweating men had to face an irate management that demanded nothing but perfection all the time.

The melting-shop managers were our only contact with the higher-ups, the rest were hardly a name to us. I knew some good managers there, and to respect them was a good thing for the steel one made. Then, some of one's own serenity seemed to enter the product, though I can't say that I ever heard of contented steel. But to know that a manager knew his job and that he respected one reciprocally was a good thing all round, good for the metal, good for the melter, and good for the manager. It created confidence, a most important quality, for good steelmaking was as much a frame of mind as it was a job of work.

I was twenty-three years on that melting shop before I became a first-hand melter, a man in charge of a furnace, and the goal all steelmen aimed at. There were many changes, and all for the better, in production methods and in working conditions. The furnaces had doubled in capacity, mine produced a near hundred tons each time it tapped, we had a new rolling mill that turned out rounds, joists, rails and the rest. We had a rod mill, the best in Europe, with a wire output large enough to fence the whole world, given a little extra time of course. We had canteens and changing rooms, and when we got the Second World War over we had showers and modern cabins by the furnaces. The old order of rough-clad working men going and coming on the streets gave way to neat dressed fellows, whose occupations had to be guessed at.

Though greatly improved on, the furnaces were still vulnerable, and steelmaking was still a chancy thing where the metal didn't always flow the right way up. There were still wet shirts and plenty of anxious moments for melters, and always the great satisfaction of seeing one's charge surging from the furnace to the ladle. Then the melters felt like sea captains who had brought their ships safely to port after a long stormy voyage.

It was that long voyage before each charge became steel that allowed me and my kind to exercise our skills and so to feel at home with our jobs.

On basic open-hearth furnaces the melter's craft is not in his hands but in his eyes. Through years of gazing in the white heat of furnaces he acquires a sort of secondary sight, as if his eyes have special compartments for the judging of furnace temperatures. Previous to the increased instrumentation on melting shops, the melter's eyes were almost his only guide to controlling heat. Nowadays he has much aid from precision instruments which take a great deal of strain and worry from him, but yet do not render his skills obsolete. It is as important as ever that a melter should know what's happening inside his furnace and what to do about it.

The great aid instrumentation gave me was to show me the safe temperature for steelmaking and to correct me when the temperature was too high or too low. At various intervals, especially during the refining periods on all the furnaces, the temperatures of the metal and slag were noted by a heat-recording machine. I was very grateful to it, and very subdued, for it also silently and unrecordedly reminded me of the thousands of times when my temperature control had been very poor. A good thing for me that my lack of skill had not been conspicuous by its absence, else I would have been permanently absent from the pay office window.

It was that inconsistency in heat control, for we were only human, that helped to make our steelmaking a hit or miss affair. Where sometimes we could produce a ladle full of beautiful steel within four hours from filling the furnace, there were other occasions when the same type of steel took seven or eight hours to produce. Even then the delay would go on, for the furnace bath which had taken a battering through too high temperatures, would need hours of maintenance before it was ready for the next charge to go in.

Other times the results of high temperatures were calamitous. A first-hand would aim for quick steel and take a gamble that nothing would stand in his way. Then all the mishaps of melting-shop life would pile up, cranes would break down, supplies of necessary lime or iron scalings, or even pig iron, would be held up, and the furnace and its team would be in deep trouble. The roof and linings of silica brick would drip into the bath. The bath, being a basic dolomite composition, would not take kindly to the acid silica and would start to give way. Then a huge shout would echo over the other noises in the shop, 'A breakaway.' Everyone would hurry to the stricken furnace and tap out the metal into the ladle which usually awaited below. Meanwhile the metal would still pour through the damaged part like hell's flames.

Such a happening was a poor finish to high hopes and even though much steel would be saved there was still the breakaway to disturb the unhappy first-hand. He, poor fellow, would feel like jumping into the fiery mass in his deep anxiety and mortification. It didn't help him when his team suggested that he should do just that, for they had the exhausting job of later clearing it all away.

Such a scene, distressing as it was to the melters, provided a thrilling spectacle to those not actively concerned; they even hoped for encores. It had its place in the *chiaroscuro* of melting-shop existence at the time and it helped to make the bright side positively glitter.

On cold, dark, winter mornings the melting shop itself was a glittering place. It stood out like a lighthouse, warm and inviting as we hurried along. Once there, and the taciturnity of too sudden awakenings and hurried arisings would fall from us and we would drink hot tea, the inevitable start to each day.

Each furnace was manned by four melters, a first-hand, second-hand, third-hand and a chargewheeler. The first hand was responsible for the welfare of the furnace and for what was in it. He was not a foreman in the ordinary sense, he didn't so much give orders as make decisions and his decisions were respected by his team, but only within the realm of the furnace.

The foremen proper had the overall charge of all the furnaces and were responsible for the tapping of all furnaces. They were traditionally known as sample passers and were invariably men of vast experience who had been skilled first-hands themselves.

No one ever asked me to become a sample passer though I was there long enough to be on nodding terms with Vulcan himself, and I thank heavens that I wasn't asked, and I took care that I didn't ask. It can be a limiting thing to a man's nature and outlook and I liked my melting-shop friends to keep walking towards me and not dodging round corners. When they were doing something not quite right I preferred to be a conspirator and not a policeman. Still I have nothing against sample passers, I knew some good ones.

I knew some good fellows among the melters, in fact I knew many, for mine was a friendly trade and it bred good men and it still does. It was the most common thing for the furnace teams to enjoy each other's company and when that was so the time went by on wheels. I had a particular three working with me for a long time and I was secretly sorry when they were promoted elsewhere. Apart from an odd flare-up when temperatures were an all-time, all-embracing high, we got on famously. Sometimes we talked trade-union matters, for the third-hand, Irish Jackie Rea, took an intelligent interest and attended the branch's meetings and reported back to Franko Arstall the second-hand, and little Harry Green the chargewheeler, who lived in Wigan twelve miles away, and me. We three went very seldom to the meetings except extraordinary ones.

Everyone on the furnaces and on the cranes serving the furnaces, and on the pitside where our steel was teemed into the moulds, were members of the Steel Trades Confederation. All the rest who trod the melting shop, maintenance bricklayers, fitters, electricians, were trade unionists too. Franko Arstall had been an industrial designer but had quit because steelmaking fascinated him. I was glad it did, for he was prodigiously and prodigally strong, and I benefited exceedingly when my strength was failing. Irish Jackie Rea was a strong fellow too and of an age with Arstall, about thirty-five, when they worked with me. He had a good voice and a good presence and made a lot of money on television and radio in Ireland as well as England. That he never tried full time was his wife's idea, she preferred his regular pay packet to the uncertainty of the theatrical profession. Jackie didn't mind for he liked a spot of steelmaking as well as the next man. He liked the big drink after it too, with Franko Arstall.

The two men were as proficient as I was in steelmaking and we used to go forward together to examine the furnace and the state of the charge inside it. Sometimes the furnace would be charged for a high-carbon steel, sometimes for a medium-carbon sort, and sometimes for mild low-carboned, low-sulphur steel. It was really repetitive in the sense that we had done it all so many times, but it always seemed fresh, always an adventure, and a pitting of wits against a furnace to which we often accorded human qualities, the worst ones especially.

Sometimes, if the furnace was newly charged up, we would gaze on the liquid iron busily surging round the still solid steel scrap and lower the door again with the realization that the refining stage was two hours or so away. For me there would be little to do in the meantime, but pile on the temperature and reverse the flame at regular intervals. For Franko and Irish Rea there would likely be furnaces to tap out, a communal affair along the long stretch of furnaces which were all at different stages of steelmaking and which were identified each one by a letter of the alphabet. They stretched in a line four hundred yards long from the A to the O, and silent and inanimate though they actually were, to the melters they were living and real.

An hour or two later and Rea, Arstall and me would again be giving the furnace plenty of looking at. This time the solid-steel scrap would be solid no longer and the whole charge of liquid metal, beneath its complete covering of slag, would be ready for the refining stage to commence. Irish Jackie would pick up a long-handled iron spoon, thrust it through the spy-hole in the furnace's middle door, pour its slight contents on the floor and examine it intently as it sparkled up. 'There's plenty carbon,' he would likely say, 'and sulphur to match it. Shall we open her out with iron scalings and top it up with spar all round her?' I would nod assent to anything like that and watch big Franko examining the roof and linings. His was a melter's automatic action from a long way back.

The charging machine would spread a box of iron scalings over the thick slag, and when it had well warmed in we would shovel fluorspar over it all and wait for the slag to open out and start boiling. What we were seeking was a metal that would absorb the heat of the hot flame and bubble its elements of sulphur and phosphorus into the slag. As they left the metal, we expected too that the carbon would reduce – that was why we put the iron scalings in – and that the manganese element would stay where it was long enough to help the sulphur to reduce.

Sulphur was a wayward element in our steelmaking and the only way to reduce it was to have a good fluid slag. In fact all our steelmaking depended on the way we controlled the slag. The two facts synchronized, good slag control and good temperature control was the only way to make good steel in the basic open-hearths. We achieved it daily and very often the result of it looked lovely as it bubbled away in the furnace bath. Still we all felt even happier as we watched it flow into the ladle. We knew then that we were getting a run for the money.

I always associate instrumentation on the melting shop with the time the gas-flamed furnaces went out, and the oil-flamed ones came in. That would be five or six years after the Second World War. It gave us our first control panels on the furnaces, they saved us much manual labour and were a big step towards precision steelmaking. It was pleasant to regulate the oil, steam and air flows by the touch of a button compared to the hauling we used to have on the old-time gas and air valves. It was just as pleasant to control the furnace draught, and to synchronize the regenerating chambers in the same effortless fashion. It saved a great deal of anxious labour when the oil burners replaced the old gas ports. The gas ports through which the flame entered the furnaces continually became unlevel with brick debris, which needed great exertion to dislodge. The oil burners on the other hand rarely went wrong and when they did the pipefitters soon replaced the old for a new one.

The design of the furnaces got better and better in our place and the silica brick type were replaced by an all-basic brick type, and what an improvement it made to safe steel-making. Between the basic brick furnace and instrumentation, the chancy steelmaking disappeared long before I quit the melting shop. What goes in an open-hearth furnace today, comes out safely and without great trouble and with a fairly accurate timetable.

I cannot remember even one period of bitterly conducted industrial dispute between the steelmen and the steel masters. We got little from them without fighting for it, but then we didn't expect to. There was plenty of good nature in our trade, and when we had a grievance we found sometimes that the steel masters were not without good nature too. It certainly would have disturbed my serenity to be in a bitter strike-ridden trade and I'm glad that I wasn't, and that I can look back with no bitterness at all.

My trade was a good trade and I left plenty of fellows on the melting shop who think the same as I do. The same fellows are hoping that the vast changes in steel production will not be cataclysmic for them, that the trade will still be interesting because it still will need their skill. I hope so too, for their sakes, very much so, but I wonder. The day of the open-hearth furnace, whose centenary is about 1977, I think, is closing in slowly but surely, and the industry will see the biggest transformation in its history long before the end of the century. The whole contours of steel melting shops as we know them today will go too, and I'm just a little sad about it. It is in the slowness of the open-hearth process that the melter finds the time to use his skill. How can he be skilful or why should his skill be needed when instant steelmaking gets going properly? I wish I knew the answer, but maybe it's better that I shouldn't.

In spite of all the uncertainty about their part in the future of the trade, the melters I know are tremendously interested in its vivid present. They don't bring the job home with them, and I didn't myself for long years before I quit it. They don't bring the look of it home either and I found those changing rooms quite a novelty too. Neither do they come along in the father and son tradition any more. A lot of that was sheer necessity, for lots of the steelwork towns had little else to offer. The Second World War and its ensuing prosperity did away with all that. There were plenty of jobs with better prospects than the long wait for promotion on the steel furnaces. They were better paid ones too. There were lots of young fellows who came on the melting shop, gave it a whirl and departed, it was not for them. Some of them lingered too long, they intended to go but steel got them first. They are still on the furnaces and they are not doing too badly. That is up to now.

As for me, the open-hearth furnaces served me well and I served them well, and I'm not sorry we met. They gave me the chance of a worthwhile working life in a tremendously interesting industry. That doesn't always happen to working men.

PATRICK MCGEOWN

THE AUTHOR

I was born in September 1897, in a place called Craigneuk in the West of Scotland. It was neither town nor country, just a district full of steel works, iron works and coal mines.

My parents were Irish from County Armagh, and my father was a steel furnaceman. I remember particularly noticing the steel works' huge slag tip, and my mother telling me dreamily that it was the Mountain of Mourne. I remember too my father laughing and saying, 'She means a mountain of mourning, it took oceans of sweat to put it there.'

I found out later that he was right, and before I left Scotland I helped to make it bigger still.

My first school was St Patrick's, a local Catholic elementary. After that I spent three years at a higher grade school in the town of Motherwell, one mile from home. When the First World War started I was under age, not quite seventeen, and not very brave. My classmates of the higher grade joined to a man, although not one of them had reached manhood proper. Only one came back, and he minus an arm. I shook the one he had left. 'It will do for the handouts,' he said wryly. He didn't need any, he became a prosperous businessman.

In England, and on the steel furnaces, I met a nice little girl. We agreed to marry when I had saved £20. After many fluctuations I managed £15. 'Let's marry now,' she said, 'we'll be past it before you get the other fiver.'

So we married and lived happy ever since. Once I heard her say of me, 'He's a simple chap, and harmless.' I could have told her that myself.

We have two children, both girls, and both grown up. The eldest, who is mentally retarded, is a happy little thing who lives at home and who loves the Beatles. The other is married to a television writer. They are a fine young couple and they have a fine baby, and I love just looking at all three.

In the spring, summer and autumn I cultivate an allotment. Sometimes when I'm digging my wife calls out, 'You should rest more often. You won't always be on top of the soil.' That makes me dig harder than ever, and only when she's gone do I straighten up. Then I tell myself thoughtfully, 'She's right you know,' and I lean on my spade for quite a long time.

On the Trawlers

Two or three of my pals were coming home from sea and talking about what a marvellous life it was in the Merchant Navy, and so I decided to give up school and go to sea. I knew somebody who was a chief steward on big boats, and I went through the usual routine: galley boy to assistant steward, assistant steward to second cook, and then I went cook of a big boat and eventually chief steward. From cargo ships I transferred to troopers and went all over the place, including the invasion of Sicily. At the end of the Second World War I sort of gave it all up and was at a loose end when one night I met somebody in the local who had just been demobbed from the navy. He asked what I was doing, and I said I had been thinking about going back to school to study maths and science; I wanted to be an industrial chemist, but when I went to see the rehabilitation officer all he would offer was £2 5s. a week. I couldn't live on that, so when this friend of mine said what about coming with him as cook for the trawler he was going on, I agreed.

I went on the dock with him the following day and there were two or three ships in. He took me along to the ship's runner and got me signed on. He told me to see about the food and brought out a list of what was put aboard for the crew of twenty-six; when I looked at it I thought to myself, what am I going to do with this amount of stores? Things were very tight in those days as far as rations were concerned, and we had been used on the big boats during the war to ordering as much meat as we liked when we went to the Argentine and America. When I started to ask about this and that, he said, 'Oh, we don't supply that sort of stuff. If you give good plain food they'll be quite satisfied.'

Hull, where I live, is the largest fishing port in Britain, but even so I'd never actually been aboard a trawler, so I couldn't tell at the time what it was really like. I went home after signing on and thought about getting my gear ready: whites and white coats, jackets and trousers, hat, that I'd worn when I was on the other type of ship. On the night before we were due to come away I asked mother to give me a shout at 3 a.m. and ordered a taxi for 3.30 to get me down to St Andrew's Dock. When my mother gave me a call I could hear the wind whistling outside and knew it was blowing a bit. The taxi-driver asked where the ship was laid and they told him No. 6 Ice chute, and there she was: the *Lord Stanhope*. She looked very very small to me, but smart. She had just been freshly painted up. I jumped aboard, there was no ladder or anything, and asked an old chap standing and watching on the deck where the cook's berth was. He took me down to the cabin which wasn't very big, but I still couldn't see the berth. Then he pulled open two sliding doors and showed me what looked just like a cupboard with boards, about 6 ft long and 4 ft wide. Well, I'm 6 ft 1 in. and at that time I weighed about 13 stone, so I thought I wasn't going to be too comfortable. I asked where the bed was and he said you had to supply your own from the stores on the dock. So I asked to see the galley. I had a shock when I saw it, it was just like a small kitchen at home, with a tiny coal stove and the sink not much bigger than a bucket and one small bench and a seat, and no more than 10 ft by 14 ft in all. It was clean, I'll give them that, but when I looked for the gear, the pots and pans they were strewn all over the place. I was used to shining enamel gear and these were all big dirty things. I didn't take much joy in that. I wanted to see the storeroom then and the old man said it was down below next to the cabin, so we went back down and found that everything had been more or less thrown into the place. There were one or two shelves but they were inadequate for the amount of stores, and everything was piled up. I checked the list and everything was there.

I thought then that I'd better unpack my gear and get it put away, and looked round for some drawers, but there weren't any; that was another thing that put me off straight away. I had to leave my things in the two cases I'd brought. Then I went ashore and got a bed which was about 5½ ft long,

3 ft wide and made of straw, what we call a donkey biscuit, which gets damned hard after you've lain on it for a while. Soon the chap I knew, who was the mate, came on board and the rest of the crew followed. The engineers first, they were a mixed bag, one or two straight out of the service who had been trawling before the war, and some new chaps. To look at them there were some real hard cases, but that's another story. Anyway, everybody got down and the skipper rang the telegraph and told them to cast off forward and aft and took us as far as the lock pit. We went out in the Humber and it was blowing and there was a bit of a mist over the river. We'd been going about an hour and a half when all of a sudden there was a jarring sound and we listed over to port. We were on a sandbank. We had to stop the engines because the intake for the water was sucking the sand up. After radioing what had happened a coaster came to give us a tow and the tide slung him and he also got on the sandbank. We both had to wait for the following tide to get us off. The boys had brought a few bottles with them and decided to have a party; it developed into a bit more than a party, there was a fight and one of the chaps got his head very badly split open, whereupon six of the crew demanded to be put ashore. All the time I was thinking to myself, well, this is really good, because we didn't see a lot of this sort of thing on the big boats.

When the six replacements came aboard and the tide changed we eventually got off. As soon as we left the mouth of the Humber she started to roll. I got a meal ready which went all right, but when we got into the North Sea everything started sliding about and the battens supplied to jam your pans on the top of the galley stove were insufficient; I had to get some string to tie them down. It's a wonder that ships of this class don't really get swamped because, the way they roll when the weather is bad, the top of the rail goes under the water and just scoops the sea aboard. The galley was swamped on that trip by a sea that came over the boat deck and through the skylight, and it even washed a couple of pans out of the galley. That was how deep the water was, because most of the time the drain holes aren't large enough to clear the water away and we have to use buckets.

When we got well into the North Sea we started to play cards and talk about the ship and the length of voyage. As a rule trawlers are gone about three weeks, five days running to the fishing grounds, ten days actual fishing and the rest steaming back home again. On this particular trip we were about twenty-seven days, due mainly to the weather conditions and the foul work. While we were talking the mate came down and told me the old man wanted me in the chart room. I went up on the bridge, thinking naturally that the skipper was the same as the captain of a big boat, but I was wrong there. He was a down-to-earth sort of chap and quite a character. He asked me about my war service and said he was glad to be back fishing again so he could earn some cash; he'd been one of the top skippers before the war. Anyway, after a lot of talk he said that when we started fishing I could give a hand on deck as soon as I had finished in the galley.

We got to the fishing ground after a rough passage, and for the first twenty-four hours I've never seen anything like it in my life. I had hardly ever visualized fish in the quantity in which we were getting it. We were just scooping the cod aboard by the ton. My day usually starts about 4.30 or 5 to get breakfast at 6, dinner is at 12 and tea at 6 p.m. As soon as I got everything finished and squared round, they rigged me out in sea boots, frock and sou'wester, and on deck I went. I was up to my eyes in fish, hundreds and thousands of fish. We gutted them first in the pens on deck, then headed them and washed them all with a hose before they went down the chute to the fish room. The weather was good for the moment, and the ship was steady and what with the fish and the shooting and hauling of the gear and all the activity, it was quite interesting. Time passed quickly. After four or five days a north-easterly started to blow and soon it was freezing – freezing very hard, at least 10 degrees below. Of course, fishing didn't stop, the deckies went on gutting fish on deck eighteen hours a day, though it was blowing about force 7 and there was plenty of water coming over. I was still giving them a hand, and I'd learnt to be useful with the gear, helping hauling in the nets and the different wires for heaving fish up. I was helping bring a bag of fish aboard, pushing a block over the wing bobbins to get it forward from amidships so that the bag wouldn't fall on the men, and instead of using the palm of my hand with my fingers on the outer edge of the block, I got hold of it with my whole hand. Just then the ship rolled and the wires and block came tight with the bag of fish and two of my fingers were in between the block and the wing bobbins. It was so cold, and I was wearing thick woollen mittens, that I didn't really feel any pain at all – just a slight pain, nothing more. The ship rolled back, releasing the block, and I pulled my hand away. I stepped back, pulled my glove off and my fingers were just sort of hanging. I couldn't move them. They were bleeding a bit but not a lot. I went up on the bridge and told the old man and he said I'd broken them. My fingers were still so numb I couldn't really feel them, but as soon as my hand started warming up a bit I knew all about it. They strapped them up and put a couple of splints on and I didn't go on deck again after that. After the trip I learnt that it wasn't my job to go on deck, but the skipper had just more or less told me that to get another willing hand.

I don't know how I managed to last out with the food because we were gone nearly a week longer than usual. When we got home the catch made £7,000. At that time my basic rate of pay was £5 10s. a week, plus 1½d. per £ of fish. After deductions and paying for my gear, I think I cleared about £20 over my basic pay which in those days was a lot of money. I was quite satisfied.

I stayed with my friend the mate for over three years on different ships. I was on the *Colwyn Bay* when, coming into Hull, the skipper said he had some bad news for me. I thought I'd got the sack because the slightest thing, your face that doesn't fit or something you've done wrong, will get you the sack and that's it. But he said my mother had died a week ago while we were away. Apparently they all knew aboard the ship but there wasn't one of them told me.

So I stopped home for a voyage. When I went back the skipper was having a trip off and the mate took it. It was one of the worst trips I've ever done as far as conditions were concerned. We hit black frost for a start. It is a mist over the water, hanging like steam, and anything it touches freezes instantly. I've seen fish coming over the side and frozen in a couple of minutes; if you put your fingers on to metal, any metal at all, the skin will be brought right off. Two of the chaps got frostbite, one on his toes, and we had to get them patched up as best as possible. Then it started to blow and the waves coming aboard iced the ship up. With the weight of ice she started listing and each time the spray hit the side it froze and collected, adding to the list. We had to stop fishing and lay to and chop ice. No sooner had we chopped it than the spray froze up again and we had to start chopping again. The ship was listing over badly and we tried to steam out of the frost, but it seemed to follow us; the men were working as long as they could chopping because it looked as though she was in danger of turning turtle. At last we managed to limp into Norway and even then you couldn't stand up straight, the ship was listing at such an angle. We used steam hoses to get the ice off. Instead of going out fishing again we went back home, where the firm was having a new ship built. The owners gave us five weeks off on pay while we waited for the new ship; it was a very good firm, you could talk to the owners and they would try to rectify faults, which was something that the majority of owners wouldn't do, never mind help you with anything.

I had my second accident a few years later. We were coming home in bad weather and I had a pan of semolina pudding on the top of the stove and it was boiling hot. It was a new ship built with two bulbs on the bow to increase speed and stability. When the weather is bad these ships have the habit of riding up the wave and then slapping down on it. Then the ship's stern jumps out of the water and it's very bad to keep things down on the benches or stove. I was in front of the stove when she did one of these belly-flops. She lifted her stern out of the water and the pan of boiling semolina got me. I was badly burnt on the chest and neck. We were steaming down the North Sea and the skipper belted her on and we eventually got to Grimsby where I spent a fortnight in hospital. It set me back a bit and I had quite a spell ashore, working for nearly a year as a Hoover maintenance engineer. But I decided to go back to sea, signing on with a skipper whose next trip ended in disaster; his ship, the *Norman*, ran on to a rock that we now call the Norman rock off Greenland and was lost with a lot of the crew. It was trawling's biggest disaster since the *Lorella* and *Rodrigo* were lost off Iceland in black frost and ice. The other ships could hear them talking on the air but couldn't get anywhere near them; each time they tried they started to ice up and had to get out of it. All hands were lost.

Eventually I went into a ship called the *Somerset Maugham*. She is more or less of a legend as far as fishing is concerned. A marvellous ship. I did two trips with a Norwegian skipper called Stipetic in her and they were both fabulous; he is the finest coast fisherman I have met anywhere. The first trip netted £12,000 and the next £13,000 – and then came the strike over foreign landings. The skippers came out because foreign landings of fish were cramping British markets, and some of our fish was being left on the market, which lowered our earnings considerably. This had been going on for quite a long time, but the skippers' action was stupid: they tried to book the Government, and you can't do that. Our union, the Transport and General, told us to have nothing to do with the strike and to go to sea if we were told to. So when the owners offered the mate the command – he had a skipper's ticket but had never had a ship to himself – and he asked the crew whether they would sail with him, we agreed. It was a success from the start. We went away to the Norwegian coast and made a fabulous trip; every trip after that was fabulous. We kept coming home and just topping the markets, in other words being the biggest catch and the most money. In the Silver Cod trophy for the highest annual catches, we were fourth the first year, first the second, second for the next two years, and first again the following two. Some of the luck and fame of Somerset Maugham himself seemed to have rubbed onto this ship; but as much, if not more, depended on the skipper's ability and skill. The trophy is for one man and one man alone, and that is the skipper. The prestige goes to him and so do the perks. He gets 10 per cent of net profits after expenses of the trip have been deducted. But not much is said about the crew – and the crew of that ship, and any that lands a quantity of fish, really have to work. Preparing the nets and getting everything ready for fishing operations; and when they get down to the fishing grounds it's roughly eighteen hours a day, and that irrespective of conditions. When a man has been working eighteen hours a day for ten or twelve days his actions become mechanical, he's more or less a robot. Admittedly the money is good for all hands if you forget the hours worked and the danger involved. On an average three-week trip, the crew works about 270 hours per man – 90 hours a week, for a basic wage of just over £12 a week. On a *good* trawler it's sometimes possible to make this up to £25 a week by the payment on the catch, but even so the hourly wage comes down to only 5s. 6d. If wages were compared to industry on shore – 40 hours on basic pay, then time-and-a-quarter, time-and-a-half, double-time – then the fisherman's basic rate of pay comes down to as low as 3s. 6d. an hour. And the death rate is twice as high as in coal-mining: over 9 per 10,000 employed a year on average since the Second World War.

On the *Somerset Maugham* even the engineers when they'd finished would go down to the fish room or up on deck and give a hand gutting and stowing the fish away. Often by the time I'd done my turn stowing it would be about midnight. By the time I'd got washed and had a drink of tea it was perhaps 1 o'clock before I turned in. By 4.30 I was up again. I was putting in as many hours as the crew, perhaps more. It was all hell and no notion. And though it was a success story from the start, it wasn't all success. There was one particular trip we went to Bear Island and the fishing was very prolific: we got 4,700 kit of fish, which is 10 stone to a kit. When we got home it was put on the market, there were quite a few ships in, and the buyers said most of our catch was too small for them. About 2,800 kit went to fish meal and all we made was £6,000. It was all good fish but a bit small. But ships running for the Silver Cod trophy by and large don't care about quality; it's quantity they're after because the skippers know the more fish they land the better chance they have of winning.

But there was one thing about the *Somerset Maugham*: we really used to run for home whatever the weather. There was one trip when we had to get home by 28 December to qualify the whole catch for the trophy, and it was Christmas before we left the fishing grounds. I got the Christmas dinner ready as best I could in the foul weather we were having as we belted home through everything, when the ship gave a bounce and a roll and a lurch all in one and away went the dinner. After I'd been doing turkeys and chickens and pork, the usual veg and soup and sweet, coffee and biscuits, cheese and cakes, the thought that went through my head can be imagined. I tried to salvage what I could but the same thing happened again. It was like a stew by the time we'd finished. We managed to get into Hull all right, but we missed the end of the year and the trophy by 37 kit; a part of our catch was credited to the new year because we arrived over the date.

A lot of people have said that a fisherman's life isn't hard but monotonous, but those people, the few who've been aboard trawlers and written about them, don't really realize what fishermen go through. There's not only the really hard work and the weather, there's the lack of sleep and the lack of time even to have proper meals. Men become robots, they just do their job automatically. Some of the things they have to put up with aboard trawlers are, if not beyond human endurance, practically up to that level. Often wet through, having to get changed, coming back out onto the deck and getting wet again in cold as intense as 20 degrees below zero, away from home three weeks at a stretch, with a turn-round of three days or less between trips, cooped up in a small area, on call in case of danger twenty-four hours a day. . . . Conditions that I don't suppose any man working ashore would stand, or if he did he'd certainly be getting a lot more money than fishermen.

I spent over five years on the *Somerset Maugham*, and the reward was pretty good. I bought a house and a car, and I don't owe anybody any money, and I've got a bit saved up. People often ask me how I manage, being a cook, but my wife works and she helps swell the kitty. She makes some of her own clothes, she does all her own decorating, and she looks after the house very well. I don't drink a lot, I don't gamble and so, between us, we can manage.

Still, after that long on one ship I thought it was time for a change. Since the *Somerset Maugham*, there have been practically no more conventional 'side-winder' trawlers built. Now every firm on the dock has gone in for the bigger type of ship – the freezers. These fish from the stern of the ship and they have a bigger catching power, carry more fish and stay away longer, from six to eight weeks. I was dubious about going on them because I don't like being away from home if I can help it; three weeks is long enough for me. But when I was offered a brand new freezer called the *Marbella*, which was fitting out and doing trials, I joined her. The difference between the two types of trawler is fantastic. In the galley everything is electric, a really large electric stove, two big ovens, an electric potato peeler, mixer, water heater. There are automatic dumpers, as we call them, which swill waste away instead of the buckets we used to dump over the side, and I had a second cook. On the conventional trawlers a few years after the Second World War they started putting 20 or 21 men on board instead of the previous 26, but on the freezers the complement is back up to the old figure, but with all this equipment there was no difficulty in catering for the extra men.

Everything on board the *Marbella* was really modern; the berth was good, with a spring mattress, table, drawers and everything you could want. The gear was excellent, with all the pots and pans of stainless steel. It was a fantastic change from my first ship just after the war.

We went off to Greenland; the fishing was very slack and

we sailed to Newfoundland. We'd been gone about three weeks and still had only caught about 100 of the 600 tons these freezers can hold when something went wrong with the engines and we had to put into St Johns. I rang my wife and told her we'd be away a long time because we still had another 500 tons to catch. But in three weeks, once the repairs had been done, we were coming home with a record 627 tons, the largest quantity any ship out of Britain had ever handled. The fish just seemed to be there and we all dug in to help bring it in. Within about three hours of being caught, the fish is frozen into solid blocks weighing about 120 lb. each in the ship's freezers.

But for all that cold in one part of the ship and all the modernization, there was one problem they hadn't solved: the heat in the galley went up to 90 degrees. When we got home the owners said they would have a look at it. On the next trip a week later, I've never worked in such bad conditions: I recorded temperatures of up to 120 degrees in the galley. Even the berths were 80 to 90 degrees – we were all two decks, and some three, below the bridge, and it didn't seem as though we could get the heat out. I dropped nearly a stone in weight, and that was enough for me. Though we had another record trip I left her for a trip on a side winder, and one of the older ones at that. In comparison the conditions were so poor that I knew I'd have to go back on to freezers. I signed on the *Sir Fred Parks* and we went to Newfoundland again.

Freezers are capable of going to these distant grounds. The nearer grounds such as Bear Island, the White Sea and Iceland are getting over-fished. This is why these bigger ships are being built. The Bear Island and White Sea grounds are soon going to be like the North Sea – there won't be any fish left. The fish haven't time to breed because they go to the Norwegian coast to spawn and they're caught on their way there. It's time some of our freezers started searching for fish round the African coast, as the Germans and Russians do. Britain used to be at the top of the fishing league at one time; before the war in 1938 over a million tons were landed, but in 1965 this was down to about 780,000 tons; we're getting close to the bottom of the league now.

There were 31 men on board the *Sir Fred Parks*, because about 30 tons of fish were filleted on board, and this needed more men. On Christmas Eve I was working in the galley until midnight; when I was woken the next morning at 4.30 they said we were steaming to a ship in trouble. It was the *St Finbarr*, which made news when she caught fire and 12 of the crew were lost. We got to her, but we couldn't get close to her; the waves were 20 to 30 feet high. I don't think people who haven't seen it can imagine what it's like to see a ship on fire, especially when all you can do is go round and round without being able to help. There were four men on the stern, the skipper, a mate and a couple of lads; we managed to shoot a line from a rocket gun across to her and passed some warm clothing over, but that was all we could do. While I was aboard the *Somerset Maugham* I had sort of chummed up with the wireless operator, Tommy Gray; now I heard he'd been on the *St Finbarr*, and as he was trying to get off the ship he had jumped down and missed the life raft and gone into the water. It was freezing and poor old Tom went. I think that was the biggest shock I'd had for a long time, watching the ship burning and knowing that he'd gone. Tears came to my eyes and I just couldn't stop them, and I'm not really a very sentimental sort of chap.

After we had circled her all Christmas Day the sea eased a bit, and one of the other four ships managed to get a line to her to tow her to port, though she was still burning very badly. They also managed to get the four men off the stern. But about forty miles off land she went down. I think it's a good thing she did, because to get a ship like that into port and then have to start going through the routine of finding out what went wrong, with 12 men burnt to death, somehow isn't right. It may seem heartless, but I think it's better that way.

We were gone nine weeks in all, and things weren't so good aboard the freezer. There was a lot of arguing and quarrelling. But after that length of time and all we'd gone through, it was to be expected. Some chaps can stand being cooped up and seeing the same people day after day; but others can't and they have to have some outlet, and if it comes in disputes it's got to be understood.

Fishermen are tough – they've got to be, otherwise they wouldn't be able to carry on and work the way they do. A man working ashore leaves home in the morning, goes to work, has his regular break, then goes home to his family. He may go out for a pint or a game of cricket or soccer. He has his outlets, he has a bed that's soft, there's no rolling about, he gets his sleep. But a fisherman has got to turn into a bunk, and if it's rolling he doesn't get a solid sleep and is often woken up and even thrown out of his bed by the rough seas. Fishermen are often condemned for their roughness, and I think it's wrong. You hear of chaps coming home and going out to a pub and spending £10 or £20. But they've been away three weeks or more without an outlet, and if people just tried to visualize what they've gone through to bring in the fish on their tables, I think they would have second thoughts about condemning them.

Fishermen are made rough by what they go through. You can't put up with what they have to put up with and be entirely different. There are chaps that do it. I – but then I am a cook. There are hazards in my conditions as there are for the rest of the crew, but not like those facing the deck hands. When, after that first experience on deck, I was asked to go up again, I said no, it wasn't for me. I said, the men on deck were just a bunch of idiots, those were my exact words. I mean, no man in his normal senses would go on the deck for the amount of money they were getting then, and I mean I wouldn't go now either. I couldn't stand it, and there are a lot of people ashore who couldn't stand it any more than me.

And when a fisherman spends a lot of money, it's not on himself but on other people. All the time he's got money in his pocket he has a lot of friends, or hangers-on. If some of those who are so ready to criticize the fisherman had to work as hard as he does, putting an hour into an hour and doing a full day's work for what I should say isn't a fair day's pay,

Britain would be in a better position than she is today. It's time these conditions were altered, freeze or no freeze, because 3s. 6d. an hour for a 90-hour week under the terrible conditions they work in, where you don't stop just because it's raining or you're wet, where you have to be a jack-of-all-trades, a mechanic as well as a fisherman, and where you're on call not eight but twenty-four hours a day is, by anyone's reckoning, an unfair wage.

Some fishermen are very foolish, I'd agree. They don't think about the future. They come home and spend their money, not on themselves but giving it away, throwing it away on others. They think only of the present, and that's understandable if the small amount of time they have ashore is taken into account. They have been made the way they are. And a lot of them hate the job. Who wouldn't? You hear them talking about getting jobs ashore, but until they get older, into their forties and fifties, I don't think many men could take a shore job, because once you've been to sea for any length of time it gets into your blood. It's something I can't explain. I hate my job at times, I really curse it, talk about working ashore, and yet I know I couldn't stick it. The people ashore are of a different stamp, a different stamp altogether.

They say the fishing industry isn't paying its way. The government are pouring millions of pounds into the industry, millions of pounds of public money. Yet the trawler owners go on saying they are losing money – what is certain is that the government is losing money and that means we're losing it. It's a failing industry then, but I notice the trawler owners still run their Rolls-Royces and Jaguars. I notice that they hold very big parties and have very big houses and to me they don't seem to be short of money. They don't seem to be losing at all, but there you are, they say they are and who am I to dispute what they think or what they say they think? But it always amazes me that when old trawlers in Hull are got rid of at last because they're no longer economical, they aren't scrapped but sent to one of the smaller ports. Ships ten and twenty years old, into which money is going to have to be poured, ships which are only good for the fishing grounds round our shores which are soon to be left without any fish. Why don't they scrap them and build bigger trawlers capable of going farther afield? It would pay them in the long run because I don't for one minute think that freezers are losing money. In fact I'm certain they aren't. And moreover the fisherman is getting less of a bonus per kit on the freezers than for fresh fish: about £2 15s. instead of £3 15s. This means that for every hundred tons of fish, I make about £31 over my basic wage of £13 7s. 9d. a week. The average freezer's catch is 400 tons, so I may earn about £120 in bonus; this brings my average weekly wage to about £30. But for this I work fourteen to fifteen hours a day.

If the fisherman is not making anything out of it, somebody is. Where is it going? The owners are always complaining about the running costs of the trawler, but the German and Russian fleets that have been built up since the war have ships so large you could get some of our freezers on to their boat decks. And they have practically double the number of men. Our crews are always at a minimum – if someone is ill someone else has more or less got to take on his job, with all the strain that means.

It isn't the number of men that is costing money, it's the way the industry is being run. Bigger trawlers, bigger freezers with larger crews to go to more distant grounds would pay the owners far better than sticking to smallness. As I pointed out earlier, there isn't at the time of writing a single British trawler which has been to any other coast apart from Newfoundland and Greenland.

People on the Hull Fish dock are always talking about the reduction in catching power, and yet when one firm's ship finds fish it's not as though he tells all the other ships of other firms. All you can hear on the wireless is stacks of code flying about. What is needed is common catching power, by which everyone including the public will benefit. Because now, when fish is plentiful, prices to the general public stay much the same for a matter of a few pennies. I have seen fish go across the road for fertilizer because the merchants weren't buying it. Why not put it on the market and let the public have it cheaper? It is high time the industry was reorganized because, if everybody is losing as things are now, then money is just being poured down the drain.

Recently something has been done to try to cut down the death and accident rate. Some of the deaths are the result of the sea's natural dangers and nothing can be done about them. But many are caused by exposed winches and wheels, by wires lying about, by low railings – by things that have remained the same since well before the Second World War. But the boffins and experts trying to find better ways of safeguarding the fisherman in his job don't seem to want to talk to him and find out what ideas he may have. There are some things that the 'ignorant' fisherman who has spent years at sea might be able to suggest that perhaps the experts and show people might not think of. In any case, the Norwegian death rate of fishermen is a third lower than Britain's, and there, by law, winches have to be protected and railings must be of a certain height.

Apart from deaths, the accident and sickness rate is shocking; maimed hands, loss of fingers; but excessive fatigue, as a recent study by the Royal Society of Medicine shows, makes fishermen especially vulnerable to diseases of the circulatory system and of the brain, and malignant diseases such as cancer of the lung and stomach. Fishermen run greater risks of getting these diseases than any other workers in Britain. And as newer ships stay at sea for longer periods the dangers of these diseases are likely to increase.

I am only a cook, but it grieves me to think that men's lives have to be lost or endangered needlessly in these ways, by people not bothering or big-headedness or just stupidity. But somebody somewhere needs shaking up, and it isn't the fisherman, because he is doing his part when he goes to sea. It's certainly someone ashore, lacking organization, lacking interest. All the trawler owners seem to think about is getting their ships away to sea, and having them come back with good and profitable catches, irrespective of some of the things that are going to happen – or are already happening – aboard.

PETER MARTIN

THE AUTHOR

I was born in Grimsby in 1924, but my parents moved to Hull six months later. My father was a clerk with the LNER for fifty-two years.

From elementary school I passed my scholarship to a secondary school in Hull. I played football and cricket for both schools, and also several games for the Hull Amateurs.

At the outbreak of war in 1939 I left school against my parents' wishes and joined the Merchant Navy as a galley boy, ending up as a chief steward.

My only connexion with the fishing industry was an uncle who had been a trawler owner, but had retired fifteen years before I first went to sea. When I look back on more than twenty years on trawlers I can't help being angered that, for the benefit of the country, men are allowed to go to sea to be injured and killed without any thought being given to their welfare. To make the so-called ignorant fisherman's life easier and safer, we need all the help we can get.

A few years after starting on trawlers I married a girl whom I had been to school with. We have a daughter of sixteen who has just left school and is a copy typist. I am very proud of her. She did well both at studies and sport.

In my own spare time, which is not very much, I like to play chess and go angling.

The Machine-Minder

At the employment exchange the interviewer produced the card. Machine-minding, long hours, night work. The factory runs twenty-four hours a day, seven days a week. Operatives do twelve-hour shifts, six shifts a week – a seventy-two-hour working week. The pay is 5s. 6d. an hour rising to 6s. maximum, double-time between 8 p.m. Saturday and 8 a.m. Monday. 'It's a question of staying on your feet . . .'

Envisaging some super-efficient concern where I could earn £19 – £28 a week – big money for Brighton – I went out to CBR Jersey Mills. After years of studying, I needed a temporary job and wanted to work in a factory rather than an office or shop. So many people spend their whole working lives in factories that I was interested in finding out what it was like. It seemed simple, a good enough reason at the time. A year later, as I write this in August 1967, a lot of my time is spent on a picket line *outside* the factory with fifteen others who joined a union.

But they were keen enough then to take me on. 'You can tear my hair out if he doesn't make a good operator,' a woman-director who interviewed me said. And to me: 'Don't tell them you've been to Oxford.' Filling out my form, the factory manager asked with surprise where Middlesex was.

In the knitting room where I was to spend the next seven months, twenty tall, green, circular machines stood in four rows, their half-dozen operatives listlessly eyeing me in my suit. The first day I enjoyed. I looked and felt happy. I had a place in the world, was part of production. It was my first factory job.

I was shown how to put a cone up and how to stop the machine when a cone had almost run out. The cones holding the yarn are at the top of the machine, the knitting process in the middle and the fabric accumulates in a roll at the bottom. The fabric has to be watched for faults. If a thread of yarn comes out of the needles, a line of holes is left in the fabric, a 'press-off'. These are often the operatives' errors in letting a cone run out, or in not adjusting the thread. Another fault is a 'needle', a ladder-line left by a broken needle.

I was put under George who had been there only a fortnight himself. Why was there no training scheme for trainees? I asked. 'They don't stay long enough to make it worthwhile,' one of the managers replied. Why weren't there enough sticks for putting the yarn up with? They got broken and weren't replaced. . . . I asked lots of questions about the machines at first, but often I didn't get replies. To learn, you had to find someone who would talk, and information was usually imparted in dribs and drabs, secretly. You learnt by making mistakes. If you made too many, you got the sack.

Watching the cones, checking the fabric, attending the machines which constantly break down, you're on the go all the time. If a machine stops, it must be started, and when it is going the cones are running out and have to be replaced. Hour after hour without break, from one machine to another and back, putting up ends, changing cones, starting the machines and trying to watch the fabric. The machines aren't designed for the operator. You bend low to see the fabric, and climb up on the machine to reach the arms holding the thread. To see all the cones you have to walk twenty-five feet round. Usually an operative has three machines with a total of 150 cones – many of which you can't see immediately because they're on the other side of the machines; you have to memorize which cones are going to run out. With bad yarn the machines snag constantly; it's gruelling keeping everything running.

I did what I was told. The others watched me. We were in the same room for twelve hours and little could be hidden. I stopped 'hiding myself'. At the rate of twelve hours a day I became a machine-minder.

Hey, the machine's stopped. A top red light? Find a stick, disentangle the thread – break off the balled-up yarn, put the end up, check the thread is not caught, press the button, throw the handle. Peer at the fabric – needles? lines from tight yarn? Feel the yarn as it runs, alter the tension; we're not supposed to, it's the supervisor's job but he's too busy. Change a tight cone. A red light above droppers – cone run out? press-off? A yellow light – the stop motion has come up, maybe something is out of position on the needles, a build-up of thread or a broken needle. Clear the build-up, change the needle, start the machine again. And the other machines, are they all right? One of them stops every other minute on average. Can't spend more than thirty seconds looking at one, leave it for the two others, make sure they're all right, come back to the first. May take five or ten minutes to clear. By the time the trouble's clear, another one's stopped. Break off the bad yarn, disentangle the cone, restart the machine – a few seconds later do the same again. . . . Repetitive little tasks too expensive for any machine to do, but cheap enough for underpaid labour. Machine-minding goes with semi-automation.

Many trainees lasted only a few days. After a fortnight, I thought of getting out. But I stayed on, wanting to find out more about the other operatives, the factory, how it worked and why. After a fortnight you suppress the hours and the repetitiveness. One of the operatives says, 'People go benuttered here often, then they become sane again. One has to be a bit benuttered here to start with.' After a few months you can relax with the machines. You maintain them and do jobs you're not paid to do but which vary the monotony. Change needles, which means undoing part of the machine, discovering which needle is bent or broken, finding the right type to replace it; you should call the supervisor, but he's over-worked, and it's quicker and more interesting to do it yourself. Checking the oil level, cutting off the finished roll, altering the tension. . . . Life is a lot easier if the machines are working well.

We're not paid to think, in theory that is. We're machine-minders, not operatives; that's why the pay is so low, that's why we work seventy-two hours a week. But in fact we have to think; the supervisor expects us to, he hasn't time to do all the jobs for which we're not paid. The firm has no mechanics as such; if we worked to rule, did just what we're supposed to, the place would come to a standstill. Whatever they say, it requires an operative's skill and interest to keep the place running.

The machines can appeal – the ever-running threads, the delicate three thousand turning needles, the effects traced in the fabric. The machine dominates your eyes and body. The inner mechanics are mysterious, for we don't know the technology. A manager remarked: 'Nobody told me anything either. I had to learn it bit by bit. Do you think I'm going to tell anyone?'

The machines work 168 hours a week, more than we can. When we come back from sleep, these totem monsters are standing in the workroom, still running. We machine-minders re-enter their territory.

On days supervision is close. 'The place feels bad, like as if there was barbed wire, you know.' You can't sit down. 'Get off your fucking arse.' There are no proper seating arrangements. All one can sit on are boxes of yarn – and this could damage the yarn. You think forwards to the tea-breaks at 10 and 4 and the half-hour lunch break. There's no canteen. In the last four hours there's no break. Acutest boredom is between 5 and 6, waiting for the management to go, with a couple more hours still to last out. Before 8, mark up the card, put a coloured thread in for the end of the roll. Each machine costs about £10,000, so there's £200,000 worth of equipment in here. Each machine can make about two rolls, each of 40 yards, every twelve-hour shift. Each shift's production must be worth somewhere between £750 and £900, I estimate; our wages per shift don't reach £20 in all. It's a capital-intensive plant: CBR made a profit of £97,000 in the last full financial year, ending October, 1966, more than 50 per cent up on the previous year. Dividends totalled 24 per cent. Why are the wages so low then? We go off, the night-men clock in, hello. Clock out.

On Saturday the management leaves at 1 p.m. The factory goes on. The management is proud of the plant's working seven days a week, but they're not there. It's nice to be served by others' efforts, especially when they work all Saturday on single time until 8 p.m.

I preferred nights. After 8 p.m. you measure the night's task, get the boxes of cones, find a seat and rig the machines. There's more time, and some play cards or bet on horses or on the weight of a roll. It's easier to talk when the management's gone, there's more cooperation among us. We take over each others' machines, the supervisor takes breaks himself. If one of us is tired, he may be let off easily by his mates. For the hour's break, we sleep an hour and a half on bales in the lift. Sometimes I manage to read and make notes – George thinks I'm a company spy. The bright workroom is stuporous, the machines spin, the operatives are collapsed, and outside the night is black. I begin to find out a bit about the others, not talking openly but just asking what they think about the place and why they stay. Often they come out spontaneously: 'Something ought to be done about it. I don't want to stay here much longer.' At half past four the milkman rings. The chaps drink a lot of milk, perhaps they feel the need for nourishment. An hour later someone goes for the papers. At 7, we put the colours in to mark the end of the rolls; it takes twenty minutes to come round. Sweep up, wash up. 'When you're ready, Mark,' to get him to come and cut off the rolls. The supervisor books the roll, weighs and bags. All respectable. The women clock in, the managers arrive. The card clock jumps to 0800. Out.

I get to my room at 8.20 and make myself something to eat. After that I've got about three-quarters of an hour free before going to bed. A seventeen-year-old machine-minder complains that he's got only two hours a day for play and he's too tired for it. Those who have children hardly see them on days. There is nothing else besides work. Before you've had time to recover, you're walking back. The hissing noise of the machines means another claustrophobic twelve hours. Life is a path round the machine, out the door; bed and back. One might stand it for a few weeks. Is it the way to spend a life?

After a month I wondered if there was anything I could do.

I wanted to see if there could be a counter-vailing power. I wrote to the TUC asking to be put in touch with a union. They gave me the wrong one, but finally I got in contact with the National Union of Hosiery and Knitwear Workers. The rates of pay at CBR turned out to be about half the rates under the national union agreement. A forty-hour week is standard elsewhere. I hadn't been aware of this, nor were any of the other operatives. The factory is isolated from others of its type which are mainly in the Midlands, and no direct comparison had been possible. Then some mechanics came down from Leicester to overhaul the machines and the word got round that knitters there were paid 10s. an hour or more. Got around, and then was forgotten; but a residue remained, though no one did anything. 'They're like sheep,' Chick said, 'they won't do anything, they'll just leave the job.' Passive rebellion was the commonest state. One young man, humping boxes in the basement, declared, 'This is where revolutions start.' But nothing happened.

Working seventy-two hours a week, it was impossible to see anyone outside work. You seldom had a day or a night off at the same time as another. As soon as 8 o'clock comes, we were often too self-concerned even to say 'See you'. What could be done when everyone seemed isolated? We dragged on. You can't do a job perfectly that many hours a week. 'The yarn keeps breaking, we have to fix the machines ourselves. They expect perfect operatives for 5s. 6d. an hour,' Chick said. The perfect operative, as everywhere in industry, kept by his machines the whole time, kept constant watch on the work, didn't spend a second thinking of anything else. A temporary halo fell on me. The management, not surprisingly, liked operatives who showed some intelligence; it isn't a job for the ham-fisted. They probably thought I was stupid to be working there, but if that's what I wanted. . . . If I hadn't been thinking about the objective situation and what could be done, I would probably have gone mad. On one of my days off I arranged to meet a union official at Victoria Station, and he asked me to organize a meeting outside the factory; it was a challenge. But it would have been too easy to make a gesture, like handing out literature; something else was needed. I joined the union secretly and enrolled the only three others in whom I had confidence.

We kept on working; there was some short time and it wasn't the moment to attempt anything. Just trying to keep a grip, to survive psychologically, was difficult enough. The machine dictates simple repetition. It stops, you have to move; no use arguing. A few seconds later, the same thing again. You can't fight a losing battle several hundred times a day and survive. We submit to the repetitiveness and it's no use looking for a gain of significance. Naïvely I kid myself I'm achieving something by completing a roll and I look for some significance at the end of the shift. There's none, not for us. We continue, changing cones, drudgery, withdrawn, labouring animals. Bending over the machine, we stare into the revolving fabric which reflects the blank screen of the mind . . . self-hypnotism.

Many leave, as many are sacked. Like Curly, it's easy to become 'erratic' and not bother about the machines; it's the way most people break up and get the sack. Those who leave aren't missed. The turnover is fantastic; in twelve months over 125 employees have gone, three times the number the company employs at any one time. The turnover is highest among the fifteen or so machine-minders.

About half is floating or fringe labour. Two deaf-mutes, some near-illiterates, continentals with poor English, coloured immigrants. A number of the English-born have been in the Merchant Navy, and perhaps the long hours and being shut up with others in a confined space have prepared them for this. Some of the young have recently lost a job and are working here while looking round for something else; some of the older chaps are knocked out and don't know where to get better jobs. Alan, half-French, told me: 'I suppose I'm a bit of a fool for staying here really. Why not get a decent job and get out. Eight hours a day.' I've seen Philip, a Hungarian refugee from 1956 who became a supervisor, crying with rage. About ten employees are women, engaged mainly on mending and inspecting. They are paid 2s. 9d. an hour plus a bonus of about £2 a week. The two supervisors get 30s. a week over the flat rate of 6s. an hour.

The operative patterns his sense of time by the job. If you drift too much mentally, a cone runs out. You can function quicker, better by putting the machine first and finding a secondary place for reflection. You learn to relax while running several machines. Stay cool, be quick and trust the other machines will be OK. Complexities are pushed aside to a small spare-time area. George said, 'I just go off into a daydream.' 'For twelve hours a day?' 'Yes, certainly.'

Eyes survey the cones, fingers adjust the thread; your wrist strengthens to turn the handle, thighs thicken for padding about the machines. Intelligence helps to spot in half a second what's probably wrong and try the quickest procedures. Something on each machine doesn't work: a warning light, the starting handle, a button – recurrent malfunctions. There are seven different makes of machine and each of them has its peculiarities. What's wrong here now – dropper? buttons stuck? thread out of triplites? or . . . ? To 'read' the fabric you have to be sure of the conditions for observing it successfully.

It's no use losing your temper on a twelve-hour shift. Apathy and distaste have to be suppressed. You try to have the easiest machines and other minor advantages, but there's no point in being emotional over this. You can't claim too much, fuss too much, complain about the yarn; no one has any sympathy to spare. Len used to look despairingly at me; what could I do?

Machine failures give amusement. A smashing build-up breaks the monotony. If a machine is out of action, good; if it gives you a job to do, at least that occupies the mind. The machines are cursed; their speeds are determined, we are not allowed to change them. 'You bastard.' 'What that machine needs is a stick of dynamite under it and blow the bloody thing up.' 'Between the two of us we've worn this fucking thing out for today.' Chris often used to beat the machine with a stick until the stick buckled.

Some rode along on libidinal fantasies, waiting for wifely release. Cones were used to mimic phalluses and once as cuckold's horns. The machine seems to figure as an irreducible sexual opponent. Several operators I noticed habitually scratched their arse. One said to me once, 'Have you felt his arse? He's got such a lovely little arse.'

The night the power broke down, something we had been waiting for, the sex-talk burst out. 'What are you doing, having a wank with that filthy book?' 'If you go home now, you'll catch the milkman coming out.' 'Old Sturt is on the nest.' 'I think about it all the time, it keeps me going.' 'You have it every morning when you get home.' 'You make it sound like a meal.' 'You should bring fanny with you in sandwiches.'

Many suffered from a sort of psychological degeneration and were impervious to communication. They seemed locked in themselves. One chap hardly spoke to anyone; Alan habitually turned up half an hour early and stayed behind late, as though his whole life depended on the place. Outside reality was attenuated for everyone. Once, seeing the countryside from a train on my day off, I was in ecstasy that anything so multifarious, so different from the workshop, could still exist.

One night I caught my foot in the machine. It stopped and so did the factory while the machine was dismantled. After, I had a recurrent fantasy of putting myself into the machine – a protest symptom, a way of getting out with dignity? We had to be physically and mentally tough to stay on, for we were selling our health.

I recall our bleats and half-jokes. 'What a life, eh!' 'It's enough to drive you potty.' 'Mrs Evans won't get her mink this Christmas.' Alan confessed that the biggest mistake of his life was to pass over a post-war job in a cemetery. Mark told me he'd got through two and a half volumes of *War and Peace* in ten months. Having lived an isolated life until then, I found myself becoming increasingly involved with my workmates. I kept trying to find out more and more what they felt, and discovered that the one thing we could talk about was our resentment, resentment at being treated like dirt, expendables, brought in as objects and pushed out again when we had ceased to serve. Them against us. The men were interested in information about the firm, the profit it made. Without mentioning the union, I found that most of them were well disposed. But we were still on short time, and at the back of everyone's mind was the 'Labour', the dole. We run the bloody machines, I thought, and they take what we make. A factory is an instrument of social humiliation. We're not greedy for money, we just want a place in the world. But we can't find it here, that's why so many quit. Meanwhile, we're outcasts, under necessity: to clock in, to labour. Clock out – to live?

On the lavatory wall someone wrote, 'I hate the CBR.' 'Why do you work here then?' 'Because of . . . short hours and good money, ha-ha.' 'Barmy cunts.'

Chris said, 'I feel like an educated sort of animal that has been taught to run a machine.' Dick told a director: 'You treat us like a load of shit.' But nothing happened.

The technical director addressed us: 'Those of you who've been in the services know that the only way to get things done is to all muck in and help each other. Leave the machine as you would like to find it, that's the spirit.' Others were more explicit: 'You've got your jobs to think about. Jobs aren't two a penny now.'

Although much was beyond the operatives' control and depended on the supervisor, it was the operatives who were blamed for bad production. We complained about the yarn, but the management refused to go into details: we were semi-skilled. Something could always be found wrong with any machine or fabric. 'I can get anyone the sack before I get it myself,' one supervisor said. 'Girls' work', a director called machine-minding. At the 'Labour' someone remarked: 'How much do you pay for boring a man to death?'

When production reached 9,000 lb. a week and the faults averaged four per roll or less, a bonus was paid; it was rare that both targets were reached, once every five or six weeks perhaps. My bonuses ranged from 1s. to 18s. at the highest;

since the operative's individual faults were deducted from his bonus at the rate of 1s. 6d. per yard of needle, 1s. 6d. per eighteen inches of press-offs, the bonus was a bad joke, if you can call it a joke.

Perhaps these hours and conditions were normally considered reasonable for short-term employment. Perhaps we were being given a favour by being allowed to work. But if this were so, shouldn't the effects of labour on the person be considered? If operators were under strain, did they give less trouble because they left rather than complain? Maybe the men, closed in on themselves, isolated from each other, accepted these conditions for the pay packets.

I wrote off again and the factory inspectors came round in November, 1966. The Factory Acts were posted up, holes in the floor mended. It was something, but not enough. After I was sacked I asked the factory inspector what provisions should be made about safety guards which some of the machines then lacked and he said he would look into the matter.

I prepared invitations to a union meeting. None but the three men I had already enrolled was to know about it until I handed the invitations out. I planned the meeting for forty-eight hours after the invitations, to give as little time as possible for counter-attack. I wasn't all that confident I could organize the men, wasn't absolutely sure what their reaction would be. I was sure only that, from being an isolated individual, I had to try to forge a community by assuming its values. Most important, I had to try to organize things so that the men could talk more openly about their situation. Only a couple of them had ever been in a union, and then not as active members. None of them belonged to any political organization, and I had only in the past few days applied for membership to the Labour Party.

Early on 3 April I wrote:

These trundling machines, measuring the hours of production,
Like sand-clocks running out,

The rumbling beat that cumulates in the mind,
Leading to expectancy of end of shift,
Or the end of this repetitive subordination?

At 6 a.m. I started to give the invitations out. I believed it might get me the sack and, through routine subordination, I was afraid. At the same time I was relieved: my relationships were now direct and straightforward for the first time.

'That's the best thing that ever happened to this place,' Alan said as I handed out the invitations to the day staff.

'It's easy for you,' he joked to the others as they took the invitations.

On the evening of the next day, Mr Clive Roffe, the firm's founder and managing director, asked us to read and acknowledge a letter which stated: 'This is a small family firm and a trade union has no place or position in it.' The technical director said to me: 'In your letter you say that every person has the right to join a trade union. In the same sense every firm has the right to employ whom it chooses.' 'Everything's back to normal,' someone said on the floor.

Fifteen attended the meeting the next day. They were interested in discussing CBR with a union organizer who knew the industry. The technical director stood outside the meeting place. The following evening, 5 April, Geoff Killick, one of the first whom I had already enrolled in the union, was dismissed. The factory manager confided in him: 'No one would have done for those men what you have done.' (He disliked the set-up almost as much as us and left the firm soon afterwards.) At 8 p.m., as I started the night shift, the technical director said: 'The firm no longer requires your services.' I was given my cards and a week's money in lieu of notice. No reason given. 'You can go away now and do whatever you would be doing instead. I don't know, we do what we can for you chaps,' he added. I shook hands with the others before I left.

In the four days between handing out the invitations and our getting the sack, about fifteen people had signed application forms to join the union. For the first time during those days I was able to talk openly to the men on the job and tell them that the only way to get better conditions was to have the union in, and that the National Union of Hosiery and Knitwear Workers was the right union. 'Everywhere else there is a forty-hour week, rates of pay are about twice what they are here. This is the only way to improve the place.'

After our sacking, we went round to see the others at home, persuading them to join the union straight away. Eighteen joined, including the Hungarian supervisor. One or two were scared. While we had still been in the factory, we had occasionally talked about improvements that could be made; now we worked out proposals which would have brought in an eight-hour shift, systematic training to run the machines, fewer men per machine, reducing wasted time and higher earnings. But we weren't able to present our demands.

On the evening of 17 April I was getting home when a car drew up with six from the night shift. 'We've been sacked, the lot of us. We've to get our cards tomorrow.' They had been asked to sign over a sixpenny stamp a document declaring that they were not members of any trade union. They had refused and been sent home. The men had held to the proper values.

Within a few days, all eighteen were dismissed; there were no operatives left. The managers and the one supervisor left ran the machines, and advertisements appeared in the local press offering jobs at the factory.

The dispute was officially recognized by the union. Though my sacking was just an event, one I could foresee, when the others were sacked I felt a responsibility to them, and started organizing the protest. I remembered while still in the factory telling one of the men, an educationally subnormal chap who had been frightened of joining the union, that if we got the sack we'd organize protest marches, have television cameras outside, and get in the papers. It had seemed a bit far-fetched at the time, but now it all started to happen.

From the beginning I saw my role as keeping the local end up, ensuring that the men kept together, leaving the wider issues to the union. Fairly early on we decided that to keep together we had to meet once a week as a group so that everyone could have their say on anything they wanted to raise. These meetings are frank and democratic and often lead to rows. Yet when they end we all go out together; six months after the lock-out we're still fifteen on the picket lines.

Four have left for various personal reasons; and a scab has joined us. When he asked what he could do, we told him that BBC TV was going to be outside the factory the next evening. 'We want you to tell them what it's like to work there.' He did just that, and three days later he got the sack. He's now on the picket line with the rest of us.

At first we had a voluntary rota system for picketing which didn't work too well. People tended to turn up late, so at one of our meetings we voted to fine late-comers 5s. an hour from union benefits. The first week two men forfeited £2 each voluntarily. Since then there has been no problem over manning the picket lines.

Every evening at eight when the shifts change we have a demonstration outside the factory, with help from our supporters, Young Socialists and students from Sussex University who have been among our most vocal supporters. (The Students Union has passed a unanimous resolution condemning the management of CBR.) While drawing the line at physical violence, the verbal violence is intense, and many who have quit work at the plant have admitted that they couldn't stand the abuse which met them at the start and finish of twelve hours' gruelling work. About forty or fifty operatives have come and gone since the lock-out. And of about 400 people who have come for jobs, a good half have turned away when they heard our case. But there are always people who take a job no matter what.

Many people give support and sympathy but, unless they are members of a strong union, they don't necessarily have much pull. You can't achieve a mass organization unless you go through the key, militant trade unionists and shop stewards in the area and outside, on a personal basis. The unions being bureaucratic in structure, and ours rather small, it has become apparent to us that we have to take more initiative ourselves. We were slow to realize this and it might have made a difference if we had realized it earlier.

Demonstrations outside the factory itself are important; more important still is to go to other factories at lunchtime and hold meetings to explain our case, activate the workers and build up awareness. This, and contact with shop stewards' committees up and down the country, is vital, especially for blacking. By and large this can only be achieved by personal contact, I've learnt. When I went to Stockport during the bitter strike at the Roberts Arundel factory, the AEU district secretary, with whom I had a long talk, picked up our black-list; he hadn't seen it before. Within minutes he had picked up the phone to a company doing business with CBR and extracted a promise from the union representative to black work. We wouldn't have achieved this if I hadn't gone there, because there is no national organization for militants.

The CBR management view me as 'Taylor, MA, a graduate from Oxford University who, despite his education and degree, took an unskilled labour job and whose motive for this became apparent when he secretly and in collaboration with union organizers began to enrol members.' Explaining the dismissals, the company said: 'It was necessary to discharge certain employees for good and sufficient reasons which had nothing to do with their being, or not being, members of any union.'

The men have all been impressed by the trade-union support we have received. Isolated, many not knowing that trades unions existed, they had never thought there was an organization that could do anything about the situation. But once there is an organization, people become involved because it is there.

A convenor at a Crawley factory wrote, 'The shop was appalled at the conditions under which you have been working. We congratulate you on your courageous decision to join the trade union movement and fight this kind of employer.'

To do so, the men endure hardship. They are living from hand-to-mouth on union money, unemployment benefits and hand-outs from our appeal fund if anything is left over. We get less than half what we were making under the previous sweated conditions, but we are fighting for something: the dignity of labour.

Postscript: May, 1968

We held out for nine months, picketing the factory twelve hours a day to keep away newcomers who answered the ads the firm put in the local papers. During this time many things happened: their development throws light on the problems of struggle.

On 28 April, about ten days after the lockout, the company talked about re-instatement, and asked the NUHKW to call off the picket. The union took no action, and CBR then declined to discuss re-instatement further. In due course, the NUHKW asked other unions to help black CBR, and later the TUC was involved. Our union appreciated that this was a fight on principles, and though it did not mobilize its rank-and-file, sending an organizer down from Leicester once a week, and then once a month, its benefit pay was generous and we were able to continue the fight.

An appeal fund launched by Brighton Trades Council raised £1,700, but the Trades Council was not successful in mobilizing local trade unionists, and our most numerous supporters continued to come from the University of Sussex. On 14 July, we issued a 100th day Manifesto. 'The workers of CBR claim their rights under the United Nations Universal Declaration of Human Rights, 1948, Article 20(4): "Everyone has the right to join and to form Trade Unions for the protection of his interests."

'We claim protection for the CBR workers under ILO

Convention 98, 1948, ratified by the U.K., which states: "Article 1.1. Workers shall enjoy adequate protection against acts of anti-Union discrimination in respect of their employment. 1.2. Such protection shall apply more particularly in respect of acts calculated to (*a*) make the employment of a worker subject to the condition that he shall not join a Union or shall relinquish Union membership; (*b*) cause the dismissal of or otherwise prejudice a worker by reason of Union membership or because of participation in Union activities."

'CBR is only a strikingly flagrant and blatant instance. We ask for a law within the terms of the ILO Convention, that every employer should be compelled to permit his employees to join a Trade Union if they want to.'

Meanwhile, day after day on that drab corner of Shanklin Road, the men picketed, tackling anybody who went into the factory. In return for the bitter psychological war we waged on the scabs, some replied: 'Why abuse us? We were desperate for a job.' 'All I know is that I've got a job and it's cold outside.' These men were fellow-workers, we knew; but we knew also that the system pits worker against worker. Many jobless men, aware of this also, refused to scab.

Some of the scabs claimed that unions were weak and had let them down in the past. 'I believe in freedom and individualism. You are trying to force us to join,' was a fairly typical comment. 'Trade unions are no good anyway. They only get people into trouble. I've seen enough of trade unions,' was another. 'If you were stupid enough to join a trade union and things didn't work out, that was up to you,' said some.

But amongst us on the picket lines, a comradeship formed which we had never known inside at work, and we were heartened by the support we received, for instead of being isolated victims we had come to be at the centre of a nationwide movement. Geoff Killick's remark was a fair reflection of our feelings: 'Anti-union prejudice screens people from the reality and so they remain ignorant. I used to think trade unions had too much power, but CBR changed my mind. In fact, I'm amazed by the lack of strength the unions seem to have in a case as blatant as this.'

Anti-union prejudice amused me. I heard one lady say: 'They knew the contract of employment. If they didn't like it, they should have left without making a fuss.' Another lady said: 'CBR, that's where the employees did something they shouldn't have done, joining a union, wasn't it? I think it's shocking preventing people from going to work when they need a job.'

The factory manager left; the chief clerk also left. We picketed the TUC in September and the Labour Party Conference at Scarborough. On the 250th day of the lock-out we received a message from Bill Jones, London busmen's leader and member of the TUC General Council: 'Certainly it is not a story of this day and age, but of an age we thought had passed. The struggles and determination of these lads is to be applauded, supported, and given the utmost credit. But what credit is due to one of the most powerful and united trade union movements in the world to have allowed this small employer to cock a snook at it for so long? The time is long overdue for the leaders of our great movement to lend a hand.'

Ernie Roberts, Assistant General Secretary of the AEU, asked: 'Why isn't the strength we possess used to compel these employers to recognize trade union organizations and workers' rights?'

In autumn, 1967, we urged the NUHKW to increase its pressures, especially by second-order blacking and by more open appeals to solidarity. The President listened to what we said, but didn't answer in detail.

In November, the union informed us of a tentative agreement with CBR to end the dispute on nominal recognition without re-instatement. The agreement had fallen through, however, because the NUHKW had tried to get negotiating rights. We said that an agreement without re-instatement was worthless.

On 8 December, the President informed the men that an agreement with CBR had been reached as follows:

'1. It is a fundamental right that workers may belong to a trade union. Both parties accept this.

'2. It is understood that one of the functions of a trade union is to negotiate on behalf of its members.

'3. During the dispute, sufficient labour has joined the company for the plant to be fully manned at present and therefore no employment opportunities exist.

'4. The parties agree to use their best endeavours to reach a better relationship.

'5. On the basis of the above understandings the parties agree that it is in the interests of all concerned that the present dispute is now terminated.'

We expressed our opinion, the union leaders listened, but there was no interchange and no vote. In our view the agreement was meaningless and should not have been made, and a vote would have shown this. But the agreement existed (and was already approved by the union's N.E.C., we were told); placed before this fact, the men were offered sums of up to £200 each by the union if they signed a statement acknowledging that the dispute was ended. Realizing that the dispute could not be continued with inadequate funds, the Lockout Committee advised members to decide individually whether to accept the money. Geoff Killick and I refused, maintaining our disagreement with the settlement and our belief that those who for eight months had borne the brunt of the struggle should be allowed to discuss and vote on the terms, even if later our decision were overruled by the N.E.C. The fact that all signed was taken by the NUHKW as acceptance of the terms of the settlement, though we had never been asked to accept or reject the terms of the settlement itself. The union's General Secretary, with whom I took this up, maintained that the men had acknowledged the termination of the dispute and had therefore accepted the terms on which the dispute was terminated, and that it was a quibble to make a difference.

After nearly eight months of picketing, thirteen of us were left. Of these, all but two continued to picket CBR for six weeks. On 19 January 1968, we ended the unofficial dispute with a demonstration outside the factory and a final statement.

Since then the men have scattered to other jobs: one is running knitting machines in the Midlands and earning over £30 a week; another is trying to start up his own business making light-fixtures; yet another has become a trade union organizer. Subsequently CBR reported a loss for its financial year ending October 1967, of £79,531. 'Adverse trading conditions and shortage of raw materials ... were aggravated by the labour dispute. There have been some improvements: week-end working has now stopped for the time being, and some rates of pay have increased slightly. But CBR is still in control.

In our final statement we maintained our belief that the union's agreement invalidated the reasons for the strike, maintained our hostility to the denial of trade union rights and rejected any settlement that fell short of re-instatement with recognition. But we also tried to draw the conclusions of our long struggle:

'We know now that there is no effectual remedy for a 72-hour week at half union rates, which must therefore be regarded as a normal part of working conditions under the present economic and political order.

'Even under a Labour government, we cannot believe that the working class is in power, for if it were, the CBR lockout would never have happened, or would have soon been over.

'In the present situation, we believe a trade union must be militant, that is, using methods of opposition. We believe that a fight on principle means involving people in the wider issues.

'For us, the CBR lockout has been a profound experience. We have understood the limitations which keep British labour in an oppressed condition. We have felt the deep loyalties of trade union solidarity. Towards a united trade union movement, and justice for the working people of Britain.'

MIKE TAYLOR

THE AUTHOR

I was born in 1933 at Hornchurch, Essex. My father, who was of working-class parents, was an administrative officer in the National Coal Board at the time of his death. I went to grammar school and Oxford where I read PPE.

I did my National Service in an infantry regiment and the intelligence corps where I studied Russian. Feeling that my academic studies were incomplete and that it was necessary to be clear on values and spiritual problems before engaging in politics, I spent the next eight years – until taking the job as a machine-minder – studying psychology, philosophy and sociology privately. I lived at home in a small village on money which I had been able to save while in the army.

My studies resulted in a 600-page manuscript called Happiness in Political Community. *It was concerned to show how people lose an objective sense of values and become involved in subjective social norms, and how personal reintegration is possible in community organization.*

The book, which is unpublished, was politically deficient. I have since learnt that capitalism is psychologically entrenched, and that it needs community organization in which people, who are afraid of accepting the underlying economic forces, can encourage each other to speak out. This is what has happened to some extent in the course of our present struggle. I hope to be able to re-write this book, using the practical experience gained in the past year to modify my earlier theoretical considerations.

My parents were socialist in outlook, but I had no particular left-wing convictions. Until joining the Labour party at the time of the lockout I belonged to no political organization. I am single. For a time I thought of teaching philosophy, but I realized I wasn't good enough. I am now a full-time trade union officer.

The Convenor

The voice of the city is sleepless,
The factories thunder and beat,
How bitter the wind and relentless
That echoes our shuffling feet.

The words of the revolutionary song are still relevant to workers waiting on a cold winter's morning for a bus that is always late. But when a worker is driving to the factory on a fine morning in his own car, as I and hundreds of others in my plant do, the link at first sight may not seem so obvious. Yet if you look below the surface you'll find that the more things change the more they remain the same.

From the Coventry journeymen of medieval times to the workers of 1917 who struck for the recognition of shop stewards, our city has had a tradition of workers' struggle. We are heirs to this tradition; but today, with the development of monopoly capitalism, the struggle is more complex than ever. Attempts to alter the methods of payment, speed-up, mergers and take-overs, wage freeze, unemployment, short-time working, automation – these are among the problems which confront us on the shop floor and which form the core of our struggle.

Since our factory is part of the crisis-ridden aircraft industry, the immediate contradictions are apparent to most of our workers. Advanced technological methods exist in our plant alongside First World War buildings and antiquated managerial ideas, greater output per man is counter-balanced by growing mountains of paperwork and bureaucracy. Overall hangs the lack of planning for the industry and the threat of cancellation of contracts, short time or redundancy. But while these contradictions are obvious, the long-term answers are not so apparent to the same workers. It is here, in the influence of reactionary ideas in the labour movement – ideas that labour and capital are reconcilable, that capitalism is the best system we've got, that the class struggle no longer exists – that for me, as a militant trade unionist and communist, the biggest problem lies. For the basic issue remains what it has always been: to advance our struggle against the ruling class and, as part of this advance, to exert and extend our control on the shop floor. Despite the difficulties, I welcome the struggle, it is life; the absence of struggle is stagnation and death.

Our factory is highly organized and highly skilled. Starting as a rather paternalistic concern at the turn of the century, it has grown by a series of amalgamations and take-overs – the latest quite recently when it was swallowed up by its rival – into a combine of some 80,000 workers and technicians in plants all over the country, a size equalled only by a similar concern in the USA. Our plant employs about 4,000 manual workers, over half of whom are highly skilled, and roughly 2,000 staff workers, mainly technicians, draughtsmen and clerical workers. We make one complete jet engine and the components, including discs and compressor blades, for a number of other jet engines, including those now being tested for the Concorde.

The amount of machining that goes into the components is very high indeed, sometimes involving removing nine-tenths of the weight of the original casting or forging which we receive from sub-contractors. Much of the work is done by highly skilled operators on conventional machines – lathes, milling and grinding machines – while some of the rest is carried out on specialized machines like tape-control drilling machines and copying lathes, which also require highly skilled workers. Because the work has to reach such a high standard, there is one inspector for every four workers.

We start work at 7.30 – the time which was decided by a workers' ballot organized by the shop stewards' committee when the 40-hour week was introduced some years ago – so as to be able to finish early, at 4.15. On Fridays, because the lads like to get away early for the week-end, we finish at 3.

The management were somewhat against these hours, but faced with an overwhelming vote, they accepted them. On nights, the men voted to work four ten-hour shifts – though this was against the union officials' wishes – because they said they wanted to get the unpleasant job of night-work over as quickly as possible. In fact the struggle for a four-night week went on from 1947 in the Coventry District, with strikes, overtime bans and refusal to work on Friday nights occurring at spasmodic intervals. Both at our factory and many others, mass demonstrations took place over this question. The full-time union officials argued, correctly in some ways, that it was wrong to extend the working day or night; the shop floor argued that nights were different in essence from days and that social activity at the week-end was curbed by Friday night-work. Though in theory it was wrong to lengthen the shift, in practice the lads found it better. Union executives and the employers grudgingly conceded the four-night week in face of this argument supported by mass action.

Shortly before 7.30 I park my MG in the multi-storey car park which holds 700 cars and go into my shop. I don't have an office, just a desk and a phone; our committee is against the idea of isolating the convenor behind walls from the shop floor itself. I have a quick look at the night book to see if there have been any problems on the night shift, though usually the lads have dealt with their own, and then a glance at the press to see what they're saying about us: the *Morning Star*, the *Guardian*, the *Financial Times*. Usually one or two of the leading shop stewards will come round to discuss any problems.

As convenor, I work full time on shop-floor problems, though the 170 shop stewards normally do some production work, depending on the amount of union work they have. For some this might be only 5 per cent of their time, for others as much as 30 per cent. My day is fully taken up, usually with two or three meetings fixed in advance with management, plus the day-to-day problems that arise. These can include a very rare sacking, or rather a notice of sacking, since the company cannot fire a man out of the gate but have to follow a procedure with the union and shop floor; the normal wage claims for sections or men who are not getting the rate they are entitled to; and claims on piece-work rates which, since thousands are fixed every week in the plant, are the major source of dispute. And sometimes men will come to me with personal problems, or with problems concerning their mates in other factories in the district which perhaps aren't so well organized, to get advice on what they should do.

To be effective, trade unionism, which is the workers' basic weapon in their struggle, must be militant, immediate and democratic. On our joint shop stewards' committee we are constantly trying to improve the organization inside the plant, to raise the level of awareness of the problems to be overcome and to make a conscious attempt to work out the answers. We aren't always successful, sometimes our ideas don't work; you can't win a worker for an idea just by saying, 'Here's a good idea, let's try it,' and expect him to take it. You've got to explain, demonstrate, show him it will work and that it is to his advantage. While my endeavour is always to make apparent the links between the immediately obvious problems and their long-term solutions, it is no good being abstract or exclusively political about this. You have to win the lads for limited demands, carry them forward from one objective to the next, create a well-organized and militant shop-floor organization in which they can participate fully. It is shop-floor problems which concern the lads most immediately and broader issues must always be directly related to these.

While leadership counts for a lot, the method of payment in a factory has an important bearing on the organization and militancy of the workers inside it, for the method can help to mould the basis of activity. At our plant we work straight piecework, which means that the worker gets an agreed sum of money for an agreed amount of work, and the more he produces the more he earns. The idea is not new: masons working on cathedrals in the Middle Ages were similarly paid. But when first introduced into the engineering trades, it was a method of intensive exploitation and often of self-exploitation by the individual, who would drive himself even unconsciously. But in a highly organized factory it has certain advantages: it is direct, it can lead to higher earnings, and it gives the workers a measure of control over their production. The continual battle over rates makes the workers very militant, for when the rate-fixer comes out to argue with you, you're immediately faced with the basic element of the class struggle: exploitation, potential or actual.

Part of my time and much of some stewards' time is spent in arguing piecework prices. This usually develops into a Greek meets Greek affair. Only a small percentage of thousands of prices fixed in a week – which in itself is due to the vast variety of work and the continual modifications that are part of our industry – get beyond the operator or ganger level. A man does not have to be an all-round craftsman with a technical knowledge of everything to be a good negotiator. It is not only technical factors that enter into the negotiations, as I'll show later; in every case the end result is reached through a compromise which should yield the operator or gang earnings of about – or if possible higher than – the average of his section. This for a skilled craftsman is a few pence above the district average of 15s. 5d. an hour.

If the operator doesn't get satisfaction, he calls in his shop steward; the ratio of stewards to men is about one to twenty-five. If there is still no agreement, I am called in to meet the chief rate-fixer. We thrash it out and in the majority of cases reach agreement; if I have got the best I can, the operator will usually take it, though not always. Then it is a question of persuading him or operating the old Coventry tradition of putting the job on the floor, which means that the operator refuses to do the job until he gets satisfaction. In the case of a section dispute I'll put it to the lads that I have got as much as I can without a strike and they have to decide whether they want to have a go. Sometimes they say it's not worth it and at other times they will have a go and stop work. We have a stoppage in one or other section at least once a week. But, as I'll explain, we've never closed the whole plant down except once, and this was for three days.

If a job goes on the floor, the company retaliates immediately by refusing to give the worker another job until he does the one under dispute. As immediately we turn the attack onto the company for depriving a man of work. The section then stops work in support which puts pressure on the company and the man usually gets the bit extra he wants. Under the national engineering agreement, prices must be mutually agreed, so in a well-organized plant the company can't force a price on a man; but the same is not necessarily true in a badly organized factory, where victimization by management of one sort or another is possible.

I'm not always successful, of course. I have been criticized by the workers on a section in a dispute over a farthing. The company was offering 6¼d. for a job and the men were holding out for 6½d. In a situation like this the dispute then goes to the estimator, who is a company executive, with myself, the operator and his steward arguing his case. If this fails the dispute goes to the personnel manager, and finally to the works conference, where the full-time union official comes in. But this is extremely rare. Neither the union nor the lads want to take up time; much more often we resort to the direct tactic of letting the job go on the floor.

In disputes over prices there is one thing that is never discussed: the speed at which the job is to be done. We will discuss basic engineering problems such as maintaining certain finishes and dimensions, but not those of speeds and feeds. The reason is simple: the company must not be allowed to assert direct control over the speed at which a worker does his job. He must remain sole arbiter of that. It is part of his control over his working environment. The firm doesn't like this, of course, and would prefer so-called scientific methods such as time and motion studies etc. to determine rates, rather than what comes down fundamentally to a clash of individual strengths.

In my view the rate-fixer's job is not to fix the cost of the job but the profit margin. Whether you are making a frying pan or a jet engine, a theoretical estimate of the costs in-involved, the tooling and overheads, has been worked out by estimators (who are different from rate-fixers) before the job leaves the drawing board. The rate-fixer comes down on to the shop floor to get a price as much below the estimate as possible. Being engineers, the estimators and rate-fixers at our factory have a fairly good idea of the labour cost of a particular job; if you are machining a shaft and have to take off so many inches of metal and produce so many dimensions, the whole operation can be worked out theoretically on speeds and feeds and the tooling set-up required. But very often the skilled worker, the man who actually does the job, will improve on the theoretical set-up by the way he sets his tooling. He will often run the machine faster than is theoretically thought possible, grind his tools differently, have a cluster of tools doing the job rather than a single tool which has to be changed for another. To anyone on the shop floor it is evident that the greater part of responsibility in production depends on the workers themselves.

This is one reason why controlling the work environment is fundamental to me. While the means of production are in private ownership, it is the owners or their representatives, the managers, who determine not only what shall be produced but the machinery by which it shall be produced. And yet there is a fundamental contradiction here. Running a firm is not a matter of a few brilliant minds at the top; it is a total process in which the workers play the vital role. While management takes decisions on what to produce on the basis of the orders they can get, the method of production is modified many times before the final product is made. First of all, management's global decisions are modified by the feed-back from studies that determine how these decisions can in practice be carried out; secondly, but by no means of lesser importance, these decisions are again modified on the shop floor by the workers themselves to enable production to be carried out. It is a myth that management manages on the shop floor. When it comes down to details they don't, they give instructions and hope somehow they will be implemented. The skilled worker has to work out, from drawings, the best method of doing the particular job; he has to set his own machine, he has to get the necessary tools out of the stores, he has to grind his own tools and so on. Using his ingenuity and his skill, the worker is constantly made aware of his active and valuable role in the productive process. That his actual control over the work process should be reflected in a desire to increase his control over his work conditions generally should come as no surprise. Lest it be thought that the worker's vital participation in the productive process is confined to – and recognized only in – a highly skilled factory like ours, I would recall a recent remark by the production manager of Rovers, who said: 'Our most valuable person is the shop-floor worker.'

Earnings are one of the principal controls, but by no means the only one. Over the past four or five years, pretty much since I became convenor, a fair part of my time along with other stewards has been spent encouraging and helping workers in a department or section to form a gang. This is a powerful weapon in the struggle for control, because the employer can no longer pick on the individual worker but is forced to negotiate with a collective. Some sections of our plant, such as final assembly of engines, have always worked in gangs because this was the best for the company. So we took the decision that what was best for the company under certain circumstances was good for us all the time. At that time there was real inequality of earnings in some sections and a lack of strength in negotiations with rate-fixers, as well as a failure to be able to control labour-loading. We presented our arguments to the lads: the gang was a collective in which weaker members could be safe-guarded; everyone would get the same wage; there would be more control of conditions; and it could improve earnings when one man – the democratically elected ganger – could be almost full time on rate-fixing problems and the organizing of work. Since foremen are usually busy at production meetings, filling in forms or doing progress work, the ganger ends up by having some control over the allocation of work. Of course, this organization of the work process by the workers themselves in fact helps the company; but when it reaches the stage where the company feels it is losing control over the organization and earnings of the shop floor, it reacts.

At first, however, the company didn't react, and the gang system started to spread. Usually the most able negotiator would be elected as ganger to negotiate all the prices, and he would get to know the rate-fixer and how he was thinking. Of course, the reverse was also true, but these are facts of life in a factory and we aren't at each other's throats all the time. Yet the ganger knows he has twenty, thirty or forty men behind him; and if he tells a man to put a job on the floor the whole gang will pay that man's wages. I've seen gangs where a man has had a job on the floor for a fortnight. Everyone on the gang is losing only a few pence an hour to pay his wage and eventually the firm has to cave in. The gang is a terrific weapon in the hands of the union.

Since the company has seen this, and realized the degree of solidarity and militancy that results from the gang system, and seen what they call their right to manage being seriously affected, they have put up more and more obstacles. The company wants to retain the old system because it helps them to play one individual off another.

Recently a turning section in my own shop decided they wanted to work the gang system. The company clamped down immediately and refused. Some months before the company had tried to get us to accept a new agreement for gangs which was designed to reassert company control over such things as work allocation, labour-loading and piece-work negotiation. As we were short of work at the time and not in the best position to fight, we left the matter in abeyance until we were in a more favourable position. Now the company announced that no more gangs could be formed until we accepted their terms.

As soon as we knew this, we worked out our best strategy.

We didn't want a factory strike, but the section on its own was too weak. We called a meeting of all gang stewards and discussed what to do. All the gangs were keen to see the system extended. It was decided that from the beginning of the work week the section would start working as a gang and would no longer fill in individual dockets but record work on a gang sheet. We told the company we didn't accept the foisting of an agreement on us since all agreements must be mutually agreed. The company retaliated immediately. As soon as an individual on the new gang ran out of work the foreman told him he wouldn't get another one unless he booked as an individual. When that happened we turned the situation from fighting for a gang to the company depriving an individual of a job. I called a meeting of the shop stewards and we agreed to hold a mass meeting of gang workers the next morning. Several hundred workers attended and they voted not to start work until the company accepted the new gang under the existing conditions. We gave the company ninety minutes to reach agreement, otherwise the men would go home. As the gangs cover such a cross-section of the factory this would disrupt production, and there were certain urgent jobs the company wanted to get out.

The company dithered. When the ninety minutes were up the men put on their coats and went home. We always give the company the chance to talk while the men are still on the shop floor, but this time there wasn't agreement.

Later however, during the course of the day, the company started talking with us and virtually conceded. Without promising that the section could form a gang, they gave enough hints that if the lads resumed work there would be talks and the men would be given jobs and not have to book individually. During the talks the company said they would agree to the new gang, but they wanted to have the full-time union officials brought in. We agreed to this; though the battle is by no means over at the time of writing, we are determined to keep to the existing agreements and not allow the company to assert the sort of controls it was attempting in its new agreement. Meanwhile we have achieved one more limited gain.

We don't believe in lengthy strikes; several short, sharp stoppages are better than one long one. Our strategy is that there are plenty of other weapons than the mass strike or, for that matter, the continual overtime ban; the latter can get a firm accustomed to its position so that it can plan its production – as we have always said it could – to do without overtime. In any case, overtime is generally kept to a minimum by the trade-union organization.

In a well-organized factory where the strategy is to go for limited advances, long mass strikes shouldn't be necessary. Of course, there are bloody-minded company managements who don't care at all if they are wrong, who prefer a total shutdown to a compromise. But there are many like ours who are not basically bloody-minded and who, though always ready with strong arguments, are often willing to see our point of view. Quite a high proportion of our management is promoted from the shop floor and their feeling that the lads are right, coupled with the economic effects of disrupting production, is generally enough to make them change their minds. These remarks about our management's relative fair-mindedness do not mean that I don't believe in the class struggle, only that our sights should be set higher.

Long strikes can be demoralizing for the lads. If they start losing a lot of time and money, their fighting spirit is affected, however much the company may be suffering at the same time. In any case, even on the shortest strikes, we always have the lads return to meetings; we don't want to leave them hanging round for days on end without anything happening. Our strategy is almost military in relation to strikes: it is our job to do more damage to the enemy than he does to us. If you can get a limited objective with very few casualties, you are all the more ready to move on to the next little step.

With each such advance we secure a little more control, a little more of managerial function is taken from management.

For example, the reasons for sacking a worker have been reduced to very bad workmanship or very bad timekeeping, and the incidence of dismissals, which can only be carried out by virtual agreement with the workers as a whole, is a fraction of 1 per cent of the total labour force. Dismissal, in other words, cannot be used for disciplinary reasons. Similarly, with the gang system, management has to get the workers' agreement to engage labour, which gives the gang control over the amount of labour put on to a job and the earnings level.

Nothing is won without a fight; and the employers fight back, trying to change the rules of a game which they feel they are losing control of. Measured day work, a Yankee system, is one of the latest company tactics, which, though not tried by our management, is being attempted elsewhere in the Coventry district. Essentially it is a system that sets a norm of daily production for a fixed wage. In a car factory, for example, fifty men doing a particular job on a section of track are given a norm of, say, twenty cars an hour, which represents 90 per cent of potential production as calculated by the firm. If the men increase their production by one car an hour, a 5 per cent increase, they don't get a corresponding 5 per cent increase in money as they would on straight piecework; they get less. The lads point out that not only should a 5 per cent increase be worth a corresponding increase in earnings, but that because of management's inefficiency and bottlenecks in supplies, it is rare to be able to achieve a 95 per cent efficiency. Moreover, in its continual attempts to reassert control, the company can put ten more men on the track. If the men were on piecework they could argue that they were not going to pay the extra men out of the job and so demand more money, thus controlling the labour-loading.

Straight piecework is the only system where a worker's earnings go up at a direct rate. In my opinion it is the best system for our factory and many others, because it means that a worker can control his earnings. But what about those workers, such as labourers, storekeepers, drivers, maintenance men, inspectors, etc., who are not on direct production and cannot be paid piecework?

Under continual pressure from well-organized day worker sections, as these are called, our management and most others in the district have conceded a system of payment called the indirect bonus, which ties by a money factor the earnings of the day worker with those of the pieceworker. This means, for example, that a tool-setter gets the average earnings of the skilled pieceworkers in the factory, an inspector 90 per cent, and so on. From management's point of view, this system gives an interest in production to all the workers in the factory; from our point of view it helps raise the level of earnings of workers not on piecework and, more important, builds unity and solidarity among all sections, since the workers see how their earnings are interrelated.

Management's counter-attacks are not confined to earnings. The introduction of new, highly capital-intensive machinery that displaces a certain amount of labour is constantly with us. We are not against technical progress, we are not Luddites, but as soon as there is no control the workers are under grave attack. We have before us the example of the USA, where automation is producing tens of thousands of surplus workers each year, and the example of our own firm, which has a laboratory trying out all sorts of technological improvements.

To take only one example: the introduction of tape-control machines in our factory. These are milling-cum-drilling machines which are programmed on a tape made theoretically by planners, and which can increase output up to five times per worker. They are accurate to one-thousandth of an inch and the moment anything goes wrong the machine stops automatically. The American maker of one of these machines claims that the set-up time is reduced from 19·5 hours on a conventional machine to half an hour, the cycle reduced from 12·5 hours to 1·75 hours, and the tooling costs cut from $7,300 to $1,600. Significant savings, even if likely to be somewhat exaggerated.

The management introduced three of these machines not

so long ago. Since they gave us no prior notice they were 'blacked' immediately. They weren't even wired up and sat there, worth many thousands of pounds, for several months while the company considered our demands: that a fully skilled operator work each machine (the company wanted semi-skilled operators); that the operator be paid the factory average – just over 15s. an hour, or about £30 for a 40 hour week – because we knew that arguments with the rate-fixer were going to be very difficult; and that the operators should make the tapes. The company finally agreed to look into the question, asking us meanwhile to run the machines, which we agreed to do. Subsequently they agreed to the first two points but not the third, which is still in dispute and has been taken up at district union level. Pending settlement we haven't withdrawn the six men working the machines on two shifts, but have refused to work two more such machines they have just brought in. We know, of course, that they will introduce more of these machines, but until they get our agreement they won't be able to operate them.

The point is this: while the planners who make the tapes are quite good on theory, they don't know how to combine theory with practice. They are always running down to the lads on the shop floor to ask whether this speed and feed is right, whether the theory will in fact work. They have to come to us. Rather therefore than telling the company that we refuse to cooperate in running the new machines, we prefer to show them that our members on the floor are indispensable, that their skills are needed. It is part of the struggle to retain the skill-content of our factory; despite the tapes, a considerable degree of skill is still required in setting up these machines.

But there are dangers, and these are likely to cause a lot of trouble in industry in the next few years. For while the planners, members of the draughtsmen's union (DATA), started doing the tapes without letting us know, they are also under attack because the eventual idea is that this work shall be done by computers. Meanwhile we have to be careful to try to avoid the trap of a demarcation dispute. Personally, I think we should have one union and so avoid this sort of pitfall, but life is as it is and you don't solve problems with a wave of the hand.

Our shop-floor strength is such – and this is true of Coventry generally – that when the company introduces a new machine the first thing they say is that there will be no redundancy. All the same we have to be on guard: with the introduction, for example, of new broaching machines, which work to tolerances of half a tenth of one-thousandth of an inch, one skilled and two semi-skilled workers replace five skilled and fourteen semi-skilled. Because of the constant crises in the aircraft industry, which mean that a part of the factory can be on short time while another is busy, it isn't easy to get these men moved to other sections where the work may be entirely different. So far we have managed to avoid redundancy at our plant; but the question of re-training is immediately raised, and I am in favour of it, as long as it is not used to flood areas with labour and thus present employers with further means of exploitation.

As part of a crisis-ridden industry we have found that it is not enough to demand that our own management give us work. Therefore we are always active in lobbying local MPs and raising the issues facing our industry; among these we exert pressure to orientate our production from military to civilian purposes. Through force of circumstances, we have had to evolve a policy towards our industry, which is why our factory supports nationalization. Since our experiences on the shop floor have taught us that workers can control the productive process, we advocate a form of workers' control within a nationalized industry; only this can avoid the bureaucratic state capitalist set-up in the existing nationalized industries which seems, if not actually worse, at least no different to the worker in it than the private enterprise it is supposed to supplant. The fact that so many of our managers are recruited from the shop floor only reinforces our point that the workers are capable of running the industry.

It is often said in our industry that when the weight of the paperwork equals the weight of the aircraft she is ready to fly. The larger and more complex the concern, the more the paperwork multiplies. Even to get a simple tool out of the stores requires triplicate forms, and the amount of paperwork to be filled in each day by some workers is enormous. This is coupled with a failure by management to take decisions, and a constant reference through a chain of command before even a 'yes' or a 'no' is given. It is apparent that lower and middle management are prisoners of their own system and an awareness of this can be seen in the development of union membership among supervisors. This is very healthy and means that on certain broad issues – the cancelling of the TSR–2 is an illustration – all unions in the plant, both staff and shop-floor, work together.

Through our constant struggles the workers have accepted that the shop-floor organization must be efficient and direct. I remember once inviting a TUC official to visit our factory where storekeepers and drivers were meeting to discuss an offer the company had made to their wage claim. The official expressed surprise that a meeting and report-back to our members was necessary. We told him that his attitude and that of many union officials to the sort of activity he was seeing was the reason workers in well-organized factories got more wage increases in two years than the national union negotiators in six.

This direct, democratic approach means that the joint shop stewards' committee gets plenty of constructive criticism from the shop floor, and this is all to the good; nothing is more fatal to the labour movement than an atmosphere of complacency. Many of the gangs have weekly lunchtime meetings to discuss problems. Formal organization, negotiating ability, 100 per cent trade-union membership, are all useless unless the workers and their leaders are militant, are prepared to take action on an issue. By militancy I don't mean using a razor blade to shave a gooseberry or striking for the sake of striking, as I have tried to explain. Nor do I want to hide the fact that a long and patient process is involved in winning over many workers who have always worked as individuals to new ideas such as the gang system.

Our committee produces plenty of printed material to keep members in touch with what is happening both inside and outside the factory. For example, we publish the company's annual balance sheet, which we obtain via the Labour Research Department to which our joint shop stewards are affiliated; though proscribed by the Labour Party, we find the Labour Research Department most useful. Possibly it is proscribed because it is useful to the workers. The publication of the balance sheet usually causes some stir on the shop floor, and this reinforces our arguments for the opening of the books by our firm and all others so that the workers can really see what is going on. The recent revelations on excess profits in the armaments industry are only the tip of the iceberg. Like the speeding motorist, for every one caught hundreds get away. Of course not only the arms manufacturers make excess profits: if the housewife really knew how she was exploited what an uproar there would be. This is why the campaign for publication of all aspects of firms' financial accounting is a most important one – one that is often unfortunately overlooked by the labour movement.

Our joint shop stewards committee has a fighting fund with a total income of about £80 a week. This is raised in part by a deduction of 6d. a week per worker and a tote, of which half goes back in prizes and the rest goes to the fund. This is used to give financial aid for disputes outside our factory, such as during the seaman's strike. Although some opposition was expressed on the factory floor to the dispute, there can be no doubt that if the same scale of financial help and distribution of leaflets stating the seaman's case had been forthcoming from factories up and down the land the outcome would have been different. The majority of the shop stewards are Labour Party members, a minority are Communists, and there are a few Tories; the latter are noticeably as militant as the rest when it comes to economic issues.

When I talk to older workers about the attitude of youth in

their day, I am immediately struck by the fact that today's young workers are almost all of a different stamp. This is evident in their self-assurance and their refusal to accept things at face value. This is not to say that many young workers of the past were not the same, but they were probably a minority; today, they are in the majority. I find it hard to understand why this enormous potential is not realized by the labour movement, and especially the trade unions. The latter would have a new wave of fresh ideas and enthusiasm if junior workers' committees, working along with the shop stewards as they do in our factory, were generally adopted. Our own junior committee has been responsible for improvements in both wages and working conditions. Some years before the Industrial Training Act our factory, with the joint cooperation of management and unions, introduced universal training with day release for all young workers, thus abolishing the curse of dead-end jobs. And the impact of this over a period of time will be much greater than the question of improved training alone. Awareness that the unions have done something concrete for them has engendered a healthy and constructive attitude among the young workers to the union and workshop organization.

The result of all this is a widespread belief among the older workers that the new generation will never put up with some of the things that they had to suffer in their day.

We are fortunate in our factory in having a type of work that is very intricate, that has an interesting end product and requires great skills. This reduces some of the monotony that usually exists in factory life. But factory work under the present system is not the only work that is monotonous, unsatisfying and lacking in purpose for those who have to do it. It is surprising that there isn't a wholesale revolt against a system that engenders so much monotonous and purposeless work.

Militancy and class consciousness should not stop at the factory gate. This of course is the hardest task of all to achieve.

The same workers who will lose several hours on a question of principle will not always spend several minutes in attending their union branch and voting for a progressive candidate to give them the national backing they need for their shop-floor activity. It may be in part that in a well-organized factory this is seen by the lads – incorrectly – as unnecessary. Irrespective of this, a highly organized plant inevitably widens the workers' vision to more of life than just his workplace. Part of this widening comes from the setting up of combine committees where there are several scattered plants in a large combine such as ours. They are not created easily, for different factories often have to be won for the idea; but through the deliberate spread of information on varying wages and conditions – we, for example, prepare mimeographed sheets giving complete details of earnings and organization in our plant – pressure is exerted by the lower-paid plants in the combine to catch up with the higher. The employers do not like combine committees because they prevent them from playing one factory off against another, and some of the full-time union officials also oppose them because they upset their cosy relationship with the Establishment. The ultimate, of course, would be the combine acting as a single unit, but to date this has been rarely achieved.

Another widening area is political activity in the plant. The ideas which really start advancing the workers in a factory, though many are traditional, come from the dynamic produced by the cooperation of conscious left-wing and communist trade unionists. All the policies that have emerged on automation, resistance to sackings, redundancy, etc. that have been of any use to the working class have come from the left; the growth of this activity is the only guarantee of advance on the shop floor. One aspect of the broader work that really opens the eyes of the worker is the occasional lobbying of Parliament and MPs that takes place amongst well-organized workers. When a worker walks into the House and sees the antiquated rituals (shades of Wilson's remark about the AEU rule-book being a hundred years out of date), sees, with a few honourable exceptions, the fishy-eyed MPs who have no ideas about the problems the worker and his industry face, he comes away certainly a wiser, and often a more cynical, man. But cynicism is of no good to the labour movement, it must be changed to anger and the anger to action to end this farce in which the existing system uses the worker to get what it can out of him.

For myself, and many others like me, there is thus an additional dimension to our work. Seen against a broader canvas, the frustrations of everyday factory life tend to dwindle; the major frustration then lies in not advancing the cause you believe in enough. The satisfaction lies in not being a cipher or a clock number, but in consciously striving to do something for the present and the future.

The present means improving where we can the system we work under and of advancing new ideas; it means high wage-levels and turning the factory to look outward and participate in activities beyond itself. The future is one of building a strong and united movement to bring about a socialist society, so that the final words of the song with which I began can come about:

> Yet comrades face the wind,
> Salute the rising sun,
> Our country turns towards the light,
> New Life's begun.

PHILLIP HIGGS

THE AUTHOR

I was born in Yeovil in 1925. My father was a draughtsman and later became a chief designer. I went to Warwick school and started my working life as a metallurgical technician in an engineering plant. At the age of seventeen I joined the Young Communist League.

Balloted as a Bevin boy during the war, my political convictions took root and matured in the coal-mines through personal experience of the realities of mining life.

I joined the Communist Party in 1945. Since then I have worked in various engineering factories and have been a shop steward in a car factory, from which I was sacked for writing a satirical send-up of the management.

Since 1954 I have been in my present factory, starting there as an inspector. I became a shop steward a short time after going there, and have been a convenor for the past six years. I am a member of the AEU, the majority union in my factory.

I like travel, art, music – anything from Bartok to pop, with the exception of palm court – fast driving and the theatre, not necessarily in that order. I am a trustee of Coventry's Belgrade Theatre, whose theatre for schools has this year chosen to deal with the struggle of people in the city for freedom from feudal oppression. Among many other outside activities, like tenants' housing campaigns, I am a governor of Lanchester College of Technology and Coventry Technical College, and on the executive council of the Midland Federation of Trades Councils.

I am single and live in a small council flat in a post-war development on the outskirts of the city.

The Subby Bricklayer

At 8 a.m. the whistle blows. If it's not raining and I have to wait until it has eased, I pick up my tools and walk or climb to my place of work. The labourers have already put mortar on the boards and have bricks stacked ready. I get out a set of lines, used for laying the bricks to, set them up and start laying bricks. In eighteen years of bricklaying, beginning as an apprentice, I long ago got into the habit of counting the bricks I lay, and I set my work pace to the rate of pay.

At 9.30 or so another whistle blows for tea break. Everybody downs tools and we troop off to the canteen or whatever shelter is provided for the break. Ten minutes later the whistle blows again. We start work and I wait for the dinner break whistle at 12.30. Half an hour later it blows again. Then I wait for the 3 p.m. tea break whistle. The best whistle of the day is the going home one at 5, 5.30 or 6 – this is the one that releases me from 'prison'.

On most jobs I am allotted a number which is stamped on a brass disc and which I take off a board in the morning and replace in the evening. At 8.7 a.m. the timekeeper takes the board in to the office and anyone arriving after that time is stopped a quarter or a half hour etc. Some jobs even have that abomination, the 'one-armed bandit' or time clock. This time-counting always irritates me and, if I am on a straight hourly rated job, I always charge the firm bricks laid. A brass disc costs the firm 100 bricks a day and a time clock 200. I deliberately make sure that I lay bricks short by this amount. I can understand the necessity for rigid timekeeping in a factory where the assembly line must be manned at certain prescribed times, but not on a building site, where I can always catch up lost time. Actual production on most jobs does not start until about 8.30 anyway.

Many people ask me how many bricks a day I can lay: well, it depends on the job. On long straight walls which have to be plastered or buried in footings, I have laid 2,250 in a nine-hour day. But this is unusual. Something like 1,500 on this type of work is the norm. But on small piers or fiddly awkward bits of work, I may only lay 100. A good average is about 800.

Bricklayers always work in pairs. I find it easier to work with a man who has served an apprenticeship rather than the self-taught man who does not seem to have the 'polish' of the properly trained craftsman. The latter often refers to the self-taught bricky as a 'cowboy' or 'trowel hand', a taunt to which he is oblivious because more often than not he earns more money than the 'proper' bricklayer.

If the job I am on is on bonus, then I will be working in a gang of about six bricklayers and two or three labourers. Each of us sets himself a norm, enough bricks laid to make a reasonable bonus, but not too much or we might 'spoil it'. The constant fear is that if we have too good a week the targets might be raised by the bonus clerk. To understand why this is so requires a description of the rather complicated and variegated systems of how we are paid for our work.

First, we are paid an hourly rate of pay as laid down by agreement between the trade unions and the employers. The current rate is, I believe, 7s. 2d. per hour. In 1951 the unions, after seventy years of opposition, agreed to the introduction of 'payments by results' or 'bonus' schemes. Under this system the employer pays the hourly rate of pay as laid down, plus a bonus for work done over and above a 'target' – so many bricks laid per hour. Bonus is calculated not on individual effort by any one craftsman, but by the collective efforts of a 'gang'. The carpenters will work as one gang, the bricklayers as another, and so on, trade by trade. If the site is large enough, then the trades themselves are split into gangs. You might, therefore, get twenty-four bricklayers on a site split into four gangs of six. The labourers, of course, share in the bonus earnings.

Bonus is usually paid fortnightly, so that if a man starts work on a Monday, he will not know what his bonus earnings are for two weeks. If he thinks they are unreasonable, then he can either quit or take action on the site – strike or 'go slow'. We call going slow laying 'golden bricks'. The firm must at least pay the union rate, whatever is produced.

It is this bonus work that causes most trouble on building sites. The men are not easily satisfied and are always suspicious of being 'fiddled'. The unions have little control over piecework earnings. They leave target-setting to the employers and the men on individual sites. There is little that is consistent about targets. They vary widely from job to job and with the nature of the work. But the original agreement was supposed to allow men to earn at least 20 per cent over the union rate, without undue strain. In practice few bricklayers will be content with less than 50 per cent and many want more, including me.

Another method of payment is for firms to pay a standing bonus, so much per hour over the union rate. Currently few firms would offer less than 10s. per hour. A third system is labour only sub-contracting in which a bricklayer or a group of bricklayers will undertake to do the brickwork on a job for so much per yard super (98 bricks). A contract is signed and then the sub-contractor will employ his own bricklayers. He will pay anything up to 15s. an hour, or so much per day, never less than £5, and stamp his own cards.

In case of unsatisfactory work and to prevent the sub-contractor from quitting suddenly, 5 per cent of the contract price is retained. This retention money is supposed to be paid after a certain period, usually six months after the completion of the job. Very often this money is not paid, even if the work is satisfactory.

When I am seeking employment, I always look for the job which pays the 'biggest penny'. I may look in the building section of the *Evening News* or someone may tell me where a job is: pubs provide a useful service here as unofficial labour exchanges. I have never yet registered at a labour exchange. What I endeavour to do is to select a job which is as near home as possible. I may see a site and 'try my luck'. The first thing I ask is, 'Is there any fear of a start?' If the answer is in the affirmative I then ask 'What's it paying?' The answer may be 'bare and bone' – union rate and bonus. The next question is, 'How's it been paying?' and if over the last few weeks bonus earnings have been good, I will start. If I am the first bricklayer on the job, I inquire as to what the target rates are. If they are too high, I can negotiate and try and get them reduced, but usually I would have to wait until more bricklayers start so that I can negotiate from a position of strength. Sometimes firms will not negotiate at all. If the job is a union job we can send for an organizer to try and persuade the firm to change its mind. In the meantime, if we haven't decided to quit, we will lay 'golden bricks' and 'work to rule'.

Most men will not stay on a job if it seems likely that there will be a period of this sort of trouble. More can be earned elsewhere. Since I much prefer to work for a pre-determined hourly rate, I usually seek employment with subby bricklayers. Even on the best bonus jobs there is always interminable argument about the targets between the men and the bonus clerk (if the job is large enough). The bonus clerk is usually a trainee surveyor, a young and inexperienced lad who knows little about the men's problems. He is, therefore, usually very cautious and refers to a senior for important decisions. This takes time and a 'go slow' may be under way before a decision is made. There is a common belief among the men that the bonus clerk has to be paid out of the bonus earnings before they get their share. 'Another ponce we have to keep.'

For the past seven years I have been a labour only sub-contractor (a subby). To become a subby has certain disadvantages. In the first place I must become self-employed. To be self-employed means I lose the right to unemployment pay, workmens' compensation and the opportunity of a secure job with a building firm and promotion prospects. I am also responsible for stamping my own cards and those of anyone I employ. This is seldom, as I prefer to work on my own. The benefits that accrue are that I pay less income tax than I would on P.A.Y.E., and in the short run I can earn more money than working as an employee.

For me, subbing has certain very important non-monetary

advantages. To understand what these are requires a description of work conditions in the building industry and its work routine. Robert Tressell in his book *The Ragged Trousered Philanthropist*, which I read some eighteen years ago, described the building industry and its conditions as they were at the beginning of this century. It is surprising how little has changed in the intervening period.

As I have already explained, we are still a 'casual' industry. That is, my labour is bought and paid for by the hour. If I do not report for work, there is no pay. If I am late for work or leave the job early, my time is stopped. The smallest unit of time is a quarter of an hour, although I have been stopped an eighth on one job. The timekeeper is considered to be another 'ponce'. His job is to 'steal' time.

If the weather is inclement and I have to stop work, time again is docked. Except for a few enlightened firms and local authorities, there are no pensions or sick pay for building operatives. Holiday pay is paid by the employer stamping two cards, one for statutory and the other for annual holidays. If I am unemployed or sick my cards do not get stamped. Supervisory grades from general foremen up usually get full benefit.

Conditions are, in general, deplorable. The Working Rule Agreement of the Building Industry (the National Collective Agreement) lays down that there shall be an adequate shelter in case of bad weather and a clean place in which to eat food. Hot meals must be provided if the site employs over fifty men. A lock-up for tools must be provided and a drying room for drying wet clothing. Toilet facilities must also be provided and protective clothing for employees should be available. These are seldom, if ever, supplied and if they are, men often steal or spoil them.

The conditions we usually get are a ramshackle shed that serves the multiple purpose of eating place, shelter, tool shed, lock-up and storeroom for cement. The toilet facilities generally consist of a little hut over a hole in the ground, or an overfull-elsan bucket.

Building inspectors and union officials are supposed to

ensure that proper facilities are provided, but I have seldom seen them on sites. Building inspectors are few in number and could not possibly get to all building sites in their area. Union officials are also thin on the ground and will only go to jobs that are union shops. The same applies to safety inspectors. There are far too few of them. The last time I heard from one of these gentlemen was six years ago. He sent me a letter to tell me that I should improve the scaffold I was working on. Not only was the scaffolding not my responsibility, but I received the letter three months after the job was finished.

In general, conditions depend on the size of the project. The larger the job, the better the conditions. This is because a large project can absorb the cost of expensive temporary buildings. Firms also know that the big site will attract inspectors and union trouble-shooters. The bad conditions of the building industry are not entirely the fault of management. On a couple of occasions I have been a shop steward. In this capacity I was supposed to badger the general foreman to improve conditions. On one particular site the facilities provided were, by building standards, excellent. Even hot water was provided for washing up after work. The flush toilets were smashed by boisterous labourers and the canteen, which provided hot meals, was ruined. The hot water was ignored, the men preferring to go home dirty rather than wash first. In the end the general foreman gave up and I agreed with him.

If conditions in the building industry are to improve, it not only requires an enlightened management but a work force that cares about conditions. On the whole building workers are indifferent to their work conditions. How much in the pay packet is the sole criterion for judging one job better than another. They will cheerfully leave one job with good conditions for one with bad if the money is better. Labour turnover on any given site is usually very high.

According to the unions, if a man works for a subby or becomes one, then many of the conditions fought for by the unions are foregone. A few years ago the unions sent a circular to all members suggesting that they should not work for subbies. If they did, the unions would not be responsible for lost wages if the subby refused to pay. But in my experience, subbies always pay promptly, even daily if I have wanted it.

A surprising fact is the number of union ex-militants who are sub-contracting. For one reason or other the unions have disillusioned them and they have torn up their union cards. I can't help feeling that the unions did themselves a lot of harm when they alienated these men who, in my opinion, were potential union leaders.

The building unions are in a sorry state. Membership is declining and the branches are virtually empty. A typical branch meeting consists of six members – communists are usually the most assiduous attenders – out of a paper membership of two to three hundred. To seek office in the union, as a full-time official, a brother must be elected by the members. This entails a dreary tour of dingy branches until he gets his name and face known by a sufficient number of members who will vote for him. This can take years. Even if a brother is lucky enough to get an organizer's job, the pay will be less than he will get on piecework. The union subscription of 2s. 6d. a week is too low to pay officials properly. The unions for most bricklayers cease to exist. It is not unusual for men not to know the current union rate of pay.

There are a number of reasons for this decline. Full employment and a scarcity of skilled craftsmen has meant that supply and demand mechanisms have replaced the unions as the means of setting wage rates. For the past seven years the unofficial market rate for bricklayers has increased by about a shilling an hour per annum. The unions in the meantime spend a year to get a penny. In accepting the principle of piecework, the unions made a rod for their own backs. Another important reason for the decline is the fact that the unions have lost control over entry into the trade. Rarely will a boy today go through a lengthy apprenticeship as I did, if he can learn more quickly 'unofficially'.

Buildings nowadays lend themselves to piecework. They are designed for speed of erection. The straighter the walls, the quicker the bricklayer is able to lay bricks. Lintels are used instead of arches. The favourite jobs are the ones where the work is repetitious: blocks of flats or housing estates, where each unit is the same. On this type of work the 'big money' is earned. But although more money can be earned on this type of construction, it is also monotonous. After the initial novelty of starting on a new job has worn off, it just becomes a question of one damned brick after another. The only way to stop the boredom from becoming overwhelming is to keep busy. The time passes more quickly and, of course, piecework earnings are enhanced. The jobs I can't stand are the slow-paced jobs, where golden bricks are laid. These are usually the jobs where standing bonus is being paid. I was on such a job recently. I hadn't been on the job for more than two hours when the foreman told me to 'cut out the slashing' because I would make it 'bad for the others'. Each day seemed like a week, and time was spent doing a minimum of work and a maximum of 'wanking', general loafing about. I could only stand the job for six days and went back to work on my own again.

In the main I now try to stay away from union-organized jobs. The last one I worked on was an LCC housing estate. The target rates were fair and the bonus earned reasonable. Each day at lunchtime the shop stewards, eight of them, took it in turn to make speeches. These men had considerable eloquence and the whole thing was like a lunchtime cabaret. But sometimes the speech-making would go on past the allotted half hour for lunch and the men were stopped time, which caused an outcry. When the management tried to get rid of the stewards we were on strike. The union did not back the strike and the whole thing petered out after a few days. The men returned to work, those who hadn't quit, and the stewards remained. A few weeks later there was more trouble. I left the job. Shortly afterwards I tried to organize a job at Moorgate, but no one was interested. I was the only one there with a union ticket.

I am not against the unions as such. But the trouble is that the unions have lost the confidence of building workers.

They are out of touch with the rank and file and seem content to do little about it. Most bricklayers I have worked with have been members of the union at one time or another. I have not met one in the last eight years who still has a fully paid up 'ticket'. To most practising bricklayers the union is a joke. This is a pity, because the unions have done sterling work in the past to better the lot of the building worker. As I see it, the trouble with the unions is that they are still acting on policies more appropriate to the days of heavy unemployment. They seem to refuse to believe that men are motivated by the cash nexus. Instead, they act as if members were committed to a code that now seems outdated. They continually emphasize brotherly love and comradeship. All must work for the benefit of each other. These are worthy ambitions. But I have never encountered anything like 'brotherly' love on building sites, whether union or not. Most building workers are selfishly individualistic and only hold a union card if by doing so they can earn more money.

In spite of the uncertainties attached to labour only sub-contracting, I prefer to work as a subby than as an employee. After all, what do I gain by being an employee? As such I still lack security. I can be sacked from a job with as little as two hours' notice. This applies no matter how long I have worked for a firm. I have seen men sacked with two hours' notice after having worked for a firm for over ten years. I have never felt inclined to tie myself to a firm for any length of time. The fact that as a self-employed person I cannot draw unemployment pay does not bother me unduly, as I have never drawn it. As for accident injury, I can insure myself against such a contingency. Work conditions are exactly the same whether I work sub-contract or as an employee. As a subby I have the feeling I am working *with* the general foreman rather than *for* him; the same applies if I work for a fellow subby.

Working for myself I expect to earn a minimum of £1 per hour; working for a subby 15s. per hour; and working for a firm about 10s. I won't work for less than this last amount unless desperate. At each wage rate I adjust my efforts accordingly. I do as little as possible for a firm but as much as I can when working for myself. For the subby I do as much as he pushes for, but usually he gets more than his money's worth.

As far as I can see, the unions merely act as a sort of wages council, setting minimum rates of pay and a legal framework for the building industry. On the other side are the managers. I include in this category all supervisory staff from general foreman up. Within my working memory, a building site had only one supervisor, the general foreman. This still holds true on small sites, say up to a value of about £30,000.

On the big sites, management has proliferated. New techniques have necessitated a specialization in managerial staff. It is not unusual for a sites' supervisory staff to comprise, in order of authority, an agent, a general foreman, an assistant general foreman, a surveyor, an engineer and his assistant. In addition there will be a bonus clerk. The large job will have a resident clerk of works who may have an assistant. On top of this there will be an assortment of district surveyors (building inspectors), architects and safety inspectors who will visit the job from time to time. Other non-productive staff are timekeepers. A large project will rarely employ more than 150 men. No wonder many men feel that they have 'too many ponces to keep'.

It seems to me that many of these staff men are superfluous. I never could quite see what an agent is supposed to do that a general foreman doesn't. As for engineers, it is difficult to see just what useful function they serve. And if all this managerial staff is necessary, do they have to spend three hours in the pub at lunch time? Or roll on to the job at 9 or 10 when the men start at 8? Neither, I think, is it necessary for them to leave at 4 when the job works to 6.

On jobs that are 'let out' to subbies, supervision is minimal. The sub-contractor is his own supervisor, with money as the silent policeman ensuring that he does his job competently.

For men working on a job, the general foreman is the key figure. It is he to whom they are directly responsible after the trade foreman. A subby is his own trade foreman. General foremen are usually upgraded craftsmen who have chosen to be 'generals' rather than pieceworkers. We call them 'tired' tradesmen. They will promise almost anything to get a job done and cheerfully go back on that promise if it will save the firm a few pounds. They are, on the whole, an arrogant lot, who consider themselves superior to the men. To make a simple decision seems to take them ages and if they make a mistake, they seek to 'ring' it on the workers. I can give an instance of this. A general foreman once asked me to build a wall incorrectly. When the fault was discovered by his superior, he put the blame on me. I pointed out that it was he who instructed me to build the wall out of true. He denied it. That little episode cost me £15. Requests of a similar nature I have since insisted be put in writing. When things go wrong or work is taking too long, the general foreman never admits that some of the blame is his. It is always the lazy useless workers he has.

With employees, general foremen love to act the role of squire, particularly those who insist on being called 'Mister'. From my own experience there is a distinct correlation between the 'gentlemen' and lack of competence. We call these squires 'piss-quicks'. All generals dream of the good old days before their time when there was high unemployment. They want to employ labour for as little as possible, bare union rate or less. On more than one occasion a general has confided to me that a 'bit of unemployment would do the industry the world of good'. This would enable them to dispense with pieceworkers and to discipline the workers. They, personally, of course, would not be amongst the ranks of the unemployed.

Much of what I say about general foremen applies equally to clerks of works. They are also upgraded craftsmen, but have taken their City and Guilds Certificates. Their job for which they are paid by the local authority, is to make sure that the work proceeds in accordance with specifications and conforms to local byelaws. They are security minded men who live in a 'semi' and dream of retirement day. The worst of them insist that all work be done by the book. I always give them what they want at the beginning of a job, no matter how ridiculous their demands. The trick is to get their confidence and be sure and address them as 'Mister', because they are very status conscious. General foremen are terrified of them because a too rigid clerk of works can break a job financially. They are a necessary evil, for I hate to think what firms would get away with if there was no check on their activities. But clerks have too much arbitrary power. Their decisions cannot be appealed against. If ever there was a device for lowering productivity, I would say that we have it in the office of clerk of works.

The picture I have presented so far of the building industry is not a very rosy one. Probably my occupation is not any worse than many others and better than some. I prefer a building site to, say, a factory production line.

Sometimes the work can be very rewarding. A nice sunny day, a new job and a reasonable crowd of fellows to work with can give one the feeling, 'I wouldn't want to be anywhere else just now.' This feeling is enhanced if earnings are good. The jobs I have enjoyed the most are those where I have worked the hardest. But this feeling has become more rare as I have grown older.

The industrial psychologist tells us that there are three reasons why a man works. The first is because of the job itself, call it craft pride or a sense of vocation. The second is because of the social environment of the place of work, and the third is for money. We are told that the first man is the most fortunate and the latter the unluckiest.

At one time I would have put myself in the first category. When I was younger, I considered myself fortunate to be a bricklayer. It was a skilled occupation from which I derived much aesthetic pleasure. There were two reasons for this. I found the job itself pleasurable and I felt I was performing a social service. The latter aspect was more evident when I was engaged on housing, especially working-class housing. Slum dwellers, I thought, ought to be served first and these were mainly working-class people. At the time I felt this a Labour government was in office and we had a housing plan that was supposed to help the worst off first.

As I've grown older, the job has become more monotonous, partly due to new building techniques and partly due to years of repetition. Perhaps age has something to do with it. I am becoming increasingly aware of aches and pains that were not present as a younger man. Perhaps disillusionment comes because of the way my employers and society treat me as a bricklayer. The employers treat me as a means to an end, seldom as a person. An expendable item to be discarded like an old boot when no longer required.

I am now a better bricklayer than I was. But I know this will count for nothing if I cannot produce quantity as well as quality of work. Very soon I shall be thrown on the scrap heap or have to join the low-wage 'daywork' bricklayers. I now feel no sense of aesthetic pleasure in my job. I am competent at it because this is the way to make the maximum of money. I feel no sense of being socially useful. Society does not seem to appreciate my efforts nor can I get any pleasure from building these architectural monstrosities we call office blocks and homes. My job could quite easily be done by machines and often is by new concreting techniques. For a good many years now I have sold my skill, if it can still be called that, to the highest bidder. This puts me in the psychologists' third category, the money-motivated unfortunate.

Perhaps matters would not be so bad if I could have shared these feelings with mates on the job. To admit that I am actually enjoying my job on a building site is a fatal error. If I admit this to a general foreman it is a signal for him to 'fiddle' my money. I remember confiding in a group of bricklayers once; for as long as I was on that job I was known as 'the queer bastard'.

Like most bricklayers, I am a fiercely independent character. I owe no loyalty to any firm or any man. I will quit a job if slighted by a supervisor or if a 'bigger penny' is offered elsewhere. I do my job well with an ease gained from years of experience. On the whole I resent being where I am and the lowly social position accorded to bricklayers. I might add that there is some justification for this: building workers are a rough and ready lot. Most of them are aware of their lowly social status and comments like 'You can't get lower than a building worker' and 'We are scum' are often heard. A building worker proves his point by doing all in his power to dissuade his sons from following in his footsteps. He prefers them to have a lower-paid secure white-collar job than have them follow his example. I remember asking a bricklayer friend how his two sons were doing at school; his bitter answer – 'Bloody awful, they're stupid enough to become bricklayers' – summed up the average bricky's contempt for his own position. If I had sons instead of daughters I would take good care that they did not enter the building industry in any capacity.

In summer the job is tolerable unless it's too hot. Winter-time is the worst. I travel to work in the dark and come home in the dark. It is in the winter that pay packets become slimmer. This is due to short-time working because of day-light hours and inclement weather. During the bad winter of 1962 I was out of work for ten weeks. There is the added hazard of sickness which is always greater in the winter months. Like most building workers I have fat pay packets in summer and less in winter. I never did seem able to save summer gains to offset winter losses.

Cold weather aggravates a sensitive back and much time can be lost through slipped discs, a twisted pelvis and just plain lumbago. I have on more than one occasion hobbled into work with back trouble – I just couldn't afford to take time off. I usually have a backache of some description as a permanent condition.

As I get older, the winters seem to get colder. It is during the cold weather, especially with a numbing east wind blow-ing, that I vow that this will be my last winter in the game. Next winter sees me on another scaffold saying the same thing.

Men do leave the industry and I hope to be one of them. The critical age is the mid-forties. This is the time when a man gets past his peak performance. The kids take less looking after and the wife is free to take a job, even if only part time. Needing less money, the 'cushy' secure job seems attractive. Many a good bricklayer ends his working life as a storekeeper in a factory.

The average working bricky is contemptuous of himself for being such a bloody fool as to be in the trade, but he is even more contemptuous of his supervisors, whom he sees as incompetent policemen and lackeys of the employers. He is also contemptuous of a general public which considers him a lazy, dirty workman, which he often is.

If other aspects were better, the monotony, time routine and dirtiness of my job could be offset. I may be over-sensitive, but I resent being treated as some sort of animal by supervisors I consider to be no better than me. If management were as efficient at their job as I am at mine, I would have fewer complaints. But they're not. Like the unions they recruit from the wrong sources. Pieceworkers ought to be encouraged into management because these are the men with drive. But they would have to be paid more; a general foreman today earns no more than he would if he were pieceworking, and he resents the fact, over-looking the fringe benefits and security of employment.

In any case, some system ought to be found to get rid of piecework in the industry. I resent having to work against the dangling carrot. I do it because in present circumstances it is the only way in which I can satisfactorily work. I would much prefer to have a secure job with a reasonable wage. Something of the order of £30 a week with full benefits would induce me to abandon piecework and ensure that I would produce my best efforts. I would even endure the time regimen for this salary. But even so, I think it is an insufferable indignity that my time should be calculated in minute quantities of quarters of an hour.

Soon I hope to be leaving the building industry and with little regret. In the last six years my absorbing interests have been my leisure-time pursuits. I took an extra-mural course in philosophy which I found both exciting and interesting.

Unfortunately it made my job even more boring, but at least it gave me something to think about while laying bricks. My workmates greeted my 'hobby' with derision. 'Who do you think you are?' 'You're trying to become one of *them*' were commonplace remarks. For the average building worker a leisure activity must show a return in material terms. Evening classes in car maintenance can save money, but not philosophy. If I were to stay in the industry, I could aspire to the dizzy heights of general foreman, doing the things general foremen are supposed to do and which I've described. I know good men who have become general foremen with the express intention of 'changing the emphasis' and doing right by the boys. As far as I can see, the 'emphasis' changes them and they are no different from all the others whose avowed intention is to do right by themselves.

So I shall leave. For all that, I am not sorry to have spent eighteen of my thirty-eight years as a bricklayer. There is a certain joy in being able to do something competently with one's hands and of using muscular force with common sense to overcome obstacles, to exercise individual initiative in translating the drawings (the plan which never visualizes the snags that inevitably occur) into reality. But increasingly the plans are for square boxes, designed by square little men for square little people to live in. Perhaps this is the main reason why I shall be glad to leave the building industry. I no longer feel we are creating something worthwhile.

MAX GAGG

THE AUTHOR

I was born in Blackpool in 1930 but was brought up in London. My family consisted of four brothers (including a twin) and two sisters, Mum and Dad. Dad was a lorry driver (he died in 1955) and Mum is Irish.

At the outbreak of war in 1939 I was evacuated to Bognor Regis. At the age of eleven I won a county scholarship and a year later a trade scholarship. I took up the latter and attended the Brixton College of Building for three years.

I was apprenticed to the Battersea Borough Council at sixteen, serving four years. Then the Army got me and I spent eighteen months in Hong Kong.

Demobbed in 1952, I went back to the council, but left after a year. I worked on various jobs as a bricklayer until I emigrated to Canada in 1957, where I worked, as a bricklayer, until my return to this country two years later. I married in 1961 and have two daughters, aged five and two.

Still working as a bricky I took extra-mural classes in current events and philosophy. My philosophy tutor, A. P. Griffiths, now professor at Warwick, suggested I read for a degree. I applied for the one-year course in Trade Union Studies at London School of Economics, which I successfully completed in 1963–4. Whilst there I tried for a mature state scholarship, and achieved the interview but not the scholarship.

Meanwhile I read for three G.C.E. 'A' Levels, which I managed to get by January of 1965. With these in my pocket I applied to Goldsmiths College for a place on their B.Sc. Sociology Course, and was accepted. I commenced reading for my degree in September of 1965, have passed Part I of the degree and have one more year to go for the finals.

I still lay bricks during vacation time, as at the moment.

The Architect

I don't know why I became an architect; but then does anyone really know why they take up a particular job? Rather like a military, political or legal family, mine was an architectural one. My great uncle was an architect and even managed to become president of the RIBA. My father followed in his footsteps without signal success; considering his mediocrity, it was surprising that he kept his enthusiasm until he died. In line with tradition, it was his deep wish that one of his sons, at least, should assume the architectural mantle. This, when asked, my elder brother flatly refused to do. Fully aware of the opportunity for one-upmanship I sang out, 'I want to be like you, Daddy.'

Any subsequent doubts about my choice have been nothing to the doubt that assails me now. You see, I've crossed the Rubicon and it is abundantly clear that I haven't made the grade and never will; well, not in the way that I had visualized. I suspect that either I was never really the stuff of which architects are made or that the whole bang shoot is not what I thought it would be when I joined the club; or maybe architecture itself has changed as a source that has soured. Perhaps none of us architects realize this or are prepared to recognize it; perhaps we are all perpetuating the myth that architecture is an art and won't admit that it is simply a science of building economics. I can't be the only one to think that it's all a bloody great fraud.

I became an architect because the appearance of buildings held my interest, or to put it more strongly, because they fascinated me both visually as well as historically, not, as is usually put forward, because I had an urge to draw. I believed that in becoming an architect I should be responsible for deciding what a building looked like and thereby contribute something towards my own period, secure in my own self-confidence that I might even be remembered by what I had designed. Because I had found in history certain evidence, certain values, certain conclusions, so I assumed that architecture was a logical evolution based on traditions which were changed, altered and adapted to suit the condition of each successive age. Styles and periods meant something to me. Modern was a term to denote the style of this our own period. Architecture was basically a visual matter with the utilitarian concept secondary. It never crossed my mind that there might be a social content. At least, no one ever mentioned it. Of course, planning was important, but this was taken for granted and was merely the means by which the architect produced his masterpiece. I found precious little mention in architectural history of ugly buildings that were superbly planned, but plenty about beautiful ones that were badly planned.

I had been led to believe that I was joining a profession, admired by the public, whose members were gentlemen first and foremost, then artists; men who possessed individuality and power, men who ruled their clients as they ruled the site operatives, men who were arbiters of taste and who never stooped to criticize their colleagues. It was understood that the prime object of the architect was to build to the glory of God and that the rewards were sufficient compensation for this privilege, besides which gentlemen did not lower themselves to haggle over money nor involve themselves with the sordid world of commercialism. It was stressed that architects were balanced, well-rounded personalities, the middle C, in fact, of the piano scale where high C covered the long-haired aesthetes – pure artists to some, parasites to others – and the low bass the builders and those of similar ilk. Architecture was, above all, a sensible, practical art, practised by sensible, practical men occasionally inspired to create the divine work which would last the centuries to come. That architecture had any connexion with present-day society was apparently ignored.

This, then, was the premise on which I took up my 'life's work'. This was the ambience through which I entered the profession at the very moment when this entire attitude of thought was being undermined, had begun to topple and was so shortly to be swept away by the social revolution that followed the 1939 war. This is why I am disillusioned. Yet despite the shock that my job has turned out to be very different from what I had anticipated, the compensations have not been inconsiderable. I can't, for instance, visualize doing anything else, but equally that is not to say that I shall necessarily continue as I am. The pressures of the non-architectural aspects of the work are such as to preclude this. It is simply a matter of how long I am prepared to stand the treadmill.

When I was demobbed after the Second World War I was told that I would have to repeat my first year, which I had completed before the war. This seemed no way to treat a returning hero, so I decided to join my father's office and study on my own in the evenings. A mistake this, compounded by that of living at home. Sparks flew, I left home, grew a beard, married and had children. Finally, my father summoned me to his office and sacked me. 'He won't get another job with that beard,' he assured my mother. 'I expect him to come to heel with humility in no time, mark my words.'

I waved farewell to the chance of a partnership in his practice. It took me, after many setbacks and failures, seven years to qualify. Working in a vacuum, I came to realize that I needed contacts, for clients today often prove to be other architects, official ones. After considerable heart-searching I applied for and got a job with the London County Council in the Housing Department. I say heart-searching, for this was a step out of private enterprise into security and, as I believed, the narrowness of official architecture, the very antithesis of my goal. To my surprise, because I was as yet still unqualified, I was accepted for the post of job architect, grade 3, which was a cut above a mere assistant and was the lowest rung on the ladder of the hierarchy. I moved into a world of standardization, and learnt much. Less than three years later I was at Hertford County Council as a group or section leader working on schools and exploring this brave new world of components, modules and systems. More important still I had rectified some of my disadvantages by picking up a good pedigree and by meeting large numbers of architects, dedicated to official architecture, who are now leading the profession into the new world of industrialized architecture, which, whilst not really new, is the epithalamium of our age. Simultaneously I was forming the nucleus of my own practice, for, despite the attractions of climbing the ladder of officialdom, I was still convinced that fame and fortune and, above all, true self-respect came only when you were principal of your own firm.

At last the moment arrived. A client for whom I had done a house and a sports pavilion asked me to be architect for the new office block at his factory in Birmingham. I gave in my notice and set up an office, a one-room affair in Finchley. I already had a number of clients of some years standing – most of them school friends of my wife – and my first private job had been done some seven years before. Among those early jobs was a tricky but satisfactory reconstruction and modernization of a sixteenth-century half-timbered pair of cottages near Stratford-on-Avon. Not long afterwards I happened to be at a party chatting desultorily with a most formidable woman about architecture when I suddenly realized that she was indignantly protesting at the rape of a lovely old house near Stratford. 'And I think,' she concluded with relish, 'that the architect, if he dares call himself one, should be castrated for what he has done to the house.' Blushing with embarrassment for her as well as myself, I murmured in reply: 'If you have a knife handy, you'd better have a go while you can, for here he is before you, quite unrepentant.'

Within a few months the office-block scheme was abandoned on the excuse that it was too modern. Cap in hand, metaphorically, I was begging work here, there and everywhere. The bottom fell out of my world momentarily, but I survived. I was approached by an architect with a view to forming a partnership and agreed. At first everything went swimmingly. I began a series of school jobs while my partner brought in a factory, an office extension and several other pleasant commissions. After a while we were asked to design a restaurant in the West End. It wasn't certain which of us had obtained this commission, for while my partner knew the firm's Estates Manager, I knew the Managing Director. This caused the first signs of friction. Others followed, perhaps equally stupid, until finally I could stand no more and asked for a dissolution of the partnership. Like divorce, the grounds for complaint seemed trivial enough, especially in retrospect, but at the time they were very real. I accused him of doing no work; he countered this with a charge of extravagance. In fact it was simply a matter of incompatability; on the few occasions when we meet now we are still friends.

I picked up the pieces and began again, this time using my home as a temporary office. It was at the time that Sir Donald Gibson, fresh from his triumphs and troubles at Coventry, was busy at the War Office initiating a new building system; it was decided to try out the system on a pilot scheme for a new barracks at Maidstone. The research team sought out the help of a private architect, and the trail led to me. This was my big chance. I felt sure that a sizeable job such as this must inevitably attract others of similar size. I must not let the chance go. I found new premises, engaged new staff and, for the fourth time in four years, set off to prove that I was another Christopher Wren.

It didn't work out. Not only did no other large jobs materialize, but I had no say in the project itself; as a sort of consolation prize I was given the conversion of the officers' mess. When the whole scheme was finished, I had to wind up my organization, so laboriously formed, dismissing staff left and right, for I had nothing like enough work for twenty or more assistants. Since then I have moved a further three times, each time whittling down on staff until now I share premises and staff. After nine years, I am really on my own for the first time, and it's great fun. The relief is immense but the solitude somewhat leaden. There is no one to blame but myself, no one to vent righteous indignation on, no staff to engage or dismiss, no one to harangue, only myself. On the other hand, there is much compensation in quick decisions, no arguments and no tantrums, just satisfaction that everything done is the way I want it. But by now the carrot of ambition is growing mouldy. Mule-like the position is immovable, for to go forward or backward is to plunge into the abyss, to continue as I am to condemn myself to perpetual small jobs, few holidays and an endless treadmill of working round the clock with the time machine ticking ever louder and louder, ineluctably bringing the shrill alarm of retirement closer and closer. No matter how enjoyable, how absorbing, fascinating, rewarding, stimulating or satisfying the work may be, I cannot afford to stand still. What happens next?

How much is my personal experience of architecture reflected in the state of architecture today? My own work has been divided between personal expressions of individuality, especially in the early stages of my practice, and disciplined experiences of designing and working within a framework of a predetermined system of construction, using standard components and details tied to a bulk-purchase programme, all of which precludes more than a modicum of individuality. My own practice has been a microcosm of architecture at this moment; on the one hand a whittling down of personal liberty in design, and on the other, subjugation to the demands of a preconceived method. The irony lies in the fact that I firmly believe this to be right at this particular stage in the development of building. This is not to say that development of building is at the right stage at this moment. It is not. Industrialization is far too slow. Far too few architects, engineers, builders and manufacturers believe in it and therefore the whole process is delayed through conscious, as well as unconscious, sabotage by the very group who should be ensuring its rapid progress.

It has been obvious to all that the building industry is even now woefully inefficient, despite brave attempts to rectify this of late, and that it is only coming to grips with twentieth-century techniques with reluctance in the fear that it will lose more than it will gain. Of all industries, tradition forms and maintains a formidable backcloth to its activities. It has been said that, at its best, tradition is a major way of communicating the lessons of the past to the present but that at its worst tradition is irrational, inflexible and worshipped for its own sake. When tradition acts as a brake rather than an incentive to do better than before, then it is time tradition was re-assessed. In clinging to traditional methods, the building industry fails to realize that industrialized building is, as the motor-car industry has shown, a self-perpetuating process where built-in obsolescence ensures a repeat order far more rapidly than the laborious erection of static structures designed to last several generations. Few of those concerned with building appreciate that with the advent of industrialized buildings, the term slum will prove obsolete, for each building will only last out its usefulness, at which time it will be thrown away as utensils in a modern restaurant are discarded after use.

This process will mean that the expression 'fitness for purpose' will at last mean something. With computerization and efficient assembly line methods of manufacture and rapid erection, costs should be reduced in proportion to the greater output. The next major step, however, must be the abolition of the solid site slab and below-ground drainage and other sub-structure services, for it is wholly ludicrous to prefabricate only a portion of the building.

When fully flexible industrialized building units have been produced in whole rather than in part, then we can cease to tamper with our existing traditional cities, where at present we tear down and laboriously replace out-of-date structures, with all the attendant heartaches of preservation and destruction of historic landmarks. We can then develop the proper and suitable type of city consonant to and designed for the age in which we live. This may be the linear city, or the plug-in grid city with all services and transport above ground level, the whole containing a flexibility and range of adaptability for our needs undreamt of at the moment. If we are to keep apace of the space age, development towards this conception should be far advanced already, instead of which we have barely begun to scratch the surface; hence the gross dissatisfaction with the architecture of today, by both the practitioners as well as the public. Note that I do not mention industrialized architecture, for this would be a contradiction in itself. Once you industrialize buildings you cease to have architecture; you have styling instead. Whereas cars are given an annual face-lift – sometimes startling, sometimes merely superficial to extract the maximum sales value from the gimmick – so buildings, once fully industrialized, will undergo a similar process which, whilst possibly not annual, will certainly be in five- or maybe ten-year cycles. What was once architecture will then be just styling, and like cars, all building units will be basically the same but modified to sport the stable colours.

Art and architecture are expressions of individuality and in this brave new world of industrialization there is neither room nor need for either.

For me this means the joy has vanished from architecture, the art has disappeared with the individuality. This has been replaced by commercialism and an obsession with technique. Architecture is now a business like any other business; a public service like any other public service. The architect is an anachronism in the age of the specialist, whilst professionalism is but a status symbol perpetuating an utterly meaningless hocus-pocus of outmoded ethics as hampering as a strait jacket and as successful in its restraint, effectively binding all but the few architects who surreptitiously ignore it.

Whereas the BMA is both mouthpiece and trade union to the doctor, the RIBA is neither to the architect. Were architects to strike tomorrow, little if anything would be affected. This is a sobering thought. Not only has the RIBA failed to represent architects properly, it has actually abrogated the real role they should be playing today – that of town planning – to another body, thus ensuring the eventual passing of the profession into limbo. Through sheer inaction the RIBA has rung the deathknell simply by failing to grasp that architecture today is more a matter of environment than of individual buildings.

Single buildings are out. Brick and bodge, permanency, site work as we know it now, they are out. All, or very nearly all, buildings must and will shortly become systemized, otherwise all progression will stagnate. Where does the architect stand in this process? He is trained as a professional, not a business man. Already the large building firms are gearing themselves to the 'packaged deal', with the architect relegated to a minor role in the design process. Factory architecture brings with it the scientist or technological architect, or more accurately the industrial designer, relying on the computer rather than on art.

The general contractor and his labour force of semi-skilled operatives and 'navvies', they are out too. They will be replaced by the site organizer or manager coordinating the various stages of knocking up the packaged building. There will be no room for the inspired, on-the-spot decision. So it's good-bye to the architect, the clerk of works and the builder. What then is the future for architects? They should be controlling the environment, of course, but we have town planners already and they wield vastly greater powers than the puny architects, and in any case they won't take kindly to a take-over bid at this late stage. Architects are therefore out in the cold.

For me the realization that the future of architecture lies in prefabrication with the corollary of built-in obsolescence, that the visual is undoubtedly secondary to technique and economy, has been a shock, compensated somewhat by the belated discovery that architecture is not just a design process in a vacuum, but one ineradicably associated with people. This sounds incredibly naïve. But then my own background reflects the cocoon in which so many of us are imprisoned, until we manage to break free or are borne away from that particular ambience.

The ideal architect, that middle C, pipe-smoking, bow-tied, socially integrated personality, balanced equally between art and technique, would be, if he existed, a superman.

Most of us are either art-architects or science-architects. I am one of the former and it is this group who must face up to the realization that their work in life has changed inexorably and that they are really misfits. They should be town planners, not architects. The science-architects are specialists, and by the very nature of specialization are dependent upon others; whilst the remainder are the commercialists, and they are not real architects at all, for the great god Profit demands a subservience from them that precludes real architecture. What is really so shattering is that despite the writing on the wall, more and more students are gaily entering the prison portals, each and every one apparently totally oblivious of the denouement awaiting them.

History suggests that the architect is a hybrid creature who emerged from an amalgam of the sculptor and the military engineer, and later from the foremost artisans, particularly the master mason. Like the tactician general he was a specialist to begin with, who then found himself forced to take over the overall control and direction of the whole process. Now that this control in building has been diverted to the manufacturing process, the architect in the accepted sense of the word has found himself redundant; now that the demands of design, technique and organization have become so incredibly complex, the architect can no longer hope to know sufficient to retain overall direction. Hence the dichotomy. He must choose science, that is, engineering, both structural and mechanical, geared closely to manufacturing economics, or he must choose art, which might be said to embrace sociology, psychology, geology, town planning, landscaping and history, that is, social art and architectural history.

Can these two, science and art, ever be reconciled in the future as they have been in the past? I doubt it for, in becoming a specialist, the science-architect has thereby yielded up overall control to the manufacturer; whereas it is the town planner who has assumed the role of the art-architect in his capacity as general consultant. As industry in the future will spawn out complete and whole standard buildings by the million, as it does standard windows or doors today, so the architect must turn from the detailed considerations of the individual building to that of the individual environment.

The members of my profession, having allowed this situation to occur or rather having deliberately albeit unwittingly abetted it, are now surprised at the apparent split within its ranks and yet, instead of facing up to the facts, they frantically maintain that unity must be preserved at all costs. As a body they are clinging to the past, blithely refusing to acknowledge that training and terminology need radical alteration.

Perhaps even more than this is required. Perhaps all the professions allied to the building industry should go into voluntary liquidation and reform under new groups and banners. For instance, science-architects should join up with industrial designers; commercial architects should become simply business men, whilst art-architects should join forces with town planners under the revised title of architect. Quantity surveyors and many varieties of engineers will naturally move into the computerized world of building manufacture. And the training for all this should be adapted forthwith, as indeed it should have been years ago. The RIBA is a body crippled and blind to the fact that one leg is striding in the opposite direction to the other, yet at the same time surprised to find that it is getting nowhere and, in consequence, frustrated and bewildered. By facing up to the fact that it is ruptured and that a major operation is essential, not only would it be unnecessary to continue to pretend that it is healthy, but both its members and the country as a whole would benefit immeasurably. Until this happens, I and a host of other private architects are forced to stumble onwards towards disillusionment.

Since without work the private architect cannot function, attracting work is the key to everything that follows. Invariably the work-getter is not the best designer, but he holds the power in any partnership, for everyone is dependent upon him. However equal a partnership may be at the start, sooner or later one personality emerges as the contact man, another as the designer and the remainder as organizers. The one-man band has to be all these rolled into one. Most architects like to consider themselves first and foremost as designers. I know I do. I often wonder whether the others, when faced with an empty drawing board, the brief at their elbow, the picture of the site in mind or in photo form by their side, experience that surge of panic at the start. 'Can I do it?' This is the refrain that hammers through my mind. The doubt remains until a solution for better or worse clicks into place, remains as the sweat drips from armpit to flank as one scheme after another is rejected, remains until by sheer logic the conditions of the brief have been satisfied. But at the end of the job, when the building is there for all to see, the disappointment with that sweated solution is immense, consolation present only by the thought that the next job will be better. By the end of a job, the similarity to that original solution is remote for, meantime, other hands have mauled it, fingered it, pushed and pulled it, and finally soiled it. Like a transvestite, the design undergoes mutations as each stage is reached, as each garment is donned, until it stands there for all to see and criticize, emasculated, grotesque, a mockery of that first conception. The bones are still there, but the flesh has been mutilated beyond recognition. Repeat this process, job after job, time after time, and no wonder the urge to experiment is blunted, no wonder the creative desire becomes jaded, ceases to be fresh and, preferring to remain safe, descends from the provocative or experimental to the obvious, from the trouble-maker to the money-spinner.

The variety and scope of architecture is such that it is impossible to depict a typical day's work. There are no typical days. As an assistant, the majority of time is spent at the drawing board working out, say, the drainage scheme of a building, completing the site plan, showing the levels indicating the paving and marking the positions of the incoming main services; or perhaps preparing a door schedule with details of the frames, fanlights and sidescreens with the ironmongery required; or, as is more likely today, coding a drawing so that quantities may be taken off by computer. Whereas the former might be interesting, the latter will be a chore. The principal is lucky if he spends much time at all at a drawing board. He is more likely to be dictating letters, phoning contractors, sub-contractors and suppliers to discuss points, and belly-aching at delays, or meeting clients, quantity surveyors or engineers, checking drawings, issuing certificates of payment, visiting sites, preparing reports or checking up on building regulations. Or he may be holding a site meeting, negotiating a party-wall agreement, lunching a possible future client, checking the office accounts or sending out accounts for work completed. He might even be at his own drawing board conjuring up the first sketch designs of a new project or preparing a report on the economic viability of a speculative venture.

I try to allocate a day to administration here, to one or more site visits there, depending upon the distances to be travelled, another to meetings, and what's over to drawing. Besides meetings with the client, there will be discussions with the consultants, with officials such as town planners, fire and by-law officers, as well as representatives of firms supplying materials and special items. However tidy one tries to be in organizing a week's programme, it rarely works out as planned, for all aspects of the job tend to overlap one another. For instance, the day might start like this:

'Good morning, Jean. Did those prints go off yesterday to St Albans R.D.C. for Sandridge school?'

'Yes, Mr Gotch. You won't forget to phone the client of Liverpool Road regarding the fire-escape queries?'

'No. Bring me the file on Chiltley Lane, will you? I shall be doing some letters before leaving for my meeting this morning. Oh, by the way, is that approximate estimate for the Aberdeen Park scheme in yet from the Q.S.? No? Get on to them and chivvy them up.'

'Mr Dickson on the line for you, sir.'

'Chris?'

'Hallo, Bob, what can I do for you?'

'Look, Chris, your areas are too great. You'll have to cut them down, the whole thing is costing too much.'

'But, Bob, they are pretty well rock bottom as it is. If we cut them further you'll have a sub-standard scheme!'

'Better a sub-standard one than no scheme at all, eh?'

'Well, I'll certainly go over them all again with a tooth-comb. I'll see what I can do.'

'What about cutting out that pansy canopy of yours, Chris? We can do without the frills, you know.'

'Now look, Bob, that canopy is neither pansy, costly nor a frill. It's serving a purpose and you'll get complaints if you don't have some shelter at that point.'

'Complaints or not, we've got to lop off at least a couple of thousand. See what you can do. How soon can you let me have the revision?'

'Not before Tuesday next at the earliest, Bob, I'm afraid. I'm off to Liverpool tonight; then on to Belfast.'

'Monday? I have a board meeting at eleven. I must have it by then. Can do?'

'OK, Bob. I'll get it to you by Monday.'

I ask Jean to get me Andrew Weatherfoil on the phone as I scan the minutes of the last site meeting of the Day Nursery which I am visiting that morning. I want to ask if there's any reason why we can't shift the external duct out a further four feet. It'll avoid tearing up the existing flower bed. He agrees.

'What size?'

'Eighteen inches by twelve inches, excluding other pipes.'

'Right.'

'Now the drop to the sink in the woodwork area. I'd prefer this to be in the cupboard behind the partition. Nothing against that? Good. Bye.'

Then I get Jean to get on to Nixons.

'Mr Jackson. Ask him to meet me at Polson's next Tuesday at 2.30 to have a look at those beams. If that's suitable, ring the contractor and ask Mr Donald to attend also. Tell him we shall need to remove some ceiling panels to take moisture content readings. Thanks.'

'By the way, Jean, I want six prints off that window frame coding drawing. They must go off tonight. What number? 198/65/21/G.5. No, I can't see Axel's rep. this week. Fix it for Friday next week and phone Jimmy Wright and tell him I can't make the CGLAS meeting on the sixth. Make the usual apologies, will you? You've got the site meeting files for Liphook ready. Good. I must dash.'

And off I go in the car for a day of driving and meetings, sorting out problems on site, making decisions, chivvying the contractor, getting angry with the sub-contractors for delaying progress or soothing a client irate at delay, one day wading through mud, another glorying in the sunshine but enjoying the parry and thrust of each meeting and happy to be out of the office for a day.

Yet after a couple of days of rushing about from one job to another, dealing with minutiae of construction and gloomily assessing the results of work done months before, it is a relief to spend a day at the drawing board, providing the phone is stifled, concentrating upon the problems of design, ordering and expressing one's intentions in relation to a specific building that exists as yet only in my imagination. Even here the ability to adapt one's mind rapidly from one job to another is paramount, to switch from a sketch plan, perhaps, to a staircase detail, from a layout of a housing development to furniture and fittings. Speed is essential but nothing must be overlooked. Above all, the excitement of starting a new design is intense. First comes the marshalling of the vital factors in order of importance, then some scribbled diagrams, meaningless to anyone but myself, followed by cut-out paper shapes to scale to obtain the right relationships of areas, then grouping these endlessly to try to obtain a workable solution. A whole day can pass absorbed in what might seem to others a rather stupid game of paper patterns. Time flits by. No answer is there. Something is blocking it. Panic is imminent. In desperation, I go back to the beginning and start again, this time changing the pattern. Eureka. It works. Maybe not the best answer, but an answer nevertheless. Perhaps I can improve it tomorrow. My God! It's after midnight. If I change those bogs round with . . . oh, leave it till tomorrow. Damn, I've got two meetings. Well, the next day, or the next, well the week-end then.

In sixteen years, I have handled over two hundred different jobs, but of these two hundred, varying considerably, only about half have come to fruition. Of these, the majority have been schools, houses, conversions and extensions, interspersed by a motley of other building types such as banks, offices, factories, restaurants, interiors and the odd church hall, sports pavilion and officers' mess. Almost without exception, it is the larger jobs that have been abandoned. Fat, juicy housing or shopping developments have come and gone after hours of work and innumerable drawings. The latter lie stillborn on dusty shelves in my office or remain as memories on microfilm where hopes ran high and the subsequent disappointment is painful to recollect. There are some jobs, of course, which went sour. Few architects in private practice escape the charge of negligence at some time or other; few architects can claim never to have fallen out with a client. In this world of shifting responsibility, or group responsibility, the knowledge that one mistake can put you out of business, and perhaps out of house and home, is sobering indeed. These moments, rare as they may be, have to be experienced to realize in full the precariousness of this job. Add the stop-go financial policies of successive governments with the attendant credit squeezes, add also the increasing concentration of work handled by official architectural departments and staff architects' departments, throw in the gradual and quickening process of industrialization of building and you find that the private architect is facing a frightening work freeze as well. The smaller the office, the wider the fluctuation seems to be, as my income reflects. One year I made £5,000 and the next nothing but a thumping loss. However, averaged out over ten years of practice I have, according to an RIBA survey, been amongst the 47 per cent of private architects who have earned between £2,000 and £4,000 a year.

Maybe the joy has gone out of architecture due to my own

failure as a person. Maybe my own dissatisfaction with society prevents me from extracting the joy. Maybe my own rebelliousness foments this, allowing my obsessions to dilute purpose and effort. Who the hell cares! Paradoxically, I get a kick out of it.

If I could turn the clock back, stupid as this game may be, would I become an architect all over again knowing what I know now? I would like to yell 'No', yet when I look at other jobs, I can dismiss most of them at once. What do I know of their pleasures and disadvantages, their excitements and boredom or for that matter my own capabilities for them? Nothing, of course, so it is back to the bank of the Rubicon for me to ponder on whether it is not too late to recross and try again. Clearly in architecture this is possible. But it is not something that you slough off without a qualm, for it is part of you. From the very start it is a drug that hooks and hooks irrevocably. Why else would we be so mad as to pursue the unattainable?

CHRISTOPHER GOTCH

THE AUTHOR

The youngest of three, I was born at Kettering, Northamptonshire, in 1923. Until the age of five I played hide and seek, much as I have been doing since, in the ample grounds of the family house before being dispatched, presumably because I had become an embarrassment to my parents, to boarding school. There I remained in seclusion until a road accident and the outbreak of the Second World War forced my father to economize.

Freed from the hell that was Marlborough College, at sixteen my father forced me into the LDV (forerunner of the Home Guard); that and the early blitz and a year at home were sufficient to induce me to falsify my age to join the RAF in 1941. After a year's training, mostly in Canada, I joined a fighter squadron as a tenderfoot commissioned pilot, only to be wounded at Dieppe a few months later. In 1943 I was posted to the India and Burma theatre; a squadron leader at twenty-one, flight commander of a mosquito squadron, I was wounded again.

I qualified as an architect in 1953; my first private commission came two years before and more followed until by 1958 it was clear that I had to decide between remaining a salaried architect or developing my own business. Since 1960 I have practised alone.

During this period I became involved in the local community life of Hampstead, where I have lived since 1947, believing that it provides the most nearly perfect urban environment of anywhere in Britain and one especially suitable for children in their early years. Realizing that architects cannot work in a vacuum, I have over the years been instrumental in forming the New Hampstead (Civic) Society, the Camden Society of Architects and, rather of a different nature, a professional Opera Company, Group Eight. As a consequence of these activities I am now an itinerant, persuasive lecturer on architecture, a pontificator on the environment in a local weekly paper, and have been an RIBA award and Civic Trust award juror.

Author of five books, only one of which has been published, it's clear that I am an arch-dabbler, for I also paint and sculpture in wood, and when disgusted with all these pursuits turn to rug making. These are of inordinate size and occupy me for years – a sort of permanent labour of Hercules. Opera is an obsession and keeps my wayward emotions at bay, while photography panders to my frustrated creativity.

Through studying Robert Mylne, an obscure eighteenth-century architect and engineer, on whom I have published several articles and am now considered an authority, I discovered the canals of Britain, a different section of which I explore each year by boat in an orgy of getting away from it all.

The Town Planner

Nine o'clock on a summer morning was a good time I thought for an interview in a northern town. The day starts with zest, with decisions, a decision to employ or not to employ a new man. Do that sort of thing at 9 o'clock, and who knows what will be happening by 11.30. Interview is over at half nine and the day clear for business. Time is valuable, even that half hour from 9 to 9.30 when others might be collecting the bits of themselves or queuing in the gents.

Perhaps it was 9.15 before the panel assembled to check if I had dirt under my finger nails or observable deficiencies. Fifteen minutes wasn't long enough to eradicate the first impression. The idea lingered, the idea of things happening, of things being accomplished.

The chief officer leaned back, connecting the tips of his fingers across the arms of his chair and belly. There was work to be done, he explained, a great deal of work. As he hoped I had observed for myself the problems were considerable, the legacy of the industrial revolution and so forth. He gave it to be understood that nevertheless these problems were not insuperable, given energy, application, time, hard work, etc. It was the front line but then the front line was a good place to be; that was where the things were happening. His authority were doing more to reclaim and rebuild than any other authority. They had a fine record and they were proud of that, but they were not going to rest on their laurels. Not by any means. There would be no rest until every slum and slag heap had been rolled away. Rehabilitation of the environment, if I knew what that meant. It was a question of building for the future. We must have town planners for that, and what did I do with my spare time if he might ask, and did I have strong political views of any sort as that could be difficult if I understood him.

I arrived at the County Office one Monday morning to everyone's mild surprise. Someone found me a place to sit and something to read. I was asked what salary I was to be paid, what grade I was on, and what section of town I was to live in. It was my second job as a town planner, and my first in local government.

Before I decided to opt for town planning I worked as a teacher and helped to run a small business. I gave up the first because I wanted to live and work with persons over the age of seventeen. Someone told me about town planning, or land-use planning, as I prefer to call it, and sold it to me as a real attempt to improve the physical surroundings in which we live. I read the Buchanan report and it seemed I had found something worthwhile to do, and which paid well. An exciting and new profession in which it looked as though very shortly things would happen.

You come into planning in two ways. You can take a degree course and get a job, or you can take a local government job and either do a part-time course or sit the exams of the Town Planning Institute. At present neither method achieves satisfactory results, which is an almost dishonestly mild way of putting it. Once a qualified planner, you can join a private firm of consultants, or the planning department of a county or town. Jobs with consultants are few, and they usually require you to be an architect also. As an alternative to local government, there is the Ministry of Housing.

Working with a local authority the principal business is the production of the development plan, which is how the authority intends that land shall be used during the period of the plan. Once you have the plan in theory the problem is mainly one of seeing that other people stick to it. The plan is supposed to incorporate what land shall be developed or redeveloped for housing, industry, shopping, transport and other major land uses, as well as methods and means of achieving the ends you are planning for. On top of this you have the day-to-day issues that require investigating, because they were not allowed for in the plan, because circumstances have changed, or because there is not enough information. For this you need economists, land-use planners, architects, land agents, engineers, lawyers and coordinators. The latter are all-important, because if they can't do a job the rest are wasting their time, and this is equally so if the co-ordinators and land-use planners, who are often the same people, do not know what to ask for or how a job should be done. The people who are doing the organizing or managing have to know how a job can be done and what it is that needs doing.

When I took this local government job, I didn't expect too much. But I expected to work hard, I had a lot of energy and interest, and I had no trouble getting used to the absence of time sheets; 'the system', though baffling in itself, was much the same as other systems. I cannot remember just how my interest and energy evaporated, perhaps the effect of creeping inertia, perhaps because I expected something other than meetings and consultations that get nowhere, decide nothing at all.

One winter afternoon I came back from the movies, put my feet on the desk and continued with the book I had been reading. I think it was that day that I saw what had happened, though not why, perhaps still not why. There were no letters to check out. I had not been missed. Very little was moving on the corridor. No phones were ringing. The office was cold, narrow and dingy. It smelt of socks and cigarette smoke. The light was bad and there were too many in such a small place. As I say, there was nothing to do. One of the jobs I had been working on had ground into some semi-administrative difficulty. Another had entailed a faintly unorthodox approach and my superior, a something-over-£3,000-a-year man, had found the derisory responsibility to be too much for him. A third job on which a report had been written was lying about on somebody's desk waiting to be read, as it had been for nearly three months. The reason for this last was not that this fellow was working too hard, but simply that he asked me to report for some baffling personal reason and had no interest whatsoever in the result. When eventually it returned it included some neat pencilled rewriting of phrases, pure idiosyncracies of style. Nevertheless the typist had to plod wearily through the thing again before the report went into a drawer somewhere. If there were really work going on there would not be time for these things, the most petty would tend to be brushed aside. It is only because we are playing patience with ourselves shuffling around the files, the reports and scraps of paper, that we allow ourselves to wallow for hours in humiliating trivia, new forms to be signed by someone to carry out a perfectly simple operation.

Perhaps the most depressing thing is the impossibility of getting a decision on anything from the smallest to the largest, and this is just within the organization itself. Things go round and round, or don't move at all. It's like being on Crewe station on Sunday night surrounded by dozens of porters of all grades of seniority, including the station master, and either they don't know or won't tell what time the next train is or if there is one at all. Occasionally one gets near to telling you, but at that precise moment he stoops to pick up a bit of waste paper and that's that. You decide that if you stay on the platform long enough you'll find out. Graham Williams did a fine economical plan and for two years shot flies with rubber bands waiting for a decision. He left, and a month later all his work was dredged up and used. While he was there not a damn was given about the work he had put in, not a glimmer of interest. He and his work were all part of the file somewhere, and he was only shooting flies in our room instead of lying flat in a filing cabinet because he was human, not paper.

Town planning covers such a great range, hovers so uncertainly between design work and unadulterated administration, that, according to aptitude or chance, you may find yourself spending the day in front of a drawing board, a telephone and a pile of files, or an adding machine, graph paper and the Digest of Statistics. Our office in fact has no drawing board, though with trouble you can assemble one when necessary, at great inconvenience to everyone and some mirth. At my last office we did some drawing-board work every day; here most of the time is spent in drafting reports, amending and re-amending them. The design work is a small incident before or during the administrative process, and designs themselves mean nothing unless you can persuade, cajole or trick your way into getting them carried forward. The best planners are fixers with some design training.

Writing this depresses me a good deal, perhaps because from day to day you don't think of things too much; things, details absorb you. The habits of a place take your attention. You know that thinking about it won't help. The personal humiliation I mind most of all. I can bear being highly paid, six pounds a day from public funds, incompetence, administrative delay. But the humiliation of not being able to pretend for more than one day a week that I do anything of even modest value I find bad for pride. I like to be able to pretend at least.

Others are in the same boat. Jimmy Toland has gone now, but I think he suffered most. He angered a lot of people because he complained so often and so vociferously, and the rest of us were trying to live with ourselves and forget. But he was honest, forcing himself all the time to go, cutting the ground off from behind him, never letting himself get used to or accept the way in which he was forced to work. Henry Mars is older, tougher, but still not reconciled to what he calls the feeling of rotting all the time. And I think that if we didn't all feel this, George from across the way would be less inclined to probe my increasingly melancholic humour with tales of what the whore would have blushed at saying to the sailor.

Somewhere in the region they are talking of staffing problems, shortages of qualified men, particularly planners, and in the newspapers there is a report of all the glowing improvements it is intended shall be carried out in hot haste. Only the smallest fidget of anything is happening. The other side of the jargon barrier, the pronouncements, the glossy forecasts of slum-free, slag-free, pollution-free existence we are told to expect some time just before or just after 1981, we are doing nothing of any consequence apart from giving the computer the opportunity to calculate our pay slip.

Within this nothingness is buried our predicament as planners, assuming as I must that our outfit is representative.

We are not responsible for anything, only indirectly for what other people do. If something goes wrong, nobody can get at us, nobody can say that my deficiency as planner caused this grave mishap, as they can about an architect or an engineer. We do things on paper and others carry them out, if there is anything. The councillors through whom we are responsible to the electorate find it very difficult to get at us, even if they know how and want to bother. They don't know what questions to ask, or what the department could do if it had the will. You have the elected representatives, the professionals and the electors, and practically no contact or understanding between these groups. The result is that the people in Littletown don't know what could be done in the way of economic improvements, they aren't aware of an alternative to what is now. You might say that even if they did know you would still have the problem of bringing pressure to bear to get anything done. The gap is vast.

I think about all the things planners could do one morning, as I stand counting the traffic on the intersection of a small town, sniffing the pollution, deafened by the roar of the trucks and tankers that come past. A woman with a pram busies herself wondering what I am doing stork-like and cold on the side of the road. She just gets off the road in time to avoid the last of fourteen wheels on an articulated lorry. There is barely enough room on the pavement for her with her pram. All the shops are on different sides of the street so that you must cross it constantly. The school children go back and forth across it to school; no doubt they learn to be clever with the traffic. There's a pleasant little square in the middle with a pub, a market cross and the post office, but the traffic makes it uninhabitable, an area that you are denied. The bypass is fifteen years away. Even so there is a great deal that could be done in the meantime to make the place more pleasant, just as is the case with old housing areas. Places like this need care and attention and a lot of first-rate public relations.

Planners are idealistic people, opponents of *laissez-faire*, believing that with study, organization, analysis of alternatives and planning we can arrange things better than they would be without these things. Those soured by the uphill struggle say that the administrative machinery stifles all chance of success. They say that society does not really believe in or want planning. The planners would go ahead if they could, it is the politicians, and administrators who control the politicians, who block them. They have a point. Maybe chance, which is a sort of abstract fate, is better than planning when suddenly we become responsible for it all. Perhaps a town is only acceptable if we can't do anything about it.

How do you test a plan for a town or a village or a residential area? Does a plan work if the services are adequate? But then how well and against what standard? Few bother to ask, though so much of the community's money is spent on physical development. This is why planning can so often become plain paternalism. Quite reasonably, people completely misunderstand what you are trying to do. It's just another bloody bureaucrat messing you about, denying the rights of individuals for some obscure, unrecognizable purpose. There's little contact between planners and public, little explanation, little attempt to carry the public along, persuade it, interest it, bring the event back to the people involved so that they too are carrying out a policy, so that it becomes real because people want it. Sometimes there are a few self-conscious, usually inept, publicity performances, cosy little talks, half-hearted, grossly under-financed, paternalistic and stuffy. Like the public, even the press is not expected to ask questions and will always be fobbed off with arid and meaningless rubbish. There is no two-way process. The authority hands out recommendations and information, and with that the matter is closed.

The other week Henry Marsh wanted to organize an exhibition in a small town to explain what the plans were. It required a great effort on his part, persuading people in the department to do some work for it, design the boards, get the photographs and stands, and man it. His immediate senior's resentment expressed itself in the form of refusing to allow people to man it. 'It's your bloody exhibition,' he said, 'you man it.' In the end Henry fixed it, but even so it went off at half cock because nobody understood it. The best thing about it was the suggestions book, which people used fairly uninhibitedly. One kid of eleven-odd wrote that he didn't understand the exhibition at all, but it showed they were doing something, wasn't that so? We both laughed, but not at the same joke.

Calmly in control of the administrative machine, working within the inflexible system, we walk the corridors somehow many, many removes from land and people. Nobody can get at us except through the organization, and only then in an approved series of moves. Equally we cannot get at anyone, cannot even write a simple report that is not ground through the mesh of six to eight approved censors and channels before it begins to circulate among other local authorities for comment. Our power lies in the fact that no one else can do anything, least of all the people and communities for whom in name we are working. We work in a great no-man's land of the machinery of negotiations, consultations, meetings, paper as complex and inhuman, and for all I know maybe as necessary as a traffic intersection.

The planner is scared of people who have property, for they have rights and therefore will defend them at law. Who else can cause trouble? Who else can say anything that will have effect? The owner of property will get his due whoever else misses out. Those of us who use land and property less directly have few rights. The public's interest is in the hands of the planning department, which will represent it when it sees it. Very often it doesn't. The department is remote, not all that interested, perhaps unwilling to dispute with another department. Seeing the public interest means trouble and work. The organization will fight when forced to by some accident, but it has no grit. When it does, it will fork out its reasons in such a way that the general public can scarcely comprehend them because they are inadequately explained. In any case it will not go on and on fighting a particular issue. It will pack it in for an easy life and say knowingly that 'the Minister would only do such and such anyway'. On the other hand, the owner of property will always fight, his profit is at stake, his personal interest obvious.

Doubtless the planning machinery reflects the sort of society we live in. It protects the rights of property meticulously, but deals only remotely if at all with the interests of communities and people, especially if they are economically or socially in a disadvantageous position. I don't say all this in the department, but some of it gets through. 'You're in the wrong job,' they tell me. It certainly feels that way. Silence and delay are the tactics used every time anything is suggested that is not a routine action, a routine thought, a routine way of doing something. No discussion, no anger, no derision, no hope, no experiment, just a blanket of protective silence, a relentless smothering.

There are days I go out on site inspections, to see if tipping should be permitted and with what safeguards, or to see how an open space is being used and maintained. On the way I stop off at some new housing development. There are two or three in the area that make me believe in planning again, give me pleasure and fortify me for days at a time. They are not just houses dumped like prefabricated garages along a road. Somebody has thought about what they will look like from different places, has arranged them with care for their total appearance, has brought into the development some mystery of place. You don't just look and know what all other parts of the development will be like. There's something about it that makes you want to look further, to walk among the houses, within the spaces, down the walks, into the garage courts, around trees. All this means a great deal to me, maybe because I am trained that way. Do the people who live there get pleasure the same way? Is the development a planner's creation and pleasure, or does the pleasure exist for other people? If it's the first then it's planning paternalism again, and if it's the second then it's worth much greater efforts, particularly of public relations.

Where there's muck, there's brass and full employment. If planners take away the muck there will be no brass and less employment. Try to get the NCB to clean up some of its mess and of course you might as well save yourself the time, as it would put up costs and that would make the operation less economic, which in turn would throw miners out of work. So miners and unions object to improvements in their areas, certainly if they threaten the precarious economics of a pit. It's an extreme case, but works to a lesser extent elsewhere where people put a low value on appearances and prefer to spend money in other ways. We are up against a widespread lack of interest in community improvements. Either you jack in the attempt or you try to convert. As long as you get paid it's easier to jack it in, and if people don't want it maybe you'd be better minding your own business. Could you say the same about education?

However good your intentions, the incredible time it takes to get through the smallest procedures usually kills an idea before you begin. With our planning machinery and the Ministry of Housing and Local Government you start with a minimum of two years and work up till you reach the never-never land when you just don't bother because you'll have retired or be too weary or dead. The system stultifies you, kills the idea of action, so that before you cut the grass at home you wonder whether you oughtn't to check it through with the field mice. Since everything has to be referred to ceaseless other bodies and hierarchies, sat upon, inquired upon, consultation comes to take place for its own sake, becomes a substitute for actually doing anything. Meetings are fine, the more people the better, as then decisions are much harder to come by, much less likely to materialize. There are exceptions, and I think that new towns and certain particularly energetic authorities represent these exceptions. Those of us who retain any hope for planning are busily trying to get jobs where we know these exceptions exist.

Fairly typical of this was a meeting we had recently to discuss the reclamation of an eighty-acre site. There were eight people present. It was agreed that a minimum of three years was necessary for getting through the administrative procedures before the dozers could get on to the land. As two small sections of the site were in the town map for industry, both scrap metal merchants, the town map would have to be amended. The site was highly unsuitable for any other type of development, and was in full view of a housing estate. The Coal Board owned some of the site, the shale heaps in fact, but were not going to part with it as they wanted it for storage. We arranged to exclude this part. The land was thus suitable for nothing, and a knock-down price could be expected. £25–£35 an acre. Nothing of the sort. Being on the edge of a large town, near an estate, the owners were not interested in selling at anything less than £200 an acre. Somebody wanted the land, didn't they, even if it was the local authority. If it weren't derelict the local authority wouldn't be interested in buying it to improve the neighbourhood, would they? Thus the land's sheer unsightliness created a value. It was argued whether the land was worth reclaiming when it was only for public open space, hillsides at that, not even playing fields. And when reclaimed it would have to be maintained, and nobody would do that from year to year. The residents had lived with it this long, they could go on doing so. Someone mentioned that an attempt had been made ten years ago to do something about it. That finished it, especially as the NCB claimed to have some low-grade fuel deposits, though it had generally been forgotten just where. The preliminaries of this exercise took nine months on and off, and involved a dozen meetings and wranglings between different departments and authorities.

I expect too much, I say to myself. It's always been like this and it always will be. I must cultivate my suburban garden. I think if I did not see others near me as impatient with our total impotence, if I did not measure my self-respect against that of others who are more effective and are paid less, I might do that.

Someone else announces they are leaving and casts a great gloom over the office. We are all reminded. If Mike can do it there is less excuse for us. He has declared, in effect, that though he has every reason to believe that one place is as bad as another he has sufficient energy and hope to try elsewhere.

This leaves us more restless, finding less justification for our particular brand of time-wasting. We traipse back and forth with letters and files, and slips of paper to be signed, and talk about what will be needed for 'committee'. We commence consultations, and reply icily that we are unable to help so and so 'due to pressure of work'. Meanwhile a power struggle is revealed which takes the bizarre form of seeking additions to staff, making up the establishment, which has more to do with the prestige of this or that department or departmental head than the amount of work. There is too little of that already. Presumably 'committee' will shortly be authoritatively informed that we cannot do all the exciting things forecast for the area due to shortages of staff. The landscape architect puts another beautiful plan into the drawer and dreams of an aesthetic dictatorship where landscape beautification has priority

Mike ridicules the latest blown-up drama. He is happy. He can laugh at things easily, without bitterness, without caring too much. The only people in the department who, like him, can be themselves during working hours are the heads and their deputies. In most professions they are disciplined by the end product, by responsibility to something. In the case of planning, as I have said, there is so little responsibility that they can do as they like, can drive their departments as they think fit, like a glorified car for their personal entertainment. So you are the servants of someone's whim, there's no overriding idea to which the self-respect of staff can refer. We can't even point to something as indisputably objective as that such and such a policy led to losses. There we are, stuck somewhere on the ladder, hemmed in by inflexible procedure and a galaxy of other people, living off each other, pushing paper, being pushed around, holding consultations, suspending decisions until more information is available, disguising our tracks. And on Friday night everybody tells everybody it is the week-end, and spends the evening on their private method of recovering their own personalities – children – liquor – the garden – the car. The heroes are those whose personalities survive the next week until Friday.

Well, what more do you want, you're being paid, aren't you? Answer – self-respect. To do a good job, to work for people who know how to get a job done and who are not afraid or ashamed to be seen to be responsible. I'll take that for a start, for if it all came right out in the open there would be enough stink to keep every one of us busy.

JON RODES

THE AUTHOR

I was born in Hull in 1939. My father returned from the Middle East in 1945 to take up his chemical broking business and send me through the ideal middle-class system – prep school, public school, Oxford. The first was a gruelling para-military establishment with fives-bat beatings; the second was an improvement with a site that in summer was immensely beautiful, and allowed me to spend three years as an almost professional cross-country runner. Oxford demonstrated my athletic limitations and gave me a second in history.

I spent the next three years in a variety of jobs: bar-waiter, antiques in the Portobello Road, teacher in a deep-litter grammar school, apartment clerk to an establishment in Washington, D.C. As a result of this last, I married into an Irish American family. I returned from America to hear a barman call me 'sir', to see a decrepit Macmillan welcome Kennedy at Gatwick Airport, and with Wimbledon on the telly.

On a hot day in Hyde Park I read the Buchanan report and it seemed that I had found what I wanted to do with myself, found an avenue for effort that not only paid well but was of value.

The last two times I voted for a Labour government, and shall in future vote against whichever of our conservative options seems most objectionable on election day.

Managing Science

Shortly after graduating in chemistry at the university, I heard an eminent scientist say: 'If you want to deal with people you go into production, if you want to deal with ideas you go in for research.' My experience as a plant manager in the chemical industry and as a research manager in the Atomic Energy Authority suggests that the statement is an over-simplification, and when one begins to look at the role of senior people engaged in both fields, it ceases to be true. Though I spent a good deal of my time as a young plant manager looking after the organization of shift labour, it was technical problems and their solution which taxed my mental powers and gave me status in the eyes of my immediate superiors. Later in my career when I turned to research, I found it very important to be able to get on well with all sorts of people and to inspire younger, more junior scientists and technologists to perform creative work. The contrast between the two jobs is vivid, and not least because one was in private enterprise and the other in a publicly owned organization. In contrasting them, however, my experience is necessarily subjective and too many generalized conclusions should perhaps not be drawn from my account.

At the age of twenty-seven I was appointed plant manager with a large chemical combine with factories in the north of England, at a commencing salary of £500 a year. It was 1948, and the advertisement had specified that applicants should have 'a good honours degree in chemistry and a few years post-graduate experience of an appropriate character'. I soon found I carried a good deal of personal responsibility in this job, and this pleased me because in my previous post I had had very little. I had been with a firm which felt it ought to have graduates, but when it got them, it just didn't know how to use them to get the benefit of their scientific training. Non-graduates could have done much of the work which was being done by university-trained personnel. And in any case I had so little work to do, even after repeated requests for more, that I used to spend a great deal of my time studying chemical engineering and preparing for the professional qualification A.M.I.Chem.E. Several of my colleagues and I used to go to night-school lectures in the subject. I was glad to find that my qualifications were to be needed in my new job.

The raw material we processed in the plant for which I was responsible was ordinary, common, table salt; obtained cheaply from the brine which was pumped to us from certain wells in the area. The process ran night and day, and consumed an enormous quantity of electric power – about 4,500 kilowatts an hour. This energy was needed to split the dried salt crystals into their component parts – sodium metal and chlorine gas. Every week we turned out about 70 tons of the former and 105 tons of the latter chemical, both of these being important commodities in the 'heavy chemicals' industry. I suppose the annual cash value of the combined products from my plant was over half a million pounds in those days. Once a quarter, I received a statement of the various costs of production making up the plant cost of the product. If any figure was up on the previous quarter, one was expected to offer some explanation to a small committee which looked at the production costs. If an item was down, it was usually because we had introduced some technical or operational change for the better; if we hadn't, then the figure would probably be very high next time.

A considerable physical effort was required from shift teams of tough process workers, which with the day force totalled about seventy, all devoted to keeping a hot, sometimes hazardous, plant in full operation. It was necessary for men to keep their skins covered from head to foot whilst carrying out any process operation, even including inspections; hot sodium can play the very devil with any part of the body with which it may come into contact. Workers never seemed to mind the hard effort, which resulted in a good deal of sweating since they were working on a hot plant and were well wrapped up. The leading hands, chargehands and foremen seemed to take a great pride in their jobs. They always looked keenly forward to seeing the shift or day's output figures when these were totted up at the usual times and recorded in the plant logbook. I shared an office with three other plant managers in the main administrative block of the works. On arrival each morning I used to study the plant logbook, which was sent over from the plant in time for me. Thus I could judge how things were right away, and be all ready to deal with the inevitable phone calls from the six to two shift and day men supervisors who wanted to pass on their worries and problems to me as soon as they could.

My immediate superior was the area manager, who would come into the plant managers' office and sit on a radiator to warm himself on arrival. He would look over my shoulder at the log, if I was the particular victim, and to my intense irritation start telling me in great detail what he would do about the plant's operation. Sometimes it was a colleague who had to suffer this indignity. We all sighed with relief when he took himself off to 'morning prayers' in the works manager's office – a daily meeting which the latter held with his area managers and heads of departments. Free from interference, the plant managers could then get on with their day's programme. The logbooks were accompanied by record charts removed from various instruments on the plant by instrument technicians; thus there was an accumulation of technical data, which was processed for us, routine-wise, by a pool of clerks each with a desk calculator. I could summon my clerk by pressing a bell push hanging over my desk. Side by side with this was a second bell push to summon a typist from the typing pool. The clerks and typists were all pleasant people and there was usually a good deal of friendly banter when several of them happened to be in the plant manager's office together. Football, dating (or mock dating) and jokes about the works' senior staff were the usual topics of conversation. At ten o'clock we would troop out with our half-pint mugs for the strong, sweet, canteen-brewed tea which was dispensed for us by tough, somewhat coarse women who pushed the tea trolley round the administration block.

Shortly after, the plant managers dressed up in old clothes to visit their plants. I used to wear old flannels, rubber boots, dust coat, and an old trilby hat encrusted with salt. I had a pair of goggles with sewn-on face cloth slung around my neck, and carried large cotton mitts in one hand, notebook in the other.

As I walked along through the works I often felt a sense of excitement, passing under the pipe bridges, watching the variously coloured vapours pouring out of process buildings, with the clank of buffers, hiss of steam and roar of machines in my ears. The ever-present reek of chlorine was like being in an over-dosed swimming pool. Although the products of our factory, going out in drums and cylinders standing in railway trucks, or in tank wagons, looked dull and unimportant, one knew they were important commodities in a chain of production which had as the end point such diverse commodities as nylons, household bleach, plastics, insecticides and pesticides.

Although in the early days the men working on my plant did not get any bonuses for output or when the process operated at a high stage of efficiency, they liked to see things going well. The process tended to be a bit temperamental at times, the mood of chargehands and foremen tended to change accordingly, and human relationships generally throughout the plant were affected.

One evening the electric power supply to the plant failed, just as my area manager was paying a surprise visit to see what happened at the factory at the time of the 10 p.m. shift changeover. A power failure was just about the worst catastrophe that could happen to the sodium-making process, because there was then nothing to stop a slow freezing up of the plant due to lack of heating. Certain emergency measures could be taken to retard the freeze, all involving hard physical labour, while the power station staff struggled to get the generator going again. On this occasion, the 2 to 10 shift stayed on through the night to help and my area manager worked alongside them. (Incidentally, he was not the person who used to sit on my radiator reading the log.) At 6 a.m. he rang me up to tell me about the crisis, before going home to bed. I hurried through breakfast and dashed off to the works to take over direct supervision of the team.

The power came back on at about midday, to everyone's relief. I don't think I have had such a wet shirt in all my life, but it was a unique experience, sharing a common purpose with those tough men, all of us devoted to saving a valuable unit of production from complete destruction. Of course there was overtime pay that week, but those men seemed to work twice as hard during all the hours they put in at the factory, because the aftermath of the power failure involved much hard work for a day or two getting back to normal efficiency of operation.

Afternoons at the works were spent on non-routine matters – e.g. long-term planning, safety committee and works council attendance, performing technical calculations, holding liaison meetings with representatives of various works departments such as labour, engineering, power, instruments and analytical laboratory. Thus the greater part of most days was spent in talking to people – plant supervisors and workers, technical specialists and clerks, other managers. I had no difficulty in getting on with these various types of people and indeed I enjoyed being with them all.

Although I saw my area manager for a brief while on most days, the works manager was a person apart. I am sure senior shop stewards saw him more frequently than did the plant managers. On the last working day before Christmas each year he used to have each of the management staff into his office in turn just for a few moments, in order to hand over letters which had come from head office. These stated what each of our salaries would become on the first of January. Such information was very personal and individual, there were no fixed annual increments and we never confided in each other about our salaries. Thus, once inside the firm, the management virtually did what they liked with us regarding pay, and the only thing we could compare our fortunes with were the salaries quoted in job adverts in the technical press. (Our company never stated salaries in its job adverts.)

Some of the plant managers and works engineering staff had been there years. Occasionally a youngster not long out of college would appear on the scene for a few months, but before he could be expected to make any impact on his job, he would be whisked away to some other part of the company organization. When I commented on this practice in the office, long-service staff would merely shrug their shoulders and point out that he was another 'blue-eyed boy'. This meant he had been picked out by a director, or someone quite senior to the works manager, for rapid promotion to high management posts. I was puzzled to know how someone in such an exalted position could even be aware of the existence of individual plant management staff. And I couldn't believe it was based on any confidential reports which might be written by works managers or area managers, because 'blue-eyed boys' didn't stay long enough for anyone to be able to form any valid assessment. Did these people get an asterisk against their name on joining, commending them to the attention of the top brass in the company? What qualified one for such singling out on interview – speech, poise, a super-personality? Oxbridge degrees? Or an excellent golfing record? Or perhaps a public school and family connexions?

In my second year with the company I was able to make some valuable improvements concerning the technical efficiency of the sodium process and my area manager indicated to me that I had reason to hope for a good rise at Christmas. When the time came, I received a paltry rise. I expostulated about this to the works manager, but was told that it would perhaps come next year, sometimes head office staff were a bit remote from the factories. . . . Indeed, our factory was well over a hundred miles away and visits did not take place very often.

I have already implied that the factory had a works council. When I heard that I had been appointed to this for a year I was delighted. But disillusionment set in after a few months because of all the paltry, pettifogging matters we discussed: when would there be new gates on the company houses, should steel-toe-capped safety shoes be allowed out of the works if the men had actually bought them, what about moving the bus stop a few yards nearer, should men on hot plants have lime-juice or salt tablets, or a mixture of them. The works managers took the chair, the labour officer was secretary. There were councillors from the payroll staff in each department, some of whom were shop stewards though the majority were not. One councillor who had least to say at council meetings was a senior shop steward of the AEU. He merely sat there with a cynical expression on his face. I think the one thing he and the works manager had in common was that they both knew what the company's idea was in having the works council. Afterwards we always had a ham and chips tea on the company before dispersing to go home about 6.30.

During my second year with the company I spent a month on a management training course along with several other young company executives. This was very interesting, and very convivial, because we were all resident in a country mansion which the company owned. It was stressed to us during this course that we should all be planning well ahead in our job, years in fact. Even the foremen should be planning weeks ahead, the chargehands sorting out daily problems. What a mess things would soon get into in the works, I thought, if we all tried to stick to this idealistic method of working. It was clear to me that head-office types had no real idea of the calibre and capabilities of our foremen. They had put them through foremen training courses, and assumed they were able to practise everything they had been taught. However, reading between the lines, the message was that we were expected, first and foremost, to achieve the maximum output possible from our plants – the market was unlimited; and yet we must do this with the optimum economy in labour, raw materials and services (steam, electricity, etc.). But, and there was a big 'but' here, in achieving these two aims, we must not break two golden rules. The first of these was that one must not kill men in the rush for high output, in other words, safety first – the works and plant safety committees were always regarded very seriously by the higher management, and woe betide any junior manager who was flippant about safety matters. The second rule was 'don't for heaven's sake ever let a strike start in *your* plant, or your career is finished before it gets under way'. We weren't given a set of instructions on how to avoid this calamity. But as plant managers we had, I think, a built-in safeguard in that we were in direct daily contact with our small labour force and any worker with the slightest grievance knew he could go up to the manager on his daily plant inspection and have a private discussion. And since the bulk of the labour force were old, experienced hands with a great respect for sodium and a first-hand knowledge of its latent, vicious powers, I had no great difficulty avoiding a breach of 'the rules'.

I was well on top of my job on the sodium plant, indeed I was beginning to realize I had some intellectual slack which the job was not capable of taking up, when one day a 'blue-eyed boy' arrived at the works and I was told to train him up as sodium plant manager. This I did over a period of some weeks. He was an exceedingly pleasant fellow and until a new desk arrived for him in the plant manager's office, he shared mine. Quite by accident, I saw one of his personal letters, addressed to him by his Christian name, and coming from one of the company's top men. I noted, to my great amazement, that his salary was 30 per cent higher than mine. Eventually, when I was able to tell the area manager our newcomer knew all the routine, he was allowed to take over from me. I was then told that since I was a bright lad, and was one of the few people around on the works who had studied chemical engineering, I was going to be used as a trouble-shooter, a sort of manager-without-portfolio. This idea was all right in principle, but in practice no plant manager would ever admit there was anything he couldn't cope with on his own plant. Thus, a considerable effort in public relations was required on my part before I could even begin to concentrate my mental powers on the technical problem. However, I found great satisfaction in sorting out a variety of technical problems throughout the works, and I began to think of applying for a job in research and development. I liked playing with ideas. By the end of that year, I had a good offer lined up from a new government-sponsored project in atomic energy. A house to rent was going to be available and this was a great attraction when one had a growing family. The thought of living in the Lake District was also very attractive. When the works manager handed me over another paltry rise that Christmas I knew exactly what to do. I resigned.

Fifteen years have elapsed since I forsook plant management in industry for a research career in the public service. In terms of a career, these have been years of progressive advancement, starting out from a salary of £1,200 per annum, finally attaining £4,350 as head of a research group containing about twenty scientific staff.

Perhaps at this stage I should say what in fact we have been trying to achieve by our researches over the last fifteen years. How has society gained from the efforts of the establishment, indeed the organization, of which my team forms only a small part? Well, we have put atomic energy on the map so far as its peaceful uses are concerned. We have not only established ways of harnessing nuclear fission to generate electric power, but we have made it possible to do so more cheaply than when one produces electricity from coal or oil. I sometimes meet people socially who start back when I mention working in atomic energy. When I assure them I have nothing whatsoever to do with weapons or any defence applications, they look relieved. I just couldn't have wasted fifteen years of my life in so applying a scientific training.

Although the organization I work for is a publicly-owned one, its achievements in technology are as great as anything ever obtained by a private enterprise. Let no one doubt that state enterprises, where the profit motive is absent, are capable of working with vigour and enthusiasm, in fact working as though everyone was a shareholder. (Indeed, they are in a way!) Professional people rising to a technical challenge are a formidable force. Rarely have I contemplated returning to private industry, and if I did leave my present job in the future it would probably only be for the purpose of taking up a university teaching appointment.

What does managing research mean? It obviously includes the planning and direction of research projects; but it also includes the selection of particular items of research to work on. The most senior people in research management are mainly preoccupied with deciding what proposals for research should be adopted, what should be rejected, what level of effort and expenditure is appropriate, and when research projects should be terminated. In other words, establishing the broad policy within which junior research managers can plan and execute pieces of research. My own job involves a certain amount of looking for new research projects to work on as well as gaining approval to put people onto them, but it also includes controlling actual research investigations which are in progress.

There are two kinds of research investigation – basic and applied. The latter type often originates from the need of some new large engineering project to obtain background technical data. The basic work is usually fairly long-term stuff, although a programme of work may have begun in association with some direct project work. People get ideas of their own to work on, without being sure of the ultimate application; what they are sure of is that they are adding to the general store of scientific knowledge. A certain proportion of the work going on in my laboratories is of a basic character, although much of our work is directly associated with the development of new engineering constructional materials. When some new material is first synthesized or discovered, its advantages may be proclaimed on the basis of having made and tested only an ounce or two. Before engineers can design a plant to manufacture the material, they need a whole lot of technical information – scale-up data, as it is sometimes called – to make this feasible. The properties of the new material may vary according to the particular technique of manufacture, even according to the scale of production; small pilot scale plants are sometimes built in our laboratories and operated to obtain a supply of realistic material for further scientific evaluation. Thus we have engineers (chemical and mechanical) as well as scientists (physicists, chemists and metallurgists) all working together in project teams, so that the construction of advanced nuclear-power reactors can proceed based on an adequate store of technical know-how of the right kind.

The layman often has a peculiar image of scientific laboratories. Films and television plays often represent a very naïve picture. The majority of scientific equipment is so complex these days that specialist engineers – electronic, instrument, mechanical engineers – are required to design and install 'rigs', as they are called, for scientists to operate. We find it very frustrating at times, awaiting the commissioning of new apparatus; sometimes one is held up for delivery of a particular instrument, sometimes one just can't see why the rig won't operate properly. Often time is spent trying to pump the gas out of an apparatus, trying to create a vacuum, before an experiment can begin. Sometimes we think the experiments are going fine, and don't realize that impossible results have been obtained until the computer has done the calculations for us. But we get there in the end, and the boys in the teams do find life interesting when finally experimental results are obtained which fall into a predicted pattern. The positive outcome perhaps being two-fold: the individual scientist gets a paper out, over his name, which adds to his professional credit, and the engineering design teams get their guidance on which way to proceed.

I tried earlier to give the reader some general idea of the daily routine of a plant manager. This would be impossible for a research manager since there is no routine. I cannot even say how many hours I work a week. I am at my desk by 9, but leave the establishment at any time between 5.20 and 6. I frequently only take a snack lunch, lasting thirty minutes. But of course work is often taken home at night in a bag, depending upon the particular work load.

A good deal of one's time during the day is devoted to talking with people. Talking in my office, talking on the phone, talking with people in a technical committee meeting, talking with research workers standing in front of an experimental assembly. Always there is talk and discussion going on, sometimes I feel too much. I would like more time for just thinking and studying. But all this talking to people means it is very important to be able to get on well with them. It is constantly necessary to be perfectly honest, direct and concise in these verbal interchanges, where views are exchanged, ideas developed. The team leader must maintain morale at a high level, so that an atmosphere of work can be maintained in which people will produce new ideas, will express themselves, and help each other unselfishly with such enthusiasm that they sometimes ignore the clock and work on regardless. I am now describing what is perhaps the most important responsibility of a research manager, the need to encourage and drive along the teams whose job it is to create and innovate as well as carry out routine laboratory and workshop tasks from day to day. It follows that a large number of meetings and encounters take place at short notice. It is perfectly possible, in principle, to make people wait until tomorrow, to let them book an appointment as it were, if they are junior to myself. But in practice, experience shows it pays to be very accessible to all members of the team. A man may have a good idea today; if it is not fostered and developed straight away, it may wither away. Again, a small worry today may have become quite a big problem within a day or two, so one listens to it, deals with it as soon as possible, and thereby clears a man's mind for more important matters. This is quite a different management atmosphere from the one that usually exists in production units, where more rigid discipline generally operates. I am happier, more relaxed, in the easy-going, less rank-conscious, more informal atmosphere of a research organization. Although there are depressing days when nothing seems to move very fast, there is often an excitement in the air when people see new experimental apparatus completed, when experiments go well, when the results of experiments plot out in a significant way, or when the computer sends back an unexpected answer.

In the environment I have described, it is difficult to

anticipate just what one will be doing at any given time of any particular day. Always there is 'paper work' awaiting one's attention. A continuous flow of memos, letters, documents, papers and forms passes through my office. I really wish I could cut down the time I have to spend coping with this pile of paper. Technical and scientific journals also tend to pile up in the office; one is reluctant to pass them on unopened for fear of missing something new and interesting. There is also value to be gained by merely flicking over the pages of a lot of technical literature in order to get the 'feel' of how things are moving in science. The main aim of all our work is the preparation of scientific reports and papers. These are published by our internal organization in the first place, and later, when patents have been taken out, perhaps published in international technical journals or the proceedings of a scientific society. Sometimes the latter organize conferences at which scientific papers are read out and discussed, and my scientific staff often attend such meetings. Sometimes, when the conferences are held abroad, this means we get a foreign tour, since a trip to the U S A, for example, is costly on fares, and having sent a man over there, it is sensible to extract the maximum value out of the exercise by arranging visits to laboratories, centres of learning or industrial enterprises. Of course, when scientific papers are written, a good deal of editing or 'polishing up' is necessary, and frequently several drafts are prepared and circulated at different levels of management. Sometimes, the junior people experience frustration when drafts are sent back to them for minor, detailed modification. One of the defects of our system of working is that we frequently ask the staff to commence work on new experimental projects before the writing-up of the old ones is complete; a period of overlap often occurs. Scientists then find it difficult to spread their nervous energies over both types of work at the same time and since young people's enthusiasm usually shifts on to anything new coming up, the writing up of old work tends to suffer. We research managers press for good reports, written quickly, and I think we expect to have our cake and eat it. But this is the system we try to work and personally my sympathies are with the junior scientific staff.

Still on the theme of paper work, but at the other end of the scale, there are the innumerable bits of paper that require a signature for approval. Each member of staff is authorized to sign for work or goods up to a fixed maximum level. When he wants to go above this level, he has to make a case in writing to his superior officer. So at any time I may be authorizing chits for staff in my own department, or handling chits for submission to the branch head, my direct boss, for approval by him or by his boss. This all takes time, of course. Very large sums of money require approval by high-level committees which don't meet every day, so the process can become time-consuming and frustrating.

Although we are not part of the civil service, our systems of administration, organization, staff structure and regulations are very similar. Two exercises are carried out every year to ensure that the promotion welfare of everyone is safeguarded and to make sure that there is equal opportunity for all. Firstly, there is the system of ACRs – Annual Confidential Reports. Everyone is reported on in writing by their supervisor, who has to allocate markings against a list of qualities and attributes. Suitability for promotion to the next higher grade must also be commented upon. Each report then goes to the next higher officer in the chain of command for further commenting. The ACRs are kept in a central filing system by the establishment branch, and are made available to the promotion panels. The second exercise carried out each year is the promotion review. In the case of certain grades of officer it operates twice yearly. Everyone on the staff whose age brings them conceivably within possible range of promotion is considered at these reviews, and if their own department consider the time ripe, their name is submitted to one of the central panels which conduct oral examinations. In the scientific fraternity, these interviews are almost entirely technical, often lasting from half an hour to an hour. Candidates are not only expected to describe their own work, but are frequently expected to know why the work is being carried out, and the general policy backing programmes of work. General mental alertness, an ability for creative thinking, and a good knowledge of scientific principles and modern laboratory techniques are expected, to a greater or lesser degree depending upon the particular rank and grade of the officer. Although this system is frequently sneered at by some civil servants and more particularly by exponents of private enterprise systems which have no formal structure for promotion whatsoever, I, with experience of both, much prefer the civil-service system, because it reduces the 'blue-eyed boy' and 'old school tie' rackets to small proportions. One interesting feature of the civil-service promotion system is that it is an example of 'worker participation' in management, since virtually all officers of the non-industrial civil service partake at some time in their career. The system I have described does not rigidly apply right up to the highest management posts; the method applies to some degree, though less formally. A man who has not proved himself very capable of sustained effort and achievement in a middle-management job for a number of years is very unlikely to attain the highest positions of authority in middle age and beyond. Critics of this system must contend with the fact that the establishment I am writing about has an undoubted international reputation for high-grade scientific research and achievement. So our system must be releasing a high proportion of human talents, energy and enthusiasm.

One of the weaknesses of the system is the difficulty in getting a man transferred from one class to another – a 'class-to-class' promotion, as it is called. There are three main classes of scientific worker, each corresponding to a certain level of paper qualifications. If a person improves his qualifications on paper to such a level that they equal those of people in a higher class of scientific workers, then a case can be made out for transfer to that class. In practice, this can be very difficult to achieve. Anyone who can gain an interview panel for a class-to-class promotion must already have an impressive record of achievement and service. Anyone who can pass such an interview panel will thereby demonstrate that he has talents and capabilities of a very high order. Successful candidates are rare, but it can and does happen on occasions. I would like to see the system relaxed a little so that 'late developers', who perhaps never went to a university, can have more opportunity of catching up those who started off their career in the service with an honours degree, or an even higher qualification such as a doctorate. To sum up, the meritocracy of my present organization is much to be preferred to the autocracy of the company I worked for in my younger days. Although the former system has its faults and could be greatly improved, it is inherently fairer and hence more likely to draw on a wider range of talents and liberate more total work-energy from people than the latter system, which depends too much on the hunches and intuition of one or two people in high places.

R. ANDEMANN

THE AUTHOR

I was born in Yorkshire in 1921 of working-class parents. At the local grammar school I gained a major scholarship to read science at a Yorkshire redbrick university, from which I graduated during the Second World War.

I went into industry, consolidating the practical experience by studying chemical engineering at night school during the late 1940s. By this time my wife and I were rearing a family of four boys, the eldest of whom subsequently gained a scholarship to Dartmouth and the second went to university to follow my profession.

(In case any professional colleagues read my article, I apologize to them for the title I've chosen. Since a great deal of discussion takes place on what we mean by such words as science – applied and pure – technology, research, development, engineering, engineering research etc., and even scientific and engineering people can't agree completely about the final distinctions, let alone laymen, the title is no more than a convenient way of conveying some sort of an impression to most laymen of the work I'm discussing.)

After working to re-establish a Labour government, subsequent events have made me feel somewhat disillusioned with politics. A few years ago my wife and I became members of the Society of Friends, and this has come to mean much to us.

I often find myself regretting that I can't seem to find enough time to paint pictures, listen to music or take photographs. My wife, who is a magistrate and involved in social work, is also busy, but one of our major pleasures is when we occasionally manage to get away on a foreign tour.

Child-Care Officer

I was twenty-two when I became a child-care officer, and I worked in the children's department for three years. It began when I was sent as a student to observe what went on. I discovered I enjoyed being with children. Warmth and noise hung over the room from which the work was done. I was drawn back there when I left university a year later. I hadn't taken the specialized training course in child care: only a few in our department did have the professional qualification when I started six years ago. The picture has altered gradually, and now many more people are being trained.

Child care is, of course, a branch of social work, working with people. A child-care officer is involved with a child and his family because they are separated or there is a possibility of their separation. It means knowing people one would not otherwise have known, not knowing them because it is a job.

Nobody can know what it means to be John, a child separated from his parents because they are sick and unable to look after him. But one person's wanting to try to understand him now, as he is, might help. It might perhaps enable him to express some of his hopes and fears, and so become more familiar with what is his reality. If the child-care officer brings anything that someone else might not bring, it is some acquaintance with the people, events and places that have been, and are, important to the child. And also a small amount of theoretical knowledge of the possible influence of past relationships, especially first relationships, on the present. On the other hand, some elements usually inherent in a relationship between two people, companionship, the overt expression of mutuality, and individual choice, are missing. I didn't choose John or his family, nor did they choose me.

Because child care is concerned with the relationship between people, it is involved in movement. Immediately there are shifts in mood, and in the quantity and authenticity of communication. In the wider sense there is movement in the growth or the diminishing of expectation, need, awareness, involvement, knowledge and concern.

What is also at the core of the job, apart from the network of the child's relationships, is concern with the outer world, the concrete condition in which John lives. And the work is involved in the administration of certain statutory provisions, which interlock with the other components.

It's simplest to begin with the statutory definition. It is the aspect of the work with which it's often hardest to identify, but it's this legal framework that has general application.

Child-care officers work in local authority children's departments, which are ultimately the concern of the Home Office. Various statutes give the department its responsibilities. The act which created the child-care service was the Children Act of 1948, which made it the duty of the local authority children's department to care for a child whose parents are not able to care for him, and whose well-being appears to make necessary his reception into the council's care. The act instructs that as far as possible the individual needs of the child should be provided for. If a child is received into care under section 1 of the act, and that is commonly the case, then the arrangement between the child's parents and the local authority is a voluntary one, and his parents can ask for the child's return home at any time. Indeed the child's going back to his family is to be facilitated by the children's department wherever that is possible: the Children and Young Persons Act of 1963, which applies up to the age of eighteen, increased the provisions for work with a family to prevent long-term separation of the child from his parents.

There are other sections of the Children Act which may operate and which will then alter the nature of a child's position in care; and some children will come into care through the court, not as the result of a voluntary arrangement. But section 1 of the Children Act provides the general pattern.

What the act also provides for is the financial assessment of the parents of children in care, and their contribution towards the child's maintenance.

One way to trace the involvement of a family and a child-care officer is to recall a woman's first visit to the children's department. It's a narrative of my experience in seeing her; incomplete therefore, telling nothing of her despair that has gone before, the moment of hope or hopelessness that brought the family here. Nor does my viewpoint transmit the feelings that accompany having to ask for help, the particular hazard to identity in seeking help from unknown officials: these things belong to the part that's not expressed.

In our room the internal phone rings. It's my day to see people who are coming to the department for the first time. Jennifer, the reception clerk, says: 'There's a Mrs Pegler here with three children. She lives at 32 Crispin Road. She hasn't been here before.'

This is someone new, so the chances are there's nothing to look up; in any case I usually don't read it because I'd rather talk to the person first. Sometimes it will all go wrong, because I don't know something I should have known, but that's how it is.

I go down the corridor and see that, as sometimes happens, the waiting-room is full. It is small, anyway, and each of the straight-backed chairs round the wall is occupied. One or two persons are standing. Although this is a new building, there's no window. Grey distemper. There is a child or two playing underneath the small wooden table in the centre. Otherwise it is quiet. No expectancy. I ask for Mrs Pegler and a woman, standing, in a brown coat, nods after a moment and takes one child, a girl, by the hand. Two other children, both girls, follow, and we go into the interviewing room.

There are three interviewing rooms. They're very small, each one with a table across the middle. You can move the chairs round a bit, that is all. The smallest child gets on to her mother's lap. The two older girls stand by the window and do not speak. One has glasses; she runs her fingers up and down the sill.

People are upset by the time they get here. At times they seem tranced and acquiescent. Sometimes a man or woman might be angry, and bang the table and shout: 'You've got to take them. You can have the kids because I can't stand it any more. What's the bloody council for then?' But it is the exception. Some people cry. Usually someone will talk a little, or speak in spurts, or occasionally say only one phrase and repeat it.

I think that I'm seen only as an official on first interviews like this. The perception stems from the place itself, the atmosphere of officialdom; and from everything that has gone before, all the previous encounters with the establishment that have caused the person not to expect much. I must also contribute to it now, anonymous in the bureaucracy. Sometimes it is almost as if I myself am not here at all. There are exceptions. Once in a while a person will look up, glancing round the room. One might say: 'You don't look old enough. It's an officer we want.' But it's not often.

I ask Mrs Pegler what seems to be wrong, and she doesn't say anything, doesn't answer at first, but takes one of those brown envelopes out of her bag, and passes it over the desk. I read the letter and she turns slightly to look behind her at the girls by the window.

Dear Madam

Mrs Pegler, 32 Crispin Road

This patient is suffering from depression, and is to be admitted to this hospital as soon as possible. We understand she is unable to make arrangements for her three children, and would be glad if you will receive them into your care. Yours faithfully.

So I thank her, and give the letter back, take one of the yellow forms from the box on the desk, say I have to ask her some questions, and she nods. She's full-faced and pale, and her features are heavy. Dark hair, dull, flat to the head. Brown eyes, look as though they don't see a lot, and that perhaps is the depression. She is broad, and sits heavily on the chair, moving her hands sometimes as she holds the child.

The form is called Application for Reception into Care. It

is divided into parts. It needs details about parents. About children. And so on. I don't like forms. Who does? I ask myself.

She answers slowly, with effort at first. She is Sheila Pegler, aged thirty-six. Her husband is Raymond. Also thirty-six years. His occupation is long-distance lorry driver, and his hours of work are irregular. The children are Hilary, Hannah and Susan. Aged seven, six and three. Hilary's taller, yes. That's Hannah, with the glasses. Baptized Church of England: but she's sorry, they don't go. It's St Mark's Road school. They have two rooms, furnished. There's no one to help, not a soul, her parents are gone, dead. Her husband can't be off work. Or change his hours. She doesn't know the neighbours. Anyway, they wouldn't have room for hers, would they?

Susan's always chewing. . . . She chews like this, she's chewed holes in the covers of the chairs. . . . Red plastic. . . . And Hannah rocks a bit. . . . In chairs yes, and in her bed at night. . . . She's downstairs, the landlady, and hers have grown up. . . . Bangs on the ceiling with a broom. . . . What can you do? No garden. . . . Always telling them, 'Be quiet', but they have to move. . . . Been on the council list for years. . . . Since Hilary was born in fact. . . . It will be too late if they ever do get a place, they'll have grown up by then.

She doesn't know how long she will be in the hospital. They said something about the shocks, electric shocks. . . . That would do it probably. . . . Doesn't want to go, because of Ray and the girls. Needs the rest though and that might do it. . . .

Beside a space on the form there is a heading: Reason for Application. I fill it in. Mrs Pegler is being admitted to South Square Hospital for treatment for depression. Mr Pegler works irregular hours, and there is no one to care for the children. Accommodation is limited.

Where the form asks for Recommendation, I put: Receive into care under section 1 (1948). Afterwards I'll give the form to my senior, who fills in the section headed Decision.

There's one more space on the form. Report on Home

Visit. Actually it comes before Recommendation. So I say to Mrs Pegler that it does seem as though the girls should come into care while she is in hospital, and perhaps I can call on her at home this evening to talk about it a bit more.

'All right,' she says; she has grown quiet again, shut in on herself. We go out of the room, and Hilary asks where the toilet is. Remembering, I ask Mrs Pegler if she minds if I phone the school and the health visitor about the children. She shakes her head. People hardly ever do say they mind. The lift comes; she gets the girls into the thing, and as the door is closing she says: 'Their father'll be back about six.'

'I'll be there about six thirty.'

I make some phone calls; the hospital, the school and the health visitor. 'Oh yes, I had heard, what a shame; they're a nice little family. Quite good standards too, considering it's Crispin Road.'

I ask about vacancies and there are none because everywhere is full. Because our area is the decrepit sort, other authorities make available to us provisions which they are not fully using themselves. Our department also shares some large children's homes with other hard-pressed authorities, and uses places in homes run by voluntary agencies too when that is possible. Altogether we make regular use of foster homes, nurseries and children's homes scattered over five counties, sometimes going further afield, and yet I can never remember being able to choose where the children go at a time like this, or being able to offer choice to anyone else. Perhaps by tomorrow something will turn up. But probably the children will have to be split, two to one place and Susan to another, and a long journey is not unlikely. At the weekend Mr Pegler will have to decide where to go to first, the mental hospital twenty miles away, or the children's home in a different direction.

In the evening I go round and say if they ring tomorrow it should be sorted out, the question of where the girls are to stay. There are medical forms to fill up, wonderings about what's going to happen, questions about special toys to take, and so on. The administrative officer will be sending them a form for financial assessment. In the other room, where they sleep, Mrs Pegler points out the marks on the wall, where Hannah rocks the bed; and this here, this is where she has stood banging herself against the door. These are the holes that Susan has chewed in the covers of the settee. Just look at the place: it must be overcrowding.

Mr Pegler, tall, dark-haired, a narrow angular face lined around the mouth, bends to unlace his boots and says: 'All kids chew stuff, don't they, it's their nature. It's nearly half seven.' He goes across the room in his socks and switches on the television. Mrs Pegler says that the others never made holes in things. Hannah takes off her glasses, and rubs her eyes while she tells me: 'I'm an elephant.'

I ask her why, and she looks away, stands on one foot, pulling a thread from the hole in her sweater.

'Susie's only a little mouse.'

Hilary, close to the television, asks: 'Mum, is that the woman from the welfare?'

They live in two rooms, the Peglers. It's a worn-out terraced house, and they have two rooms on the first floor. The furniture is hard, very shiny. There are two families on the floor above, and the landlady has the ground floor. There are two families in the basement. The place is on its last legs. It is a strange thing, going into people's homes, and I don't think I enjoy it all that much. When I get to a place I sit down straight away: too quickly, but otherwise someone might start to tidy up, as though that was what one waited for, and it would add to the feeling of intrusion. It is much easier after two or three visits: it's the first one that is especially difficult.

There is another aspect of visiting people at home which hasn't appeared here. There are some people living in such isolation that its impact is almost overwhelming.

In a day or two Mrs Pegler will take the girls to the children's homes. One of the large ones, probably, for Hilary and Hannah; and for Susan a nursery or a short-stay foster home – we have a few couples willing to have small children to stay with them temporarily. In about two weeks I'll go to see them. Those who are looking after the girls need to know particularly about Susan's chewing and Hannah's tendency to rock. If I have time I'll visit Mrs Pegler in the hospital. Or I might call on Mr Pegler. Perhaps in a couple of months Mrs Pegler will have been shocked and jolted out of her depression, in the absence of time and resources for her to find a more meaningful way through it, and then she'll come to arrange to take the girls home.

Once they have come back, I'll visit once or twice. Sometimes children find it difficult to settle down when they have been away, and these perhaps are girls who might easily become upset, for whom separation might have considerable significance. Whatever the circumstances, whatever the child is told to the contrary, it is possible that she will feel punished and rejected at going away from home, unsure of being wanted back again.

If all goes reasonably well, I'll tell Mrs Pegler I won't call any more, and the case will be closed: I'll write an account of what has happened, and the file will be put away. If a family should return for help after an interval of a year or so, they'd be seen by the child-care officer with whom they first had contact.

There was not much doubt that the three Pegler children needed temporary care. It might be more complex.

Mrs Julie Quickendon, aged twenty-three, separated from her husband, and doesn't know where he is: she is living with her parents-in-law, and looking after her son, Dennis, aged two and three quarters. It's terrible; there are rows all the time. Dennis wakes up screaming in the night. She can't go on any longer. She's going out of her mind: she has to get away. Today, right now. She needs Dennis put away for one month while she sorts things out. She has a sister in Reading who can get her a place probably. Then she'll get a job and have Dennis out: he can go to a day nursery then. She can do it easily in a month, oh much less probably. If someone doesn't help her now, she'll end up in the nut house. She might just walk away and leave Dennis.

She is beside herself and maybe she is going out of her mind: or by tomorrow she might feel more able to go on. Perhaps I could talk to her at home, try to see what is wrong, whether there is another way of looking at it. Or perhaps she could get a place in Reading: that might be a solution. On the other hand Dennis might be haunted by monstrous phantasies of guilt and desertion in the children's home. If there is a vacancy. And perhaps it will drag on and on, and Dennis will know himself as a person who has grown up in an institution, and so not know himself at all. Dennis's father: where is he, and what does he want?

Endless questions: no easy answer. Neither the material provision nor the time for much flexibility. I could have shown the application form to my senior and asked – What do I do? But I was the one who had seen Mrs Quickendon and felt her agitation.

An abandoned child would be a rare event. But if Mrs Quickendon had walked out, gone out of her mind, could not be found on that day, Dennis would then have to be looked after. Had his grandparents been unable to help, had Mr Quickendon seemed to be lost, Dennis would have been received into care. And because it was an emergency a vacancy would have to be found, miles away perhaps in the country or down by the sea. So one of the others would have helped, driving there with Dennis, trying to explain what had happened. We would have stopped at a café because by that time it would have been late. I would have tried not to think, since thinking might be painful. I expect Dennis would have been tired, and fallen asleep.

The area from which the families came was about four miles away from the office; and there the houses, fronting dingy streets, were shabby and decaying, full of people. In patches, the council had built estates of flats. Some blocks had been constructed before 1914: red-brick piles divided by stone stairways into depressing fractions. Our area was an immigrant one, with a high proportion of West Indians: it was the sort of place that many people might pass through, and get away from if they could. There were hardly any trees. The only colour was in the market that ran through the middle.

When I first saw it I was dismayed that people lived in conditions like that. But it takes time and proximity to guess anything of the stunting and passivity that dreary dilapidation brings about. And there is the trap of withdrawal, seeing nothing, of psychologizing and finally forgetting that the collapse of a family has anything to do with the neglect amidst which it existed.

The homes and nurseries to which the children went if they were taken into care might sometimes be ordinary houses in suburban streets; or mansions sunk in the country. The old institutions lingered on – and are there still – with their own clothing stores, primary school and chapel; and three hundred children within. Even in the largest homes there were houseparents who were somehow able to understand. But residential work seemed exceedingly difficult, and good intentions could fast be corroded by the institutional milieu. Human brightness then leaked away, and staff didn't have much to offer.

Schools, reception centres, hostels, hospitals, remand homes; doss houses, prisons, mother and baby homes: the things seen in three years are only details from the world of institutional living. Particularly conspicuous amongst this collection seemed to me mother and baby homes, for their nurture of asphyxiating patronage and shame.

I sometimes went to the homeless families unit, which was run by the welfare department of our council. At first, families were evicted from the unit if they failed to keep up payments for the communal accommodation provided, but then pressure was exerted by the press and television, and the evictions stopped. Amongst ourselves we had grumbled, talked of writing letters here and there, but that was all: we'd done nothing more. The place smelt of sickness, veneered with the disinfectant with which it was vainly hoped to kill disease. Men were not allowed to stay (though now that at least has changed). When mothers went into hospital from the unit, we took their children into care. They had to go to specially designated nurseries and children's homes because they were always infected, always with dysentery and usually with something else. The hostel welfare officer would ring up to report with old-style vigour: 'Got two children for you here: to go into care. Woman's gone into hospital – dysentery and pregnant. We've got, let's see yes, we've got measles here.'

It wasn't much more than the shell of a place. After a few days women took on the bent head and shuffling gait, the pinched and bewildered look bestowed by institutions at the end of the line.

There was a lot of homelessness in our area. Every year the council's housing department allocated a number of places to us in the children's department, so that it was possible to nominate a few families for priority rehousing. Only a very few: there was some secrecy about the exact number. In my experience it always worked: the family was rehoused, the children went home, and they stayed together. It was something one could feel really glad about.

Each day at work was unlike another. That was the nature of the job. At first the unpredictability was exciting: later I wished sometimes that the work could develop a more certain rhythm. It didn't, of course, because it never could be like that, and because there were not really enough of us to go round. A caseload of fifty-five or so children – it was a great improvement on the position of a few years before – meant insufficient time to anticipate and to do the sort of work one would have liked.

Our office was in a new cement and glass block set at the junction of five main roads. Not only in the rush hour, but at any time some ticklish manoeuvring through the circling traffic was necessary to reach it by car; those coming on foot required a lively mind to negotiate a complex subway system. Ours was not the place imagination would link with children and their families.

About thirty-six child-care officers worked there, divided into groups of six. Our room was noisy. Eruptions of revelry safeguarded us from becoming bent on doing good. Entering, it was not unusual to find a diversion in progress.

Probably its beginning had been peaceful enough. A few stray reminiscences of Joan's... No, she had never really found it difficult, speaking in front of others, provided the cause was right. She had been fifteen the first time. That was when she had been invited by Harry Pollitt to address the gathering when he visited her home town. A little nervously, she'd started her statement of how things seemed to her. Actually an unfortunate thing had happened that time. After a sentence or two a voice had come from the back. 'Come down off there,' she was ordered, 'making an exhibition of yourself.' It was her mother, out for a walk by the sea. She scrambled off the platform; and one or two had laughed. Crying and humiliated, she had to follow her mother along the prom.

'You gave up!' Peter was triumphant, hoping at last to prove his claim to be the only working-class representative among us because he had worked on the buses. Anne, the thoughtful one, was always ready to arbitrate gently when called upon, though Joan seldom needed defence.

'Since when have I not said what I thought: it was just a very slight lapse. Not like the rest of you. Just look around. What a pathetic precious lot. Ask a social worker for a straight answer and what do you get? Nothing.'

Anne was inclined to agree. They might be a force to be reckoned with if they were articulate.

'It's our ability to see both sides,' Michael was banging on his desk, 'our capacity to understand ambivalence. When social work is recognized as a profession it will be different. We'll be in a position to say more then.'

What did the bloody profession have to do with it? The noise grew louder. In the end it was interrupted by Peter. He'd lost interest, and was rummaging in the pile of stuff we kept in the corner for emergencies. 'How's this for size? Do you think it suits me?'

Straw-hatted, he regarded himself, draped in a blanket, while the rest of us made guesses what he might be, druid or corpse. 'No, a polar bear. And I need a woman to hug!'

It was the signal for a scramble round the desks, and five minutes' uproar: the excitement was lovely, and we lost ourselves as children do. Then we pulled out our chairs and started to work. Michael's was the only voice, on the phone.

It wasn't altogether gaiety. We also behaved in that way because sometimes we were anxious, and because we were, after all, regarded as children are often regarded, to be kept apart from what is going on. And the outbursts were more likely to occur when George, who was our senior, was missing from behind his corner partition that we called the horse box.

George was quietly talkative: tall, red-haired and hyperkinetic. There were curious moments of a collective fondness for him. His hope was that the time would come when our area would be cleaned up and freed from sin. He remarked to me gently one day, 'What our world needs is God, not psychoanalysis.'

Like ours, each group had a senior, and a clerical officer, and each one covered part of the total geographical area for which the department was responsible. The structure was a hierarchy, a simple pyramid, with a children's officer at the top, then the deputy, six seniors, and the child-care officers. Thus the only ones who had contact with the people who used the service were at the bottom. The seniors gave advice, allocated cases from the court, and could authorize bits of spending. They tended to be somewhat serious. Mostly they had been there for a long time. They often met together, though no one really knew why.

As the department grew larger, so did those right at the top of the structure recede and become inaccessible. The children's officer put up a notice reading Private on her door. We hardly ever all met together. Our opinions on policy were not asked for, though we were the ones who saw need and who witnessed failure of provision. Sometimes there was a duplicated news sheet. . . . Bulletin No.6. Once a year someone came from the committee to give thanks for services rendered and, unless you'd gone out, shook each one by the hand and said Happy Christmas.

When I first went to the department, a colleague explained about the hierarchy and I thought it very funny: it sounded like the army. A little solemnly, he said it was the weight of responsibility to be shared. But afterwards I came to wonder how truly I could share responsibility with someone who had not seen what I had seen, because it seemed to me to depend on what I selected to tell him, how it was put. Thorough discussion might certainly have clarified what was at issue, but that didn't very often occur. What each of us needed in the job was the awareness to know what people were really saying, or trying to say, and to then decide how we could help them. To be assigned a role in a hierarchy contributed nothing to that.

Some took it quite seriously. Some referred to the children's officer as The Boss, as though the place were a production line. A sort of leaden dependency could develop: then the humour wore thin because what was happening was not compatible with the work we were trying to do. The whole structure was a drag on growth and change – in us and, through us, in those we were trying to help. I think that a naïve expectation that things would eventually be seen my way was fulfilled; within the limitations of knowledge and provision I wasn't prevented from doing what I wanted to do. There were others who weren't always as fortunate. Time was squandered in the cause of procedure, and discussions were trifling and petty. I did nothing about it: I didn't know what to do, felt unhappy when I made a lot of noise and could fall back on doubting the value of criticism when there was so much work waiting to be done: but I felt remarkably cut off from anything that might have been going on. Perhaps that's what it was: perhaps in our department not much was happening.

Quite a proportion of any day might be taken up with recording. Mine was never up to date. On another floor there were six shorthand typists, but they were always in demand and, I don't know why, I don't like dictating. Recording took up a lot of time, however one did it. You could never be sure what would happen. For one or two children, the only certain knowledge about their early lives might one day be contained in the department's files.

And telephoning. Always on the phone. You rang a charity and asked nicely: 'Please, have you got a little mattress? I have a family where the child is sharing his parents' bed, and he wets in the night, you see.'

Very sorry, no: they are so sorry. Perhaps some money could be got from somewhere then. You didn't say so, but sometimes he wetted the bed first, before he got in. Had enough, probably. From time to time, on the outskirts of the city, someone would remark to you: how rewarding it must be.

I seldom spent a whole day in the office, apart from my weekly turn to take applications. When I felt depressed I thought that my work was nothing more than a constant flight; time here, there, achieving nothing. Worse, invading private worlds and presuming to understand: propping up the status quo. And then some new thing would happen and it would be lovely: I'd noiselessly appropriate all the credit for it.

In the afternoon I might have arranged to see Roger, eight years and Marion, aged five, at Becketts, a children's home, one of the large ones, consisting of twenty or so houses.

Their father, Mr Underwood, one of a family of five, raised in the north. Unemployment and ill health in the family. Admitted to a children's home when he was twelve, and had to leave there when he became fifteen. Worked with various firms of house painters and decorators, living all over the country, married when he was twenty-two. Little is known about Mrs Underwood's background. She is said to have one brother. Married when she was twenty.

Roger and Marion were born in a furnished room in Somerset Road. The family was given the chance to move downstairs to a larger flat – two rooms and a kitchen. The rent was increased. Another child was born but died. Some months later Mrs Underwood applied to the department for help, saying she could not manage on money from the National Assistance Board. The NAB considered her rent excessive, and so would not meet the full amount. There were no grounds for the children's reception into care, but an officer visited Mrs Underwood from time to time, and tried to offer support. Six months later she had to be admitted to hospital, and Roger and Marion were placed at Hill Mount Nursery. While away on convalescent holiday, Mrs Underwood got pneumonia, was readmitted to hospital and died. Mr Underwood is now serving a two-year prison sentence, and the child-care officer plans to visit him about every six months. Roger and Marion believe that he has to work away, and that he will come back.

At the nursery the children seemed quiet and withdrawn. Aged five and two they were transferred to Becketts. They seemed to settle well, and Roger has since made good progress. The child-care officer is considering plans for the future.

Considering; but I couldn't decide what to do. Many would have suggested a foster home, but I was not very happy about fostering. I knew that it did work sometimes, appeared to provide very happily. But it seemed to me that it must be an enormous transition for a child to move into a highly interdependent family situation in which he had no origin, to find himself in the midst of a pattern of living which initially was shared by all but him. A foster home would mean a new school, new words, new ways of behaving, talking, eating, dressing, aspiring. Of course, it brought changes for the foster parents too, of whom a tremendous amount was asked, and for their own children. Change, it might have been remarked, is inevitable; and if you didn't feel hopeful you wouldn't be doing the job. But it didn't alter my feeling that the direction of change could not be taken for granted in an individual family situation: there could be no certainty that the foster home would be there as long as the child needed it, no sureness his world would not collapse again. And in any case, there was society's way of looking at it; the tendency to give thanks that a foster child was being given a home, a turning away from the venture as a mutual exchange.

Not long before, Mr Underwood, slighter, diminished now in prison stuff, had leaned on the table in the stony place and agreed, quietly and apologetically, that the children might be better off in a foster home. Then he relaxed, and smiled as one with a good idea. He'd been wondering if I could find a family where he would be accepted as a visitor when he got out.

I wasn't sure that I could. Not very many people offered to be foster parents: perhaps some potentially good ones were put off by the low allowances made. There were some who wanted a little girl for Christmas: but they hadn't thought about what it meant. Little research had been done on fostering: there wasn't much to go on. I did put one of those advertisements in a weekly. . . . An understanding foster home is needed for a brother and sister. . . . Actually, fourteen families replied. But although I talked it over with each of them, I did not feel very happy about it.

I wondered about a family unit – eight to twelve children, living with a housemother or houseparents in a suburban house – though vacancies were scarce, and it would mean a wait. Or should I leave them where they were, find an uncle and aunt who would have them home some Sundays: see what Mr Underwood was thinking.

What worried me too was that children might be jettisoned from place to place. It just happened. They left a nursery, probably feeling rejected, not knowing that they left for the reason that they were now five years old. They subsequently showed difficult behaviour in the children's home, and the housemother, who was tired and overworked, asked if they could go somewhere else where they could have more attention. And so it could go on, spiralling. Sometimes, thinking about what had happened to a child, I felt that the healthy thing would be protest: he ought to be protesting about it. But his protest was likely to be something that involved him in a new difficulty that could lead him to approved school, or something else that set him apart from others of his age. If a child accepted what was offered, one wondered if it was because he considered himself worth nothing more. If he rejected it, he was likely to be stamped as deviant.

At Becketts, where Roger and Marion were cared for, there was the absence of male figures which characterized most children's homes. Fortunately, in their particular house, there was an enthusiastic housemother. Short, round, free from fuss, and sympathetic. The children called her Auntie Elizabeth. She told me that she worked in a bank until she was forty; one day it seemed absurd, she gave in her notice.

Miss Harper, Auntie Elizabeth, had been very nice to Mr Underwood when he had been there. One wished it were always like that.

Blueberry Cottage, Becketts. We go into the sitting room. Roger wants to sing a song he has learnt at school. He is tall and thin, dark hair, blue T-shirt. Standing with his hands behind his back, he sways with the song, then loses the words and pretends that he hasn't. It trails away; and he's saying he's got a new teacher...

Marion, sandy-haired, in a summer dress, is shy, and crawls on all fours behind the chair, looking round as she goes and wanting to be trapped in the corner. She squats on her heels and says: 'Got your car?'

It is early, but we go out for some tea, to the place we have been to before. Others have varying opinions on the value of outings. Certainly it's not our job to come as benevolent bringers of treats. Sometimes I take the children out and sometimes I don't; it depends on how things are, and what opportunity there is for making contact with them in the children's home. It's often limited, to my mind.

Roger's favourite is fish and chips. He has found he loves *coffee*. Questions rattle out: 'What's grey, got four legs and a trunk? Oh no, it's not. Guess, it's a mouse going on his holiday. *You're* wrong.'

Marion does not know what to have. She sits and wonders.

Aged five years, such difficulty is not surprising. But if she stays in the children's home it's possible the confusion will be no less when she's fifteen because she won't have had the customary amount of practice. She might not have as many words as other children, and lack their capacity for abstracting: deprivation can neatly become self-perpetuating.

They talk about Dad. They ask about the place where they were before they came to Becketts. I tell them it was Mrs Allison, their first child-care officer, who visited them at the beginning; I came to see them when she had to leave because she was moving away from the city. The nursery was called Hill Mount: it was Auntie Sally who usually looked after them. It had seemed to me that their special friend was a boy called Trevor.

'Oh no, I had a girl friend. She kissed me. Her name was Sophie. Lots of friends I had there.'

Marion says she can remember that place too, but Becketts is nicer.

We go back, and they want to drive past the other houses, blowing the horn, shouting to the children. It is as though we have been on a year's journey. After talking to Miss Harper I say good-bye; I'll come again in about two months. . . .

Asked at the beginning why I did it, I would have said that I wanted to help people, because it is an easy thing to say, and there is a sense in which it was true, though then I could not so readily have seen that helping is being helped. At the very beginning I thought too that the job would give ready-made the things to say. It's a concept which allows little for deviation from a pattern, or indeed for any exchange at all, and it must have been that my sights were set on telling people what to do: I think that is what social work seemed to me to be about. The first visit I made was to a woman who was sick at home, and from whom some information was needed: consciously I took on a part and played what I thought was the social-worker game. Role-play like that is empty, and it petered out: I had to go again in order to ask the necessary questions. It takes much longer than that, though, to see people whose experience of life, whose words and behaviour are different from one's own, as people – at least it's taken me longer – and there is a sense in which one doesn't, and never can, because it's a job that is being done. Despite that – and the limitation is always present – there's every reason to strive for understanding.

NORMA VINCE

THE AUTHOR

I was an only child, and I grew up in the suburbs of London. My father spent the first years of his working life as a railway ticket collector: late in his twenties he became manager of a large department store. In 1943, when I was four, I started school, at a Catholic convent, where I stayed for six years. Subsequently I went to a small private school, a girls' high school and a grammar school. When I was eighteen I took a shorthand and typing course at a college in London, and then worked for nearly a year in a publishers. Afterwards I went to Exeter University, where I studied social administration for two years. I spent the next three years working as a child-care officer; and when I left the children's department I went to the Greek islands, where for about nine months I worked for a family, mostly looking after a baby and cooking. Later I worked in a mental hospital in Surrey, as social worker in a unit for adolescents. I was there for the best part of a year, and then took the mental-health course at the London School of Economics. In October 1967 I started working with the Family Service Units in North London.

The Schoolteacher

I teach in a large London comprehensive of over a thousand boys. The school is surrounded by pre-war LCC flats where tarmac and concrete separate red-brick buildings four stories high. The area is used completely for living in, so there are few green spaces or parks. Every morning I walk through this area with its grim and dead environment no matter what the weather; it's here that the boys I teach live.

The school itself, except for a near-by old people's home, is the newest construction in the area. It is a building on three floors with classrooms like boxes either side of long corridors on each of these floors. At either end are art rooms and science laboratories. Gymnasiums and workshops are separate from the main building. An older building, which occupied the site in pre-war days, is used by upper-school boys. Whether it was intended or not, the school's physical layout gives the impression of compartmentalization, with the outer buildings occupied by subjects of inferior status. There is further subdivision, because teachers in a particular subject department work in rooms adjacent to one another.

The classroom I teach in is thus near the classrooms of all the other English teachers. Specialization and an academic division of labour is encouraged so that, though I once taught History, I now deal only with the one subject – English. Added status is given to a 'specialist' teacher and few chances of special allowances are held out to the non-specialist. Teachers of remedial classes who cover most subjects with their pupils, despite their obvious teaching ability, are, like their classes, accorded low status within the school.

I remain in my room virtually all day except at break and lunch time, when I meet other members of staff. In this room I am faced by thirty-two desks and chairs. My desk faces them. Boys come to me for six or seven periods a day for the five days of the week. They sit in the desks and face the blackboard, my one basic item of teaching equipment. I have the possible use of a record player, but have to change rooms with another teacher to do so. There is no real access to a tape recorder. I use films as an aid to my class teaching, but this means moving my classes through the building to a room which is fairly tightly time-tabled for use by other classes. Recently the school added to its range of teaching aids such equipment as cine-loop projectors, TV, back-projectors, and 8 mm. cine equipment, but with a staff of eighty who might use them, their number is pitifully inadequate, and opportunities for their use by any one individual are obviously limited.

On one side of my classroom is a large window; another side holds the blackboard and the other walls have spaces for items to be pinned up. I use them for showing some of the boys' work; the rest can display information for the boys and my own exhibitions.

Unlike a primary-school teacher I teach only the one subject in this room and so cannot adequately relate what I am dealing with to other subjects. Boys come to me for a set period lasting forty or eighty minutes and then they move on. Just as I may see seven different classes in a day, so a particular pupil may be taught by seven different teachers for seven different subjects. No interplay exists between subjects, so lessons concerned with 'communications' like English, French, German, Art etc., are considered separately from one another. Even connexions between the 'sciences' have to be inferred by the boys; and preparing for separate examinations called Mathematics, Physics and Chemistry reinforces this division between disciplines. Connexions between History and Geography tend only to arise by chance: once, whilst we were talking about the 1917 Russian Revolution, a group of boys informed me with surprise that they were also studying Russia's geography. Furthermore they had not expected the two subjects to reinforce one another and give an added interest and meaning to the facts under consideration.

Thus I teach English in isolation and refer outside the subject to other areas when I can. Teaching English for me involves helping the boys to become 'articulate' in a broad sense – it entails giving them direction in acquiring the ability to express orally or by writing basic information, their opinions on various subjects, their own feelings or ideas; also I aim to help them understand, enjoy and perhaps evaluate all sorts of reading material; and finally I want to get them to see the use that can be made of books. These are wide and vague aims and when translated into reality in the environment of the school it is difficult to keep them in view.

In the classroom situation there is myself, the boys, the blackboard, their textbooks and exercise books. This is by no means a rich and varied educational environment and provides no adequate contrast to many of the boy's homes, especially as the books quickly become battered and defaced, the paint-work spattered and the general furniture chipped. It would be more satisfactory to have a classroom as a place for experiment, partly on the primary-school model, giving the boys the opportunity to go their own ways and do what interests them with a greater variety of media to work with. The present classroom situation tends to encourage a rigid teaching method. The basic approach remains 'chalk-and-talk'. The thirty-odd faces staring towards me expect this, and the military line-up of desks is hard to break away from. The lessons often proceed by what amounts to a lecture or by the time-honoured method of question and answer between teacher and class. Both of these methods cut down the participation of the boys to a minimum and it is small wonder that there is inattention, with those large windows drawing eyes away from what is going on, bad behaviour, little involvement, or no motivation to work. Maintaining interest therefore almost inevitably rests with the personality of the teacher concerned, and so I stand in front of each class performing and living up to the teacher's reputation of being an actor *manqué* in order to keep that small spark of interest alive. So far I have had a measure of success in this direction because, I believe, many of the boys like me and are willing to give what I have to say some of their interest and occasional enthusiasm. But on the other hand I know that in part this response to me is a reaction against the authoritarian approach of other teachers, whose attitude to their pupils is that there is little hope of success for even the most intelligent and that the job is a routine bore anyway.

As the majority of my teaching life is spent in the classroom situation it naturally gives rise to most of the disappointments and frustrations of the job, besides its excitements. For the boys this procedure provides training for their later working life. Involvement in their work at school is low, whilst it is in their non-work pursuits that they really become alive, a dichotomy likely to be carried on into their later life.

A contrast also exists between home and school. Any interest that may develop in school work can rapidly be upset because the home environment, even of sympathetic parents, works against the values of the school. Lack of space and the attractions of TV help to discourage the completion of homework, and parents, rather bewildered by what their sons are learning at school, are unable to help their children or may positively discourage interest being taken in things they regard as unnecessary. These factors I have found become real problems for boys faced with an examination for which they need a fair chance to prepare. For other boys the local youth clubs, discotheques, cinemas or street corners provide attractions which their whole cultural background does not equip them to resist. Several boys I have talked to have revealed a considerable, probably superficial, sophistication gained through these experiences. Still other boys, sons of widows, of parents whose lives are carried on outside their homes, or in one case of parents so unstable as to leave the other partner regularly after a tremendous row, have had to take on some of the responsibilities for a family, and this naturally distracts them from any attachment to the school or its purpose. Yet other boys have fully adopted their future adult characters based on their parents' model and no longer consider the school a significant place for them. One of my pupils had become an almost obsessive gambler by the age of eleven and would attend the dog-racing track twice a week to work out complicated bets with a skill that contrasted sharply with his performance in school mathematics. And yet, when the opportunity to vary the teaching approach arises, interest rapidly wells up, though these occasions all too often have the appearance of being a special 'treat'. Thus boys have shown me they really do feel and understand things. Sometimes an individual or a group will respond vividly to something we have been discussing. On another occasion a 'backward' class, who all seemed very moved by the atmosphere after the death of Sir Winston Churchill, with great enthusiasm compiled a scrapbook on the man's life and funeral, bringing newspaper and magazine articles and pictures to complement their own writings. Yet another similar group produced an excellent book for me on the 'Wild West', for which they researched at home and in the school library for several weeks to extract relevant information and illustrations. This group, like so many other remedial or backward classes, tended to be ignored or ill-cared for by teachers not ideologically committed to their welfare, but given encouragement and opportunity they proved they could do as good work as the more favoured groups in the school. Another remedial class I have taught fell enthusiastically into making a cartoon film with bits of 16mm. stock we had available, and were full of their own original ideas on how to approach the job.

The school follows the principle of 'streaming' classes. We have therefore an eight-stream entry, but the loss of grammar-type boys to the local grammar school has produced the general feeling among the pupils, and especially the older boys, that they have failed or that they are second class and not being given a fair chance. Even so, the school has had many successes at O and A level with boys who would never have been given a chance to sit these examinations if their eleven-plus grading had been unquestioningly accepted. Boys in the upper part of the school also prepare for the CSE examinations and various craft exams.

Streamed groups, and the subtler divisions of 'setting', are adopted because they are believed to facilitate learning by grouping boys of similar abilities, but I have observed that the method inculcates the boys with a competitive approach and reinforces their feeling that some of them are better than others; this happens despite staff attempts to assure parents and pupils that class divisions are made so each individual can get the training he needs. I have found the boys are interested in who goes up or down because going up the ladder is positively valued, whilst going down means that a particular individual is no good and 'thick'. The boys very rapidly weigh up the situation and are not fooled; so streaming remains a ranking device which shows the school's assessment of the worth of an individual. Those at the top of the ladder receive the attention and encouragement of many staff members whilst the rest may be ignored, ill-treated and generally encouraged to become what a number of teachers expect them to be – apathetic and incompetent. It is noticeable that, as one goes up the age range and down the ability range, behaviour and interest rapidly deteriorate, so that boys leave the lowest stream of the fourth year thoroughly alienated and bitter, feeling they have wasted the previous few years.

Part of the justification for streaming is this alleged opportunity it gives the able and hard-working boy to leave his particular class and go into one more suited to his individual abilities. Yet, after the original sorting is made on entry, the proportion of boys who are actually moved is tiny. One or two boys might be taken out of a group but a disinclination to move boys down, the already very full classes, and the administrative inconvenience all militate against changes being made. It is generally only the obvious misplacement or the boy sponsored by a number of teachers who has the chance to rise, and then only into the next class; the rest are just encouraged to stay in the contest by the possibility of change held out to them. However, this is not to deny that certain individuals have made a spectacular rise through the streams over a number of years and have finally left with several examination qualifications to their credit.

Streaming in the school is partly a result of the examination system, which pervades not only this school but the whole educational system. Stratification by ability levels applies to the preparation for exams, so that top streams take GCE, middle streams (the majority) take CSE, and bottom streams take nothing, usually leaving in the fourth year. This reinforces the feeling of typing experienced by the boys, and tends to impose a further rigidity on the teaching. However, the CSE English syllabus has provided a considerable liberation in exam preparation whilst the GCE is still dull and reveals its middle-class, public-school origins. Recently I taught a sixth-year group of average ability who were hoping to take the O level English exam; but, through earlier neglect and little exam orientation, they were so put off and bored by the English-language syllabus that they almost immediately gave up hope, and no virtuous homilies on the importance of hard work could encourage them to accept the course of study as one relevant to their lives and worth their effort.

From choice I teach in all years of the school and in all ability ranges, so I have been upset to notice a further unintended consequence of the streaming method. It can be inferred from the above that remedial classes tend to be neglected or left, if they are lucky, to humane, dedicated individuals who do their best to help these boys against lack of equipment and scant consideration. But another factor enters here, because many of the boys are of foreign origin, with a high proportion from the West Indies, India or Pakistan. Most of them have only recently come to Britain from a very different cultural background so that, when attempts are made to fit them into the school, they tend to appear in the low-status classes where their chances of doing as well as their white equivalents are few. Yet in the younger classes I have observed little social tension, and one class I taught for two years showed great solidarity, with strong bonds of cooperation between English and foreign boys. However, by the time they enter upper school most of the pupils have absorbed the attitudes of their environment so that, particularly in the fourth and fifth years, a rift develops which is felt in the classroom and is very obvious in the playground, where the 'coloured' boys play their own game of football, with 'whites' prohibited. Sometimes racial fights develop but, in my experience, usually on the instigation of a white boy who professes to 'hate 'em all'.

Streaming is a reflection of the general bureaucratic structure of the school. Just as the class divisions are hierarchical, so are the staff divisions. When I began at the school my status was low because I was new and only an ungraded assistant teacher. Now my position has improved because I have taught there several years and receive a special allowance. Yet I am still unimportant. Authority resides particularly with the headmaster, who is appointed by both the local authority and the school governors, his deputy and the two heads of upper and lower school, but also with the five heads of the main subject departments and the six-year masters – fourteen individuals in a staff of nearly eighty full and part-time teachers. This group functions in the orthodox bureaucratic manner (though their organizational theory is rather out of date, because they wish to supervise the minutest details of the projects they organize). Vast piles of paper spill out of their offices spelling out in minute detail the organizational procedures the staff are to follow and the boys are to conform with. Much of the staff's potential teaching time is spent filling in forms, collecting forms from the boys, and handing out letters for parents. This paper work doubles when a special event is due. The evening when the school is open for parents to visit, meet staff and see the work follows weeks of planning and special preparation. But the communication is generally a one-way passing down of what the 'authorities' in their wisdom believe to be good policy (and often it is). Committees of these 'authorities' proliferate, sitting on various matters such as examination entry and the use of visual aids in the school. Full staff meetings are usually called to pass out information to the staff. Rarely is the democratic opportunity for comment or criticism from below given, so that frustration exists on the general staff level which is expressed in resentment, back-biting and unhelpfulness.

But one of the greatest contradictions between reality and school policy is revealed in the insistence of the latter in encouraging our working-class pupils to adopt a middle-class mode of behaviour and middle-class ideals. Emphasis is laid, especially in assemblies, on 'character training'. The boys are subjected to long sermons with such key phrases as 'honour of the school', 'self-control' and 'proper behaviour'. Infractions of the rules applying to wearing the school uniform are the subject of many sanctions; but it is not only dress: one fifth-year boy was suspended, just before his O level exams, for persistently wearing his hair long. Many of these restrictions appear petty, breed resentment and only help to confirm the opinion formed by numerous boys that school is alien to them and their point of view, and that their teachers do not really like them.

In fact some staff reactions confirm this. A small group, frequently the most vociferous, show their distaste for their job and pupils by various racial and reactionary, or intolerant assertions. Other staff view themselves as in transit and just moving through the school on their way to something better; usually the hope is to get into a grammar school. This means that only a small proportion of staff really believe in what they are doing and want to take an interest in the boys, and it falls to this group to carry out the real task of helping the boys get to grips with educating themselves and opening their eyes on the world. I regard it as an obligation on a teacher to make a pupil question and query the world that impinges upon him, rather than encourage him to accept it gratefully or reproach him because he does not do so. The text on the wall of the junior school I attended and which was built in 1855 still haunts many teachers with a middle-class orientation – 'obey them that have the rule over you'.

In several ways the school, despite its comprehensive label, is like so many other secondary schools in trying to adapt itself to the public-school model. Uniforms, the morning assembly, the class-room relationship, the emphasis on sport and the prefects are examples of this. Yet the prefects fit neatly into the bureaucratic structure of the school. They are the stratum between staff (or management) and the pupils (or workers), and they are drawn from the latter. Several of them dislike the role they are expected to play and recently one of the boys in my sixth form 'handed in his badge' in response to his uncomfortable position.

The size of the school causes it to function like any large-scale organization, but because of the close attention to its direction in the form of preparing for special parents' evenings, inter-year transfers, time-tables, etc., the individual teacher who wants to experiment unsupervised is left partially free from superior surveillance in his classroom. Here an understanding departmental head can help. I have been fortunate, because the two men who have supervised me have been enthusiastic and optimistic about their work. Therefore, on an individual level, I have had the opportunity to try various approaches in my work. With one group of boys I was able to make a film in and around the school, with other classes I have followed courses of study on films to which the boys' responses have been enthusiastic. But these experiments have only got going because of my own enthusiasm and because certain other teachers have become interested. Other members of staff have had similar experiences – something new develops because they have bothered to push it forward. All clubs and societies within the school are kept going because of the initiative of the members of staff running them, though the only activities to get full recognition are generally sporting ones. For most of these voluntary activities there is great enthusiasm among the boys in early days and then a gradual falling off of interest and attendance. A film society I tried to organize flourished and then slowly died. Other staff have had similar experiences and even the school football teams find it hard to gather the requisite number of players by the time the boys are in upper school. There may be several reasons for this, but I feel one is that the school has not made itself into a meaningful place for boys to remain in of their own accord after the hours of legally compulsory attendance.

A further occasional part of my work deals with the relationship between the school and the boys' parents. There is no P.T.A. or any organization allowing the parents some form of participation in their children's education. Once again communication flows basically one way – from the teachers to their pupils' parents. Evenings are set aside for a parent to visit the school to discuss a boy's progress and performance with his various teachers. This show of consultation effectively cuts the parents off from real cooperation in their children's education. Yet in my experience parents are very concerned about their children's welfare. They want to help and do their best for them because they realize that in our society formal education is one important avenue to a measure of personal success. But they come confused and often ill-informed about what they can do, so it is easy for the school to overawe them and block the helpful suggestions they might have to offer.

This anti-democratic procedure echoes that within parts of the school organization and is reflected in the position of the unions. Most members of staff belong to a union but, after requests for the annual subscription, very little is heard from these professional associations. When external events call for some active part to be played by union members the response tends to be negligible, despite the fact it is in the members' own calculable self-interest to take part.

When I began to teach in 1961 my net pay was approximately £9 a week. My salary has increased slowly and, with the addition of a small special responsibility allowance, now works out at around £20 a week. But I am married and have a young daughter and a baby son, besides a mortgage, so there is still little extra cash for following the leisure activities my wife and I would like to adopt. At the end of eight more years I shall have reached the end of the graded salary scale with £1,500 gross a year. Any increase then will depend on my being able to secure positions of responsibility in a school. At present I am reading for an external degree in sociology which, among other things, could improve my teaching qualifications because, to move about within the profession, an academic degree seems to be more important than the teaching skill that may have been encouraged in an individual by one of the Colleges of Education. I received my basic teacher training in one of the latter, where a certain enthusiasm for the job was generated in most of the students.

So for me teaching is important and valuable work which I enjoy doing most of the time. It is a job concerned with growing and developing individuals who are never predictable, and so provides a variety of experience which is always stimulating. Teaching is a two-way process with a feed-back from the pupils which constantly modifies a teacher's own approach and, if the danger of appearing an infallible oracle is avoided and a certain respect for the children one deals with is cultivated, the job can be rewarding and sometimes creative. Formal education is necessary in any modern society to equip its new members with the skills and abilities they will need to survive and function in that society. Yet teaching can do much more because it can help to make young people better aware of their environment and their own social nature. It can encourage them to develop, mature and find some strong satisfaction in their lives. But a school's formal structure can prevent this happening, prevent a close personal relationship developing between all its members. It can take on the form of a bureaucratic organization bearing down on the pupil, ordering, ranking and instructing him, meeting him with a set of expectations he must conform to, placing emphasis away from participant learning and personal experience and acting only as a machine for turning out more or less identically functioning parts. Being part of such a process will produce dissatisfaction, lack of fulfilment, and an alienation from what should be a humane and humanizing job.

S. G. TURVEY

THE AUTHOR

I was born in 1940 in the small north Berkshire village of Compton where my father was, and still is, an industrial blacksmith. During my childhood he worked in the local foundry until its bankruptcy. My mother was employed as the secretary of the village Friendly Society; it was her income that enabled me to complete my schooling.

My education began in the village all-age school. Then, after the eleven-plus, I made a train journey of ten miles a day to a grammar school in the local market town. From there I went to a teacher training college in Buckinghamshire. I am now studying at evening classes for a B.Sc. (Sociology) degree.

I am a member of the National Union of Teachers and a lapsed member of both the Labour Party and the Communist Party. At college I organized a group supporting CND.

I seem to have been involved in education in one way or another for most of my life to date, and the dangers in this 'exclusiveness' have become very clear to me. One of my future concerns will be to broaden my interests outside the teaching profession. Present obsessions are the cinema and communication studies. I now live in London and am married with two children, a girl and a boy both under two years old. My wife was also a teacher.

The Secretary

Because there is no space in the surgery where I work, my office is the corridor by the street door. The surgery itself is a converted shop with a flat above it, in which I was living when, four years ago, the two doctors in the practice below needed a new secretary and receptionist. The prospect of having only to walk downstairs to work appealed to me, although over the years it has proved both an advantage and a frustration. More important was the feeling – after five years of mundane office jobs begun on leaving school at seventeen – of wanting to be demonstrably 'useful', of wanting to do a job which meant something. Perhaps, too, at the risk of sounding clichéd, I wanted to meet people. To take the job meant a cut in wages of £3 a week.

The corridor houses not only me but forty-five filing cabinets containing all the patients' medical records, a narrow desk hinged to the wall, a high stool, numerous toys and generally about six children. It is about two feet wide and ten feet long, drab and badly lit. The walls are dirty green (once they were pale green) and over my hinged desk, which is little more than a shelf, hangs a naked bulb. For five months of the year winter gales come in with each patient, and in summer it is impossible to have the door open, as we are on a main road with heavy traffic roaring past all the time. Working conditions could hardly be described as adequate, though this we hope is soon to be remedied. And yet I enjoy this job more than any of my previous ones.

The reason, quite briefly, is that I feel I am doing a necessary job. But even that wouldn't be sufficient if I weren't lucky enough to be working for two such good doctors. They are both young and although very dissimilar in character – one very vocal and the other much quieter and more restrained – their views on the treatment of patients are very much the same. Both believe in treating each patient as an individual and, as far as possible, taking care of the patients themselves rather than referring them to hospital out-patients, as often seems to be the case in general practice today. Moreover, they believe in taking into account both the physical and mental factors in illness.

The practice takes care of about five thousand patients in North London. The patients range from the rich to the destitute, but are mainly working class, and include patients of over twenty nationalities. Close by is a large hostel, peopled in the most part by misfits, old people and migrant workers. In the other direction – and at the other end of the scale – is one of those streets of working-class houses which over the past few years has been taken over by the middle-class: intellectuals and professionals of various sorts.

The surgery is not run on an appointments system and patients have to come and wait their turn, which is not very satisfactory from anyone's point of view; the patients often have a long wait and it is impossible for me or the doctors to plan anything at the end of morning or evening surgery. As patients come in they usually give me their name and I take out their medical record ready to call them into the doctor in turn. One of the prerequisites of the job is a good memory for names and faces, for some patients have the annoying habit of coming in without giving their name and without a 'hello', staring at me and assuming that I will remember them.

I arrive at work at 8.30 and my first job, now that we've lost the char who used to come in, is to clean away the debris from the previous evening's surgery. Then I bring the dust-bin through the corridor from the backyard to the street and check that everything is in order in the consulting rooms. There are two of these, one of which is reached by passing through the corridor. Consequently, it often becomes difficult to move during surgery hours, when I'm trying to work. The other consulting room is off the waiting room, where there is space for about fifteen patients; if there is an overflow, which is not infrequent since an average of thirty-five patients may be attending any one surgery, the extra patients have to wait in the corridor between the street door and the filing cabinets.

The next job is to open the large pile of mail which arrives as a rule before morning surgery. This consists of two main categories: hospital letters and reports, and advertisements, mainly for drugs. The first I open and scan quickly, in case it is necessary to get in touch with a patient or to bring any relevant information to the doctors' attention if the patient should attend morning surgery that day. The drug literature is nearly always beautifully designed and on very expensive paper and must add considerably to the cost of the product; most of it is entirely superfluous and I dump it straight into the wastepaper basket.

At 8.55 I open the door and the first patient comes in. This morning it is an old man from the local hostel, wearing a battered coat held together by safety pins. He is eighty years old and lives in total anonymity in the vast hostel building. He has no hope of moving, as landladies won't take the responsibility for elderly lodgers who will probably fall ill. He comes to the surgery for a repeat prescription but most probably because it is the one place where he is greeted by name. His family have long ceased to know him.

Next comes a woman of thirty who has six children. She is very excited because the local council has just offered her a house. For the last twelve years she has lived in three rooms, one of which was the kitchen/bathroom combined. She greets me cheerfully and thanks me for the help I have been able to give her; this is one of the most rewarding parts of the job when, after innumerable telephone calls and letters, something constructive results from the effort.

Patients now begin to stream in and the telephone rings constantly: requests for home visits, people asking for the results of tests, inquiring about surgery times, wanting to speak to the doctor. I try to deal with all of these and especially the latter, as the doctors prefer not to be interrupted in the middle of consultations. But some people become extremely officious, and insist on speaking to one of the doctors personally even about quite minor matters; they consider they are being fobbed off if they talk only to me.

During all this, I have to keep in mind the order of the patients and see the new ones as they come in. An elderly lady pushes open the door. She is a regular visitor but I have never seen her smile, and today is no exception. Two Indians come to register, and as both speak poor English it takes about ten minutes to fill in registration cards. The language barrier is a frequent problem and I try hard to be patient, without always succeeding when the surgery is busy. The next two patients have called to collect prescriptions and I check that they are all right and are keeping hospital appointments which have been made for them. I write out the prescriptions myself and take them in to the doctor to sign, as this saves time. As soon as they are completed I file all the records and the letters; if I don't do this during surgery, things mount up and I don't feel I am in control of the situation. Before I worked here, the filing and medical records used to be in a chaotic state, most of them lying on top of the filing cabinets, and it gave me great satisfaction to reorganize this.

A Nigerian woman comes in. She has had difficulty in making a hospital appointment, and I offer to ring the hospital. After five minutes the switchboard answers.

I ask for an appointment for a woman who has been to the hospital before. 'Is it a new patient or an old patient?' asks the operator. An old patient, I say. He puts me through and the voice at the other end asks: 'Has she got a new letter?' I reply that she has. 'Well, in that case we call her a new patient. I'll put you through to the other appointments.' She rings the switchboard. The operator says icily: 'I asked you if it was a new patient.' By now I'm pretty furious. I ask for an appointment for a patient with a new letter. This time I'm told there is a mistake. Again I'm switched back and forth between the two departments until at last I finally manage to make the appointment.

I can understand the Nigerian woman's confusion as it is difficult enough when one speaks English well. No doubt the hospital staff are very overworked, but I don't understand why so many appointments clerks appear to get satisfaction from thwarting people.

The last patient this morning is a very bizarre man. He stands breathing last night's whisky over me. He is wearing an overcoat, sandals, a ski-cap and dark glasses. This week his hair is bright yellow. He calls me darling.

An eventful enough morning, preferable in some ways to a quiet day which can be very boring because, working in the public conditions of a corridor, I cannot get on with much of the confidential work I should be doing. This can be annoying when I know a pile of letters and reports are waiting to be typed.

I lock the door at 10.30; there are still six patients waiting to see the doctor, but at 11.15 the surgery is finished. I make coffee for the three of us and while we drink it we discuss the cases. Then I am free to start typing letters. This morning I have three to the local council's housing department. One concerns a couple with three children who live in a bed-sitting room and a small kitchen. The mother's health is suffering under the strain and one of the children is attending a psychiatrist. Low-income families like this one are, for the most part, inarticulate and need someone to present their case for them. The doctor is usually the person they turn to and the doctors I work for always do what they can to help.

After the correspondence is finished around 1 p.m., I have the afternoon off until 4.30, half an hour before evening surgery begins. But on Tuesdays I have only an hour and a half free before opening the doors again at 1.55 for the maternity and child welfare clinic.

The first woman to arrive for the clinic this afternoon comes to us for ante-natal care only, as her own GP doesn't deal with maternity cases, a common enough state of affairs in the London area. The second brings her one-year old baby. She has been told by the welfare clinic that the child is overweight and must go on a diet. The clinic appears not to have taken into account that the baby's father is six foot five and the mother is also a large woman; it is hardly surprising that the baby doesn't fit into the statistics for the average one year old. Later on another woman arrives with her supposedly underweight baby: in this case both parents are under five foot four.

All the while I have to keep my eye on the toddlers who find the attraction of the stairs at the end of the corridor irresistible. I grab a two-year old who is just about to leap down the whole lot. I don't agree with making children sit down and 'be good', but on busy days I see it has its points.

The worst thing about the clinic is the form-filling it involves. Forms for immunizations, forms for vaccinations, forms for oral anti-polio vaccine, which have recently become even more complicated, forms for maternity claims; now forms for adult vaccination have been introduced. They all take time and any GP who has to manage without a secretary must get snowed under.

The last patient is a large, noisy Irish woman who often keeps the whole waiting-room amused with the accounts of the disasters which befall her enormous family of nine. Today the youngest child got left behind at the bus stop and wasn't missed until a neighbour brought him home half an hour later.

The clinic lasts only an hour and a half, but it always seems like four and I am worn out at the end of it. Still, it is only one afternoon a week.

One of the chief attractions of the job for me is the feeling of being in charge, feeling that I matter. Patients often comment that without me the surgery would be in chaos, as it is when I'm away. After all this time I know that I'm not indispensable, but I would certainly be missed if I left. As a ten-year-old patient said to me one day: '*They* just sit there while you run around doing all the work!' I need to know that I matter, and I'd find it difficult to be just a small part of some large organization. In the four years I have worked at the surgery I have never been late, although in previous jobs I was never on time.

The evening surgery starts at 5. There is usually a queue

outside when I open the door; as they crowd in, I think that the day will never finish. This evening there are a lot of young children who all want to play in the corridor. I give them each a sheet of paper and a pencil and this keeps them amused. Two of them insist on fighting, so I send them into the backyard where there is a large conker tree. As everything settles down, the door flies open and a small man storms into the waiting-room and sits grumbling and muttering to himself. He is a paranoid schizophrenic who persistently refuses treatment while complaining bitterly that no one will help him. Every time he comes to the surgery he has a row with one or other of the patients, who don't realize that he is ill. This evening I take him into the doctor straight away. Not surprisingly, the other patients who have been waiting half an hour aren't pleased.

There are many mentally disturbed people in need of medical treatment in the area, which apart from the hostel has a large number of lonely bed-sitter occupants, and they are some of the most difficult problems I have to deal with. Often someone comes in and demands to see the doctor straight away and when, since this is not generally possible, I ask them to wait, they scream obscenities at me and sometimes threaten physical violence. As I do not have even the protection of a small desk between them and me this is sometimes frightening. But so far I haven't been attacked.

The surgery continues more peaceably. One of the patients is an old lady who lives alone and is suffering from an incurable disease. But she is always cheerful, always has a smile. I feel ashamed of my lack of patience when I see her. However, I feel no one could remain even-tempered when the waiting-room is crowded and people have to stand in the corridor. The space between the filing cabinets and the wall is about eighteen inches and it becomes impossible to move without treading on someone. It also means that people are right on top of me. My every movement is watched and I am unable to have a telephone call or do anything without an audience. After half an hour of this I feel like running away. Without the prospect of an office to myself next spring I know I couldn't face another busy winter here.

The phone rings and an agitated husband says his wife is in labour. The doctor goes immediately and is back half an hour later: the mother and baby are fine.

One of the pleasantest features of this practice is that the doctors take care of the children from birth and do all the immunizations, etc., themselves. This means that I see the children developing through all the interesting stages. I enjoy this in particular when they are learning to walk and talk and starting to reason things out for themselves. I find that, though I sometimes lose patience with the grown-ups, I never do with the children, which is just as well as there are usually about six running around.

A young man comes in who looks washed out; he is a heroin and cocaine addict who is waiting to go into hospital to attempt a cure. He has been on 'hard' drugs for about eighteen months. It is unlikely that a cure will be permanent, as once he gets out of hospital all his old friends will come to see him. 'Can I have another prescription, I've lost the other one,' he says.

'How did you lose it?'

'It fell down the lavatory.'

As he has had a prescription this morning I tell him no. He gets one daily and at least three times a week comes back with some improbable excuse saying he has lost it. These have included: the dog ate it, it fell in the bath, it got burnt. I tell him to call back tomorrow. After a lot of argument he goes. Along with mental patients, drug addicts are the most difficult patients I have to deal with. They are only treated in this practice on the condition they enter a treatment centre. Initially they all agree, but rarely keep their promise. Many ask for a larger dose than they need in order to sell the rest; the GP has to try to assess the situation and not over-prescribe. Many people malign doctors who treat drug addicts, but after seeing the problem first hand I can't understand this attitude: addicts entail more work, more effort and less reward in terms of results than any other type of patient. I think any doctor who is prepared to treat them deserves sympathy and admiration. The most horrifying aspect is that, of the twenty drug addicts who came to the surgery in the last year, the oldest was twenty-one. Unfortunately, the proposed new clinics seem either non-existent or much too small to cope.

During a busy surgery like this I often don't get the chance to sit down for two hours at a stretch. As the time is spent mainly in the corridor it is very wearing. By the end, at 7.30, I usually have a roaring headache.

Leaving the surgery this late means that I don't get home until 8 and won't eat until 8.30 at the earliest. When I first started working I enjoyed the afternoons off and didn't mind the late nights, but now I am no longer living in the upstairs flat I find it much more tiring. The few hours I have off in the afternoon don't compensate for this. However, under the new government grant system we hope to be able to reorganize the surgery in six months' time and I hope not only that I shall have my own office but that we shall introduce an appointment system. Evening surgery will start at 4.30 and the last appointment will be at 6, which means I should be home by 6.30. Living away from the job, I have found in the end, is preferable because previously I felt I could never escape it and was perhaps too easily available. Now I feel more detached from the situation.

Another thing to look forward to is my promised rise in pay in the spring. At present I earn £15 per week. GPs have recently been given a substantial grant towards their secretaries' salaries and this means I shall get a much-needed £5 per week rise. At the same time an office of my own will enlarge the scope of the job by allowing me to take over some of the small nursing jobs which at the moment I am unable to do.

Many people don't realize the extent to which GPs have to finance the facilities which they provide for their National Health patients. It is only very recently that any allowance has been made towards surgery costs. The side effect, as always, which affects me in this is an increase in paper work.

Over the four years I have been doing this job the volume of paper work has built up to an alarming amount. I have forms which have to be sent off weekly, others monthly, some quarterly. There are registration forms, forms for temporary residents, maternity claim forms; the others I have already mentioned. In addition, I prepare the wages and send off the PAYE contributions. I write all the cheques for the doctors' practice and to a large extent their private ones too. I also do a considerable amount of their private correspondence. Due to the working conditions, all of this work is of necessity done outside surgery hours. Because of the shortage of doctors and the fact that a GP's income is linked to the number of his patients, doctors are forced to maintain overlarge lists. If the system is not to collapse, it is essential that patients do not use their doctors unnecessarily. I can't help noticing that there is one section of our area which tends to do exactly that: the new middle-class street with its professionals and intellectuals. Under the guise of friendship with the doctor, they often try to arrange appointments, and if this fails and they have to wait their turn, they make sure the consultation is a long one, regardless of those who are waiting outside. They seem to think that a glass of sherry will squash any objection the overworked doctor might make to unnecessary home visits in the evening for the most trifling complaints, rather than that they should wait along with everyone else.

Almost without exception, I have found, most foreign visitors to this country are impressed by the NHS and the standards it maintains. An American patient found it hard to believe that the doctor would visit her small daughter who had a severe case of measles. In America, she told me, it was almost impossible to get a doctor to come to your home. In principle, visitors are only treated under the NHS for illness which has occurred here, although many do try to get free treatment for long-standing complaints. One Irish woman who arrived here eight months pregnant had the baby under the National Health Service as an emergency patient and then asked me for the form to claim her maternity grant. It was refused.

After four years of dealing directly with all types of people I have very mixed feelings about them. The great majority of patients are considerate and do not abuse the over-worked and limited resources of the NHS. Unfortunately the ones I see most often – perhaps three or four hundred out of five thousand – are the 'regulars' who do. Sometimes on busy days I feel if one more well-known face walks through the door I will walk out of it. So far I haven't.

In comparison with the job I had immediately before this one, the satisfactions are certainly very much greater. I worked then for a firm of quantity surveyors and was well paid and by no means over-worked; but I found it difficult to get interested in the comparative costs of buildings. I now feel involved in my job to a much greater degree. It is much more interesting to follow cases than costs.

I think I am lucky to work for two such good doctors. People who know I work for a doctor always have some terrible story of neglect on the part of the GP, but this has not been my experience in this practice. After four years I have respect and admiration for my employers and complete confidence in their medical judgements. Perhaps this is the most important factor in the job and the reason I have stayed so long.

CATHERINE DRACUP

THE AUTHOR

I was born in Leeds in 1940. My mother died when I was a month old and I was brought up by my father, who was an accountant, and an aunt. When I was eleven my father re-married.

I went to the local grammar school from the age of ten to seventeen. I then ran away from home and came to London; I regret not having gone to university as a result. For the next few years I had various jobs in offices, mainly dealing with accounts and statistics and working as a comptometer operator.

I was twenty-two when I started my present job. Despite the late hours the work involves, I make as much time as I can for reading and film-going. I walk a lot but hate any other form of sport, and at school refused to play hockey.

I worked for the return of the Labour government in the last two elections, but I'm now disillusioned with their record, and probably shan't vote the next time.

Methodist Minister

No two days are the same. On some days nothing seems to happen at all. I sit in my study from 9 to 1, trying to find a new sermon for the following Sunday, and at the end of the morning with nothing decided at all – only *possible* texts, *possible* treatments of one or more of these texts, *sketches* of orders of service, the one interacting on the other. Of course there have been interruptions – half-a-dozen phone calls, two or three of them involving long conversations about personal or administrative problems, and two or three callers, one of whom takes up half an hour with his trouble. After lunch seven or eight visits, but no luck, everybody out save one sick man and one infirm old lady, both deaf. After tea a difficult business meeting. The agenda – Shall we hold united services with another church? The result – an unresolved clash between the avant-garde and the old guard. Nothing seems to have been achieved at all.

Another day I am roused from sleep by a telephone call telling me a member of my church has lost his wife, so I go round at once to find a household stunned with grief. Home to breakfast and correspondence to be dealt with before cycling a couple of miles to a Fraternal, a regular meeting of clergy and ministers of different denominations for prayer and study and the consideration of common concerns. Back to lunch, and then ten miles by bus to see patients in hospital in a near-by city, fitting in several visits on the way home from the bus station. In the evening a week-night service to take, but first the final stages of preparation, half-a-dozen notes to be written for delivery en route or for the post, an interview with a couple about their approaching wedding, and after leaving the house a call to make arrangements for a funeral service two days later. Then the mid-week service, followed by a short business meeting (the heating system is not working properly – there are some applications from outside bodies for the occasional use of the premises). Home at 10 p.m. to find my wife entertaining her Wives Club committee to coffee and sandwiches, or a group of students or an immigrant family recently moved into the neighbourhood –just in time to help with the washing up. And so to bed at 12.

So it goes on in infinite variety. In the course of a year I meet hundreds of people of every class and kind, not superficially, but at deep levels of need and in rich moments of shared life and work, an intimate participation in every aspect of human experience: birth, marriage and death, shame and sorrow, forgiveness and joy. The tools for the job? Some psychology, some prayer, a growing experience of similar situations in the past, many contacts with other individuals and agencies who may be able to give specialized help, and, most of all, the enjoyment of the company of one's fellows and a readiness to go on listening to their concerns. It has been my experience that almost everybody is positively friendly to the wearer of a clerical collar, however little he deserves it. Denominational differences mean nothing to the man in the street. We're all 'vicars' now, whatever our ecclesiastical allegiance. I have encountered none of the suspicions or hostility, which, I am told, is endemic in countries with an anti-clerical tradition. Morgan Phillips's dictum that British socialists were more Methodist than Marxist may have been an exaggerated claim, but there is no doubt that the existence in England of non- and even anti-Establishment Free Churches, one of them, the Primitive Methodists, with working-class traditions, has sweetened relations in this country between ministers and people. But I am aware that this climate of general benevolence, in which I began my ministry, is changing, not so much due to animosity as to indifference, and the end of any special respect for the clergy as men representing some generally accepted 'good'.

Today the church is obviously smaller and weaker than it was, much weaker than it looks on those ceremonial occasions when public deference is still paid. Even church members complain that it is on the side-lines, irrelevant to the needs and techniques of twentieth-century man. How different it felt when I became a Methodist minister only thirty years ago. I was a schoolmaster, and the secretary of the local Labour Party in an outer London borough. There seemed to be little likelihood of converting the ratepayers to socialism, but some possibility of getting them to take seriously the Christianity most of them still professed. So the ineffective politician became a parson! Naïve and arrogant this may sound, but in that situation it appeared to be a realistic decision.

First of all, no one doubted the size and influence of the church. *If* the churches had practised what they preached in 1914 there would have been no war. *If* the church in Germany in the 1930s had practised what it preached Hitler would never have gained power. So we put our hopes in the Ecumenical Movement, and its conference on Church, Community and State in Oxford in 1937 was, we believed, a sign not of the defeat but of the hope of the church, not an introverted contraction but an extroverted programme, with the socialist Archbishop William Temple among others at the head. Now, I admit, this all seems long ago.

Then it was possible to grow up almost entirely in a churchly environment, with no sense of being peculiar. Schools were Church of England, the Establishment was publicly Christian. I well remember entertaining a German socialist to lunch and his disbelief when I assured him that not only a nobody like me but the secretary of the Labour Party, Arthur Henderson himself, were Methodist lay preachers. More prophets like Dick Sheppard, more organization like Life and Work (the ecumenical organization concerned with the social, economic and political witness of the churches, now absorbed in the World Council of Churches), more strength to the International Missionary Council, and the walls of Jericho would come tumbling down. Of course, there was more to it than such innocent and ill-founded optimism. Readers of the Bible – and, in those days, all active Christians read their Bibles daily – didn't need Marx and Freud to teach them about original sin and man's need of salvation. Behind all the mixed motives (in those days Reverends were revered!) and all the half-baked political idealism was the fact of Christ, and a personal commitment to him which we described as 'a call to preach'. So much account of motives at least is necessary if one is to get the feel of the work, as I experienced it, at all.

In those days, when university education was only for the well-off or a very small minority of exceptionally clever boys, non-conformist chapels, as they were called, were for many young people their centres of adult political and cultural education. At the heart of it all was our personal faith in Jesus, and a desire to give our lives to Him. So it was not surprising that quite a number of us should want to be ministers. Then the long selection procedures began; there were many more candidates than places. First the candidate had to become a local preacher (the Methodist name for lay preacher, originally to distinguish him from the full-time *itinerant* on *circuit*), after helping an experienced man ('On Note' from the superintendent minister), then take services on his own ('On Trial'), and finally satisfy the Local Preachers Meeting after written and oral examinations. Then the candidature proper, supported by a unanimous (or near unanimous) vote in the Quarterly Meeting of the circuit – the group of churches in which one was known as a person and preacher. Trial sermons and written examinations on the Bible and Christian doctrine preceded one's appearance before the ministerial session of the District Synod, the Methodist equivalent of a Diocesan Assembly. And always, over and over again, the oral 'testimony' in reply to the traditional questions: What has been your Christian *experience*? Describe your *call* to preach? These hurdles passed, the so-far approved candidates went to a residential committee of the Conference, 'the July Committee' (which always meets in June), a kind of selection board. At last the ministerial session of the Conference itself, three or four hundred men, furnished with full particulars of sermon marks, examination results and committee recommendations, makes the final decisions.

The accepted candidates are then allocated to the Theological Colleges of the church. At no point have questions been asked about nationality or finances. Most men pay nothing at all for their training. After three or four years at college (all of them are closely related to universities) the young minister is sent into circuit 'on probation'. In my day that was four years on £160 p.a., with no possibility of marriage; with full pastoral charge of anything from one to a dozen 'societies' (or churches: Methodism began as a society within the Church of England) under the supervision of the Superintendent Minister; with more trial sermons, written examinations, book lists and courses of study. So close was the fellowship and strong the *esprit de corps*, so rigorous the previous selection, that few men slipped out and even fewer were turned out en route. The full session of the Conference (half ministerial, half lay) then receives those who have completed the course 'into Full Connexion', and thereafter in a group of services they are ordained by its representatives with the laying on of hands and prayer. From now on we belong to the Conference, entirely at its disposal according to the recommendations of its Stationing Committee. In my youth the stationing was very strict, but it is now much easier. If you want, for example, to teach Religious Instruction the chances are that you can, if you play your cards carefully and pull the right strings. But in theory you are still liable to be sent anywhere from Shetland to the Scillies; and, in return, guaranteed a stipend and a manse for life. Not quite for life – retirement may present financial and residential problems. All ministers are regarded as equals – of course there were and are great personalities, like Lord Soper and great respect was and, though less formally, still is shown to those with special responsibilities, and above all to the annual occupant of what we like to call John Wesley's chair, the President of the Conference; but there is no difference of order – all are plain Methodist ministers, all are equally servants of the annual Conference, all earn more or less the same money. Whether your church is rich and famous, or poor and obscure, whether you are a chairman of a district (with quasi-episcopal functions) or a junior minister in a weak country circuit, you receive approximately the same stipend. 'But man, where's the incentive?' was an American minister's comment to me. And there are, alas, signs that American and Anglican examples are beginning to infect us.

Even this brief account of the organization of the ministry will go far to explain that 'brotherhood of the ministry' of which we used in less secular days to boast. And over all still reigns the influence of John Wesley. Like Franciscans or Jesuits, Methodist ministers know they have been admitted to an order of chosen and dedicated men. You even need the permission of your fellow-ministers to retire (to 'sit down'), though it is now a formality, provided you've reached the age of sixty-five or 'travelled' forty years. And not so long ago what we now call pension funds of one kind and another were traditionally known as 'the worn-out ministers' fund'!

All this was my experience, with one exception. As I 'candidated' late, a married man with a first child, had a university degree (in Ancient History luckily, which meant some Latin and Greek), had taught Religious Instruction in a secondary school, and then for a few years served as lay secretary in a church department, I was accepted 'for Home Immediate', i.e. sent straight into circuit on probation. But according to the book I shouldn't have been married, so we received only £180 p.a. and exhausted our little capital renting a private house. But we were young and idealistic, and I had sixteen lively village chapels to cycle round in an unusually beautiful countryside. And when my flock made their near-obligatory weekly visit to market, I was able to transact almost all the business of the widespread country circuit in one place.

But is the job really as good, as acceptable, as all this might suggest? Well, of course there is never enough money, though more now than ever before (£675 to £775 according to years of service, which is to increase to £850 maximum in 1971), and in any case I had no time for commercial entertainment and, luckily, little inclination for luxuries and none at all for smokes or drink. Ministers' wives bore the brunt of this – they had to work budgetary miracles, they had to stay at home and look after the children while their husbands were immersed in their thirteen-hour day and seven-day week, they had to live in old, inconvenient cold manses, with execrable décor which one's predecessor may not have noticed, and old-fashioned and worn furniture generously donated to the manse by well-to-do members when they replaced it in their own homes by something better. Even the crocks and the carpets were provided and chosen by somebody else. The original idea was that, like John Wesley himself, Methodist preachers should travel light – but then *his* wife left him!

It is perhaps surprising that most wives and families stick it out, for they are exposed to peculiar stresses and strains. The very fact that the minister, unlike all other professional men (save, up to a point, the doctor) works from an office (his study) in his house, and that this office is never shut, means that his wife is inescapably involved in his job. The children are 'the minister's children', and expected to be peculiarly virtuous and well-behaved. Sometimes it is difficult for the inhabitants of the manse to have a private life at all. And on top of these built-in difficulties, the wives of ministers are *expected* to help run the church as an organization, preside over women's meetings, assist in the Sunday school and youth club, give addresses on weekdays and Sundays, and generally come to the rescue. I know that my wife has done all these things and more, to my tremendous advantage. Lucky is the minister whose wife is able to cover up his deficiencies and complement and augment such gifts as he has. How often I've heard the comment: 'What's our minister like?' 'Nothing special, but his wife's charming and a splendid worker.' Small wonder if she often resents this state of affairs.

Now all is being changed. Wives go out to work, many earn more than their husbands; moves are becoming less frequent – a normal period of service was three years when

I began, now it is five, six or seven – we provide our own domestic gear, and before long, I've no doubt, will furnish our own manses. None the less, ministers' wives still have to suffer what some call the indignity of having a deputation to inspect periodically the house from basement to attic to decide what must be replaced and what redecorations or repairs need doing. Even then sometimes the occupants are lucky if such recommendations are carried out before the next inspection. And in these days it is not pleasant for wives to have to go 'cap in hand' to a committee to ask for a new set of dining-room chairs because those in use have begun to disintegrate. Some would say that of all the things we ask our wives to do, this deprivation of their own homes and their own furniture is the hardest to bear.

As with all jobs which have little supervision and no fixed hours (save, in our case, 11 a.m. and 6.30 p.m. on Sundays) and where there is indeed no financial incentive, men tend to work too hard or not hard enough – the temptations are to sloth or frantic activity. Once upon a time a great preacher could get by on his Sunday performance, from which no doubt stem the many jibes about a one-day week, but then he was the pop star of those days, and I suppose had to work harder on his two sermons than many even more generously rewarded entertainers on their top-twenty recordings. But for most Methodist ministers the temptation is to over-work and anxiety which, were it not for the support of the organization, might easily lead to many more cases of breakdown than the few of which I've heard. It is difficult to be lazy, because after all one has a built-in conscience, and even today some church members, whose weekly offerings provide one's stipend, are much poorer than oneself. And always the nagging feeling that one ought to do the impossible, practice what one preaches. To be irritated with one's wife or to ignore one's children after preaching a sermon on 'holiness' is disagreeable, especially if they rub it in! I can never forget Kierkegaard's words during his attack on the Danish Church Establishment a century and a half ago. He said that it was a dreadful thing to make a living out of the Crucifixion.

Somewhere here is the central problem of being a minister, and no amount of successful and appreciated welfare service or community organization can remove it. It would be an unbearable burden did one not know that the message is not 'Be good' but 'Even I am forgiven', that whatever the demerits of the church, the merits of Christ are inexhaustible. For the Christian Gospel is that God not only forgives men, but by this very love seen *historically* in the Crucifixion, changes them ('sanctifies' is the in-word) from non-persons to persons, from inhuman creatures to truly human beings (which is why Jesus is called Son of Man, i.e. the true representative type and source of humanity, both individual and corporate). The church's critics and opponents are therefore entitled to demand what the Bible calls 'fruits of repentance'. Methodists especially have been brought up to believe that to point men to a God *who makes no difference* to the pointer is an invitation to vacuity. But we continue to know only too well that we are never as good as our Gospel.

These fundamental built-in stresses a Methodist minister is helped to cope with because he need never be left to himself. Normally he is minister not of one church but of a circuit, so that even though he has a limited pastoral charge all to himself, he frequently visits the churches of his colleagues, and meets with them in staff meetings, and with lay representatives of all the circuit churches in many other committees and meetings. He is indeed invited by and paid by the Circuit Quarterly Meeting, through its appointed circuit stewards, two laymen in charge of the circuit finances and of its relations with the ministerial staff; the stewards are appointed by the Circuit Quarterly Meeting on the nomination of a special committee, as often as not on the nomination of the ministers themselves. On top of this he will belong to the District Synod and share in the work of its committees. And even if he is never elected a representative to the Conference, he will be very much aware of it as the expression and governing body of what is still traditionally called the Connexion. He may have served in circuits as diverse and far apart as Camborne (I didn't even know where it was when I was sent there), Uttoxeter, Macclesfield, Bromley (Kent), Exeter, Penarth, Chesterfield and Sydenham and Forest Hill, to mention my own experience, and have friends in all these parts of the country, so that he is never shut up in one local situation. He is frequently challenged and enriched by a completely new situation. One of the great pleasures of the job is going back to a former circuit for some special occasion and catching up on the news. On top of all this are Fraternals of ministers and clergy, and Councils of Churches and ministerial societies. All the time there is the mateyness and 'fellowship' for which Methodism is famous, and almost every day participation in corporate worship and prayer. By all this the minister is kept alive.

Such a variety of churches, like the Methodist ministry itself, will almost certainly contain representatives of every social class save that which is called the highest. Generalizing, the majority are probably lower middle class; but in the south, where denominational differences do not go so deep, there will be a sprinkling of professional and upper middle-class people, while in the industrial north there will be many working-class members. Indeed in some industrial towns there will still be some Labour councillors and trade-union leaders who are Methodist local preachers and keen church workers, though not as many as a generation or two ago.

Now perhaps we can begin to understand and get the feel of the day's work. Here is my typical day. It falls *ideally* into three parts: morning – in the study; afternoon – in people's homes; evening – at the church. Far from being a one-day-a-week job, it sometimes feels like a twelve-hours-a-day and seven-days-a-week one.

Morning – in the study

Often I feel a day's work has to be crammed into this morning, and that I'm the only professional man in the town without any secretarial help at all. What has to be fitted in? All that is meant by preparation – Bible study and prayer, general reading, endless sermons and addresses to be planned and made; all the business of administration which springs from responsibility for a largish organization. At one time I had immediate pastoral care of a community of some thousand people in a Midlands town, plus the management of an 'estate' of thirty-two buildings. Inevitably, there is a proliferating correspondence – perhaps a dozen personal letters to be fitted in to the interstices of organization.

Afternoon – in people's homes
'Visiting', unless one has a Women's Meeting (and only a fool would despise such a meeting, as if women are less mankind than men). This visiting I have always found to be the most rewarding and refreshing part of my job. Again and again I have started out, especially in bad weather, tired and reluctant, having already done a day's work of five or six hours, only to find myself increasingly refreshed and healed by personal encounter. I have no car, so I cycle or walk, which seems to me the best way to visit both in town and country. One can always stop and talk and change direction as accident or reflection suggest. Whom do I visit? First, of course, the ill and infirm, in hospital or housebound, of my own church and community; and then as many other homes connected in any way with the church as I have time for. My visit is, at its best, to convey the love and the prayers of the church; and all that I can say is that people seem to like this service, embarrassingly much thanks for so little apparently given. Nor does one ever know, especially when visiting 'contacts' or 'by chance', in what domestic or social or personal problems one may be involved. I don't think a minister has any greater privilege than his extraordinarily welcome access to every kind of home. I have rarely been kept on the doorstep, only once has a door been slammed in my face (and that by a Methodist official who knew I'd come to condemn his scandalous behaviour), and too often I am over-filled with tea and cakes. I keep a record of all pastoral visits made, and reckon to do some nine hundred a year.

Am I wrong in believing that not the least of the church's

contributions to the community is the provision of so many unorganized, disinterested, completely free, independent, undemanding men who move through the meshes of an ever more organized, centralized and impersonal society in this unpredictable way?

Evening – at the church

Something on every night, for which one may be personally responsible or in which one is directly interested and involved: youth club (a hundred or so teenagers with a full-time paid or part-time voluntary club leader), uniformed organizations, old people's groups (13,000 lunches served last year with the help of the Town Hall, which is very keen on 'senior citizens'' welfare), church fellowships with cultural and devotional programmes, all kinds of committees, trustees' meetings to deal with the maintenance of the premises, leaders' meetings to have pastoral care of all members, to arrange special services and manage the finances, or perhaps the Circuit Christian Citizenship Committee to consider what's to be done about an approaching general election or the growth of drug-taking among young people, etc., etc. And so home to bed; but first the phone calls put off until 11 p.m., as 'I thought you'd be in by then'.

But this kind of church organization is, of course, an exceptional set-up. Every circuit and every church is different, and makes different claims on its minister's time and talents. In many country circuits, if there is a youth club, the minister himself must run it; if there is an old people's organization or women's group, the minister or his wife must supervise that too.

But I've said nothing about Sunday, traditionally the parson's one working day, in my experience the least exhausting of the week. Obviously a minister, like all his fellow-Christians, will positively enjoy services. He knows his congregation will listen critically and hopefully to his sermon. He is the undisputed M.C. This is the one occasion when he will meet the greater part of his 'flock', and this will give him immense pleasure.

On the other hand, there will be times when he is depressed and deflated, when he knows that his sermon has been too long or too confused or too clever or too dull, and the hungry sheep have looked up but not been fed. The more he knows of his people's needs – the woman recently widowed and left with a family of little children, the youth tempted to change his job for merely mercenary reasons, the woman threatened with the break-up of her marriage, the man just told by his doctor that he has less than a year to live, the girl inclined to agree with her boy-friend that the religion she learnt from her parents is outmoded and it's time she became more 'broad-minded' and allowed him to seduce her, all the endless and complex variety of the human needs of people who've got to go on living – the more he must wonder how he can dare go on getting up into the pulpit and saying, in effect, 'thus saith the Lord'. Yes, there will be times when he wants to run away, or go to church normally and sit in the pew with his wife and family himself. Sometimes he will be effusively thanked for what he knows was sob-stuff; sometimes what he believes to be the truth will be received with apparent indifference. And all the time, vanity and exhibitionism ('he likes the sound of his own voice') lie in wait for little preachers as much as for entertainers and politicians.

But is the minister's relationship with the laity really as idyllically pastoral as this? Not entirely; his position is sometimes embarrassingly insecure. In theory he is the managing director. While he is, for example, superintendent of a circuit, he presides over the Quarterly Meeting, and is indeed ex-officio chairman of every circuit meeting of consequence. He is the recognized leader of the church, with considerable authority to organize its life. He can, however, be replaced quite easily if he has put some noses out of joint. The system works like this. When a circuit wants a new minister, the circuit stewards contact men on a list of those who are moving, or indeed any minister they'd like to have, and eventually one will accept their invitation and be formally invited by the circuit for an initial period of three years. After eighteen months he can be invited for a fourth and a fifth year; after that year by year up to seven; thereafter only by special permission of the Conference. Invitations are by majority vote, but they are rarely accepted unless as good as unanimous.

This sounds admirable, but in practice it means that at regular intervals any disgruntled layman can suggest it would be good to have a change (as indeed it might) and members of the minister's church may be 'sounded' as to whether they still want him as their pastor. Nothing causes sensitive men and their families such bitterness and heartache as such prompted moves, at times, perhaps, altogether inconvenient so far as family arrangements (education of children, etc.) are concerned. But there will always be a new circuit waiting to welcome him. And it rarely comes to a *vote* of no-confidence. All the forms of mutual respect are normally preserved, and it's doubtless good medicine for the minister's ego, but it is inclined to benefit the apathetic yes-man. Generally in such crises the rank and file of a church know nothing about it, and if the ejected minister returns for anniversary services in a year or two nobody will remember the unpleasantness of the past invitation committees.

Would I do it all over again? Do I feel it's been worthwhile? Suppose I'd got on to the local council as a first step to a political career, and like so many others in that postwar election been surprised to find myself an M.P. and, who knows, with a bit of luck got a little finger on some small lever of power? Would I, knowing what I now know, have chosen differently? How about the shortage of candidates for the ministry today? They say our young men are frustrated and, in the ministry or out of it, opt for something relevant and useful like teaching Religious Instruction or the Youth Service or some kind of social welfare or counselling work. Do I share their malaise, for malaise I think it is? No, I do not. A little knowledge of church history saves me from this impatience. Was I not told in boyhood missionary meetings that David Hill worked in Canton for a dozen years before he made a single convert. Moreover, Christ emphatically warned his followers against popularity and 'success'. But enough moralizing, an occupational disease for which I apologize.

What changes have I seen, and how do they affect my work? *In the world* – revolutionary changes known to all, but as I see it, no fundamental change. And here, forgive me, I'm bound to preach: the world is still lost, whatever Bonhoeffer meant by mankind's 'coming of age', and only Christ can save it.

In the church – well, as I have for a dozen years had the responsibility of reporting the annual returns of membership to the Methodist Conference I ought to know: continual decline. A million Methodist 'members' before the war, 666,000 in 1968, a quantitatively diminishing community, absolutely and relatively (and this goes for all the denominations – including the Roman, had not Irish and European immigration come to the rescue). The not unsuccessful enterprise of the Methodist Association of Youth Clubs cannot conceal the fact that the continuing decline in the number of Sunday School scholars is likely to make the decrease of membership catastrophic before I 'sit down' in the mid-1970s.

In my work – not so much change. I suppose I've been fortunate. The churches to which I've been sent have always had a good deal of life. I've always been in touch with more people than I could cope with, so that I have never felt I wasn't needed. I have never felt my work was irrelevant, even if it was, which may be a built-in matter of temperament. The Bible, church history and not least my non-conformist upbringing had always taught me the pleasures and satisfactions of belonging to a rebellious and self-confident minority. Of course, I have 'to walk by faith and not by sight'. One can never be sure of the results of one's work. One is concerned with intangibles. A doctor can see his cures and his failures. A minister can't be so sure of either. Nor have I mentioned yet the fundamental consideration – my belief that persons matter more than history, individuals more than states, men more than governments, people more than parties, for the simple reason that they are immortal and none of the other *things* are – which is not to say that they are without very great importance. Without this belief one would not become a minister in the first place at all.

And sometimes the rewards are tremendous. The minister is brought close to his people, at times of marriage and birth and death, as he is allowed to share their sorrows and joys. If human contact is life, then he is a very rich man indeed. Recently my wife and I went to visit a near-octogenarian minister who had been our minister in our youth a generation ago, among other things to tell him what we and dozens of our contemporaries owed him – under God the whole direction of our lives. If two or three pay me the same compliment, I shall be satisfied. If in this life I never know, I still shall be content.

DOUGLAS WOLLEN

THE AUTHOR

I was born in 1909 of pious Methodist parents in the London suburb of Woodford. At the age of ten I went as a scholarship boy (in those days a stigma) to Chigwell School in Essex, where I became literate but not numerate. My father died when I was seventeen, and financial stringency, coupled with my position as the eldest of three boys, put an end to any hopes of entry to Oxford. So I became an uncertificated teacher in the local all-age village school. Here I learned my job the hard way, took an external London degree in Ancient and Medieval History, and saved enough money to take me to Westminster Training College to get a Teacher's Diploma.

For the next six years I was on the staff of Wanstead High School, took the London MA in Education, and was responsible for the teaching of Divinity throughout the school. But my religious and political enthusiasms led me to leave teaching in 1937 and become lay secretary in the department of the Methodist church which dealt with social and political affairs. I married the same year, and have two sons and a daughter.

In 1939 I entered the Methodist ministry, and since 1958 have combined with my job as a circuit minister the office of secretary of the

Church Membership Committee of the Methodist church, which deals with statistics of membership and pastoral matters.

My chief interest outside my work is a passion for art and architecture, and for the past ten years I have done freelance writing on these subjects.

The Actor

My mother, who was my father's godmother (you with me?), was an aspiring actress at forty. My father, who was twenty, was a fledgling poet. They were both Irish. In determining what I was to become, my mother won: at the age of eight I became an actor.

Thirty-odd years later I'm still an actor, sitting here waiting for the telephone to ring, waiting for my agent to get off his arse and earn his 10 per cent. Most of an actor's life is waiting, and the suspense is killing, sometimes literally. For some incredible reason the general public finds an actor's enforced idleness amusing. People leer at you and ask with appropriate winks and nudges if you are 'resting'. A joke. Being on the dole is as humiliating and frustrating for an actor as it is for anyone else. Actors have families to support, bills to meet, children to educate, so what's funny in an actor worrying himself sick about his next job?

In my time I've done just about every sort of job an actor can do. I've worked with a 'fit-up' tour in Ireland, I've been in variety, toured working-men's clubs in the north, been in West End theatre and small theatre clubs, on TV and in films. As a way of life I wish I could recommend it.

My apprenticeship was served, I suppose, in the 'fit-up' tour. I had been invalided out of the Air Force in 1943 and went to Dublin in search of work. I was offered the tour, playing leads and stage-managing at £3 a week, and naturally I snapped it up. A 'fit-up' gets its name from the fact that the company travels with its own scenery and fixtures and you fit up the stage for each performance. We took six plays with us and presented a different one each night, staying a week in every town, village or hamlet and travelling in a lorry on Sundays. A month's rehearsal for six plays – the amount of time usually given to rehearsals of *one* play in the West End – meant that it was impossible to learn more than the essentials of each. The polish was acquired on the road.

The six plays we started with were *Rebecca*, *Love from a Stranger*, *Jane Eyre*, *French Without Tears*, *Night Must Fall* and *Wuthering Heights*. Two classics, a comedy and three thrillers, and while we were on the road we added *Anna Christie* and *East Lynne*. The last two have pride of place in my memory. *East Lynne* was played straight, and the audience loved it, but it was hard work for us keeping serious faces with such immortal lines as 'Dead, dead, and never called me mother.' In the O'Neill play I landed the part of Old Chris, who is sixty-five. I was nineteen and I had one night to learn it.

There were eight in the troupe, four of each sex, roughly; the leading lady was married to the management and was sometimes sober. As there was no director, she took care of that side with her own method, which borrowed nothing from Stanislavsky (whose methods, I believe, were basically correct, but whose translation into Method acting seems to me to have got out of hand: not every character an actor is called on to portray is a shambling, inarticulate, mannered neurotic, though you might sometimes wonder . . .). Our leading lady's direction was somewhat different: 'Go twice around the sofa this act.' 'Don't upstage, ducky.' 'Do a bit of business there.' 'Keep your hands still.' From this collection of almost meaningless clichés we tried to build a character, taking advice from one another, although grudgingly, for we criticized each other harshly, yet always, because conditions were usually primitive, with a kind of mutual respect. So primitive in fact that we often had to improvise during the performance, and once managed to give a performance of *French Without Tears* with no leading lady. The latter wanted to make a quick foray into Northern Ireland to set up some dates for us to play; as she took the lead in every play, we suggested we cancel the performance. But every penny was essential and the play went on. The audience must have been bewildered as we divided her lines among the rest of the cast, adding things like 'as Diana always says' or holding conversations with someone off-stage in which the audience heard Diana's purported and disembodied voice. In as far as no one asked for their money back, it was a success.

Our scenery consisted of about eight 'flats' – light wooden frames covered with canvas about ten feet high by seven wide, painted brown on one side and fawn on the other, which 'cleated' together with ropes and screw eyes. A French window, two ordinary window pieces, three doors and two different kinds of staircase allowed an almost endless variation of scenery. Each Sunday evening, on our arrival, we went straight to the place where we were to play: occasionally it was a real theatre, sometimes a town hall, and quite often just a barn, in which case we had to build a stage and improvise some form of lighting. When the hall was ready and the set was up, the company split up: two members were sent to look for digs – thirty bob a week all in was tops – and the rest of us went on the scrounge trying to borrow our stage furniture for the week. Tables, chairs, china, anything in fact we could lay our hands on in shops or private houses that would improve the look of the set. If we were the first touring company to visit the town for a while the job was easy; if not, it became a nasty job of begging and wheedling.

For the young actor, the fit-up was a form of apprenticeship. Admittedly, you learned a lot of bad things, tricks: how to play down to your audience, how to get cheap laughs; but you also learned to concentrate, to improvise and, best of all, to control an audience. With these things came confidence, a vital necessity for an actor. But for the older actors, and we had two who were in their fifties, it must have been, on that pittance of a salary for a twelve-hour day six days a week, a life bereft of decency and dignity.

The acting profession suffers from fantastic inequality, containing both the best- and worst-paid people in any profession. Stars receive salaries of astronomical size and bit players survive on a pittance. Mrs Burton makes a million pounds a picture and Fred Spoon, bit player, is lucky to get two days' work on the same epic to make £40.

There are now some 6,000 registered members of British Actors Equity, our union, and they are neither all stars nor bit players. Taking a middle line, an actor half-way up the salary ladder, the median wage according to the latest

Equity figures is £800 a year, less 10 per cent agent's commission – i.e., £720 a year or less than £14 a week. And there's no pension. This is for a man who, having learned his job, is in his thirties or forties with the same commitments as anyone else in any other profession.

There seems to be so much happening in London, so many plays and so much television, not to mention films and radio, that when you're in work you just cannot visualize ever being out of work again. To be idle in the midst of such plenty is enormously frustrating. And yet they are so frequent, these periods of inaction, that an actor has to come to terms with them. Some take up golf; others go to acting class to work and polish and study, since you never stop learning; others go to work for domestic agencies, charing and decorating; some write; no matter what, it's essential to do something, because there is a deadly corruption in idleness that eats ambition and drive and actual talent. So, if you meet an actor, don't sneer and ask if he's resting.

Then the phone will ring – though it hasn't as I write this – and it'll be your agent, perhaps with an audition for a new stage play. Auditions are always held, not for the stars – unless it's an American company with no knowledge of British actors – but for the rest of the cast. Your agent sends you a copy of the play with the part marked that you are to try for. You read it and go to the theatre, where there are a mass of other actors, many of whom will be trying for the same part and some of whom are your friends.

You wait your turn in the semi-dark on the side of the stage until the stage manager yells out your name to some mysterious being or beings in the front of the house, which is dark. With the footlights full on, the stage is very bright and you can't see who is out front, but you are all too aware that they can see you. You're nervous, you need the job, the competition is fierce, you've got a bellyful of bats – and you've got five minutes to convince those beings out there in the dark that you are the only possible choice for the part. You haven't had time to learn the part, so you have to hold the script in your hand, and the stage manager reads with you;

he is always terrible at this, for if he were any good he'd be an actor. If you're not stopped until your time is up it's a good sign. When you've finished, a voice calls out 'thank you, leave your name', you mumble something and somehow get off stage, surrender your script and go home to wait by the telephone. If you're lucky you'll be sent for in a couple of days to go through the whole bloody business again. . . .

I once auditioned seven times for a part in a West End play; the actor who had played the part on Broadway had been quite short and as I am over six feet the casting director couldn't make up his mind, although the part was dead right for me. This is the sort of idiocy you have to contend with. Eventually I got the part and was praised by audience and critics; however, the auditions had taken three weeks. I was then out for another two weeks until the start of rehearsals, which went on for another four weeks. All this without pay. Although a critical success, the play, *Detective Story*, ran for only five weeks, which all in all meant fourteen weeks' work for five weeks' pay. We closed on a Saturday night with one and a half hours' notice. I had some good notices to paste in my scrapbook – as though it mattered.

There is no rehearsal pay for actors on a salary of £50 a week or more; for those earning less, the pay is £7 a week. As plays often close after a week, this can mean five weeks' work for one week's pay if you are over the £50 limit – £10 a week. This is just one of the many injustices that make up an actor's life.

On the other hand, if you're in luck, you're faced with the problem of the long run, something that seems to fascinate the layman: how do you manage to give the same performance every night for a year or more? The short answer is, you don't, you find ways of keeping the performance fresh. I was in *Kiss Me Kate* at the London Coliseum for a year, playing a gangster. There was a scene in the second act which required a certain amount of urgency which was not always easy to create, and one night, after we had been playing about six months, I forgot to take a leak during the intermission. Never was that scene played with such urgency. It sounds funny, and it was only an external, but the point is that I was able to use it to recreate that urgency in subsequent performances. . . .

Of course, there are actors who try to give the same performance every night without variance, but they tend to be very mechanical, inclined to go through the motions rather than the emotions. Any actor who examines the complex of relationships and motivations that make up a play and is continuously searching for new depth and understanding will make new discoveries in the course of the run and keep his performance fresh for as long as he plays it.

Theatre, naturally, includes variety and I've worked on this side of the business. I started as an impressionist and second comic, the lowest form of life, coming on after the opening chorus number to warm up the house for the other acts. It was at the Queen's Theatre, Dublin, a variety theatre with a resident company, with two performances a night and a different show every week. With rehearsals and performances we worked from ten in the morning until eleven at night. I did everything, my own spot, either comic or straight, played in sketches, compèred, even danced in the chorus line – called unbelievably the Queen's Moonbeams. Variety, whether in theatre or clubs, is the place where you learn to do it on your own, to go on stage and make the audience laugh or cry by yourself. At first it was a very lonely and frightening experience.

Working-men's clubs have now taken over the place of variety; recently I did a short stint in some clubs up north. The difference between a London and a provincial audience is enormous, and different classes also react in different ways. To take an extreme example: Lenny Bruce, the late American comic and, to my mind, moralist, who was a relative success with a middle-class London audience, could not have played a northern working-men's club. His material would have been considered filthy and the audience would not have accepted his language, the dreaded four-letter words they use every day. This every-day language is taboo when it comes to comics whose laughs come from smirky allusions and double entendres, more anal than sexual, and loaded with racialism. At the club where I opened there was another comic on the bill and I watched his act, horrified. It was full of wogs and darkies, 'buck niggers' with enormous parts, old ladies who were 'short taken', Pakistanis living fifty in a room, dirty spades and so on, *ad nauseam*. The audience loved him, the men's guffaws drowned only by the high-pitched cackle of the women.

I opened with a couple of quick gags, then did a series of mime bits, getting a couple of laughs, sympathetic rather than amused. In one of my stories, a quite innocent one, I used the word brothel, which was met with sniggers. Dying on my feet I finished the act and went back to the dressing-room. The other comic came rushing in.

'How could you use a word like that on the stage?'

'Like what?' I asked.

'Brothel,' he said, in hushed tones. 'There are ladies out there, you know.'

I pointed out that the story was in fact quite harmless, and that his act was full of lavatories and prejudice. But it was no use, I had shocked him.

I'm not suggesting that all comics playing the clubs use this kind of material, just that in my experience there are too many who do, and that the audience laps it up. I did a month of this work and nothing would ever make me do it again, I hope. Apart from the depressing reception, the conditions themselves were hardly encouraging in the club where I opened: people eating and drinking at tables, standing at a long, crowded bar with their backs to the stage and, worst of all, rows of one-armed bandits in constant use between the bar and stage. Desperately trying to be heard above the noise, everyone on stage busily prayed that no one would hit the jackpot during his or her act; in the week I was there happily nobody did.

Television is the major source of work nowadays and I've done my share of it. As a medium its primary attraction and excitement is to let the viewer watch action as it is actually happening. The popularity of sport, outside broadcasts and discussion programmes lies essentially in this. When I first worked in television in 1956 it was still highly primitive and fun. There were no recording facilities (video-tape is a very recent innovation) and instead of today's four cameras each with four lenses, you were lucky to have three cameras with one lens each. For close-ups the camera had to go half-way down your throat, and if a different lens was wanted it took about twenty minutes to change it and you were left with only two cameras. Not surprisingly, there wasn't an enormous audience for TV in those days, for all you could see on the nine-inch screen were tiny little wavering figures in a kind of opalescent haze, and the sound was dodgy too. I remember an American director giving us a pep-talk before a show went on the air. He reminded us that we weren't playing to a theatre audience but to some vast amorphous mass out there at the other end of the camera. 'Think of it,' he cried, 'think of those thousands of sets and maybe' – bated breath – 'twenty thousand people.' We were duly impressed.

The fact that it was live gave the medium the tension and urgency that cannot be duplicated on tape. Because so many things can go wrong, the actor tends to have a horror of live television. A moment's lack of concentration can result in egg all over his face in full view of twenty million people, and that's the stuff of nightmares. But when the show isn't live it loses its spontaneity, its tension. I once compèred a panel game called *Don't Say a Word*, a frenetic game in which the panelists had to communicate with each other only by mime. Done live, the show was hard on the nerves but exciting. I had to control eight extrovert panelists and a studio audience while keeping the pace at breakneck speed, give each artist equal opportunity to shine, and bring the show out on time to the split second. Though it had no message nor much content, the show was fast, funny and good television. But from the moment we started to tape it, it lost something, as though everyone, including me, was trying to imitate spontaneity. That never works.

As a glance at the weekly TAM ratings will show, an

actor finds it necessary to do an awful lot of crap, especially on television. Recently I was rehearsing for a TV comedy show in a disused church hall (the odd and insalubrious places they find for actors to work in is another bone of contention) in Scotland. There I was, a fairly well-read, intelligent, grown man crawling round on all fours on a dirty floor portraying a Scottish samurai warrior. What a way to earn a living!

(My agent has just phoned to say that I have been booked to play in another half-hour comedy series, starting next Wednesday. My part – Jesse James. My son will be delighted.)

The opposite end of the scale, as far as success is concerned, also has its drawbacks. For about three years I was in *The Larkins*, a highly popular and excellent series of its kind, thanks to the clever scripts of the late Fred Robinson and the playing of Peggy Mount and David Kossoff. I played their son-in-law, Jeff, and though it couldn't be called art it was fun to be in a hit show. But when the series finished and I looked for other work I ran into nothing but, 'Oh, you're Jeff from *The Larkins*.' For a long time I had an uneasy feeling that *The Larkins* was going to be inscribed on my tombstone. With its love of labels and instant identity in brackets after a name, the press contributes greatly to this sort of stereotyping.

Of all acting work I prefer films. To me they are the most satisfying. The work is demanding, precise, and you have to marry technique with emotion on a fine scale; there is always excitement and pressure on the set, and last but not least, you get paid.

Film is the only medium that is not acted in continuity. In the theatre or television you start at the beginning and work through to the end; although the whole is broken into sections and you work and polish these separately, you eventually start at the beginning and work right through. This gives the actor a chance to set his rhythm, establish his relationships with the other actors, and develop his character. But a film actor may be asked to play the big dramatic scene at the end of the picture on the second day of shooting, and the next day to play a comedy scene which starts the film. In a way it is instant acting.

The film actor works to one camera, while in TV you can have as many as eight, all mobile, all photographing the action continuously. As technique, it is this which conditions the basic difference between the two media. With one camera, the action has to be broken up into tiny pieces and filmed separately, then reassembled and cut into the final print. This imposes enormous limitations, since a movie camera has a limited range of vision, and lighting plays an enormous part. The acting area has to be covered by lights, big arc lamps called brutes and dozens of different kinds of spot lamps, one of which will be specifically yours. It lights only a small section and you have marks on the floor, either in chalk or wooden battens nailed down, to indicate exactly where you have to be. Your feet have to hit these marks precisely and without looking or thinking about them; if they are missed, it means you'll be covered in shadow and out of focus, and the scene will have to be re-shot. While you don't act directly to the camera, you have to be aware of it and of the mike.

When you come to the studio – and it may only be after half the film has been shot – it can well be the first time you have seen the director for whom you're working. There is no direction of the cast as a unit or even individually until the actual scene to be shot is being set up for lighting. Some directors know exactly what they want; others don't know until it's there, which means they'll shoot twenty times and at the end decide the two or three 'takes' they want to have printed. A good film director must be first and foremost a technician, must know how to shoot and edit film; a good TV director is more likely to be an ex-actor or writer.

Because of this fragmented technique, a good film actor is always aware of whatever 'props' he is using and of his clothes. You may be shooting indoors and walk out through a door, gun in hand, left hand, cigarette in mouth, half-smoked, hat on head, pushed back, flower in buttonhole, carnation, red. The next shot in sequence is you coming out the other side of the door, but it may be an exterior shot that will be filmed months later. Yet you have to look exactly the same. The continuity girl is supposed to watch for these things, but as she is only human, the actor will himself remember each and every detail.

Filming means a long day, leaving home at about 6 in the morning to get to the studio by 7.15 in time to be made up for shooting at 8, and you are lucky if you get home before 8 in the evening. And here, as always in this job, a lot of time is spent waiting – for scenes to be lit or sets to be changed or any one of a dozen different technical reasons. I always take a book with me, but I never read a line. A film set somehow becomes a different world, with different values: the sense of time is almost foreign and you become part of a group, seeming to lose individuality, taking on the colouring and substance of the rest of the unit. In this timeless atmosphere, waiting becomes part of the whole and is, therefore, not inaction but action. And because it is large and composed of so many people, a film set is quite classless.

As in all types of this business, there is a terrific loyalty to the unit and to the management, which becomes particularly noticeable when the unit is on location. This loyalty to the management is curious. It springs perhaps from the fact that the management is taking a risk and that you're all in the same boat, which is often true; and there are many good managements which deserve the loyalty they get. But there are also bad managements, and to be loyal to these is ludicrous. Such managements take advantage of the fact that it is a hideously overcrowded profession to keep salaries to a minimum, often suggesting that an actor can have a part if he is willing to accept a low salary; later the actor may find that he has undercut another actor who has been fighting for a higher salary. In the theatre a good management knows very well when their play is going to close and will give their actors plenty of notice so they can start looking for other work. But there are many instances of an actor realizing that the play in which he is currently appearing is doing badly and of being offered alternative employment. When he approaches the management and asks to be released he is told that the play is not coming off and so has to turn down the alternative work; a week later the notice goes up and the play closes. The actor is left out of work. This sounds like sheer malice, but I could cite countless examples.

A mean theatre management is also entitled to – and will – dock the actor's salary if he is ill. This can hurt, since a theatre actor's salary is averaged on the number of performances. An actor in a straight play doing eight performances a week at a salary of £40 a week who misses five performances through sickness can thus find his pay packet reduced to £15 at the end of the week. Moreover, if an actor misses twelve performances through illness or accident in three consecutive weeks the management is entitled to dismiss him; nor does the management have any obligations whatsoever about holidays. A fair management, realizing that it is not the actor's fault, will not dock his salary for illness.

But if a star does drop out and his or her understudy takes over the part, the latter will get nothing like the star's salary. The union agreement stipulates only that the understudy shall get a minimum increase of £2 per performance, which certainly bears little relationship to the importance of the part or the star's salary.

One of the most ridiculous aspects of an actor's loyalty to management consists in an unwritten rule that actors must never discuss their salaries with each other. As there is no such thing as a flat wage for a particular job – although there is an Equity negotiated minimum for theatre actors: £12 a week – and as actors don't discuss it, there is no way of knowing what anyone else is being paid. The only people who benefit from this are the management who, keeping actors in ignorance, can keep salaries down. But it's a difficult job persuading actors of this. Working in the theatre last year I aired this proposition to another actor, who was playing a larger part and who disagreed with me. I invited him to be honest and tell me his salary. He did and I told him mine. He was shocked to discover that I was getting more money for a smaller part. The next time he worked for that management he got considerably more.

Counter-balancing the satisfying aspect of working in films are some unpleasant ones for an actor. The principal disadvantage is that your work is in the hands of others. You can go to see a film you've spent weeks working on to find the best of your work has been left on the cutting-room floor. Or the bulk of your part may never get filmed – *Blow Up*, Antonioni's latest film at the time of writing, was such an experience for me, because the director had overspent. There may be a host of reasons which have nothing to do with the quality of your work: the film may be too long, the star didn't have enough close-ups, the weather on location may have been bad. . . . These are only a few of the reasons; in short, films are neither safe nor predictable for an actor.

Location is a lovely word, since it means working abroad on good expenses with a fat salary being paid into your bank account at home, seeing the world and getting paid for it. I have worked in Italy, Spain, Africa and France; in the latter country there is a further advantage: you work French hours which, to my mind, are far more reasonable. You start at noon and work straight through without a break until 7, six days a week. I'm sure most actors and technicians would gladly forgo their Saturdays to work really civilized hours the rest of the week, but for some reason it has never been tried in England.

Club-theatre work is another gamble. These theatre clubs are usually tiny and for members only, mainly as a way of frustrating the Lord Chamberlain's censorship. Plays are tried out in these theatres and, if successful, they transfer to a commercial theatre – provided of course Lord Anachronism will grant the play a licence. Last year I did a play about Lee Harvey Oswald in the so-called 'theatre of fact' at the Hampstead Theatre Club, a small but progressive theatre. It holds about 180 people and it doesn't stint on productions; but the top salary is £12 a week. Plays usually run a month and you receive £3 a week rehearsal money, making in all £60 for eight weeks. Of course, if the play had transferred –

which for various reasons this one did not – the salaries would have increased enormously, and it would have paid off. I don't at all regret having done this play because it was a serious project, beautifully directed by Peter Coe, and it was a pleasure working with Sarah Miles, Alan Dobie and Bessie Love. But how many such gambles can an actor afford? It is essential to do serious work, but an actor and his family have to eat.

Having mentioned so many different forms of acting, it still remains to be said that what really matters is the creative part of acting. To read a good script with a good part in it for you, a part suited to your own particular talents, to know that you are going to work with good actors and a good director – this is what the business is really about. In these conditions rehearsal is exciting, a month from first reading to first night, in which to create, to fuse slowly and painstakingly the work of writer, director and actor. All three are important: the writer who provides the text, the words and ideas; the director who is the outside intelligence, the extra pair of eyes which see the production as a whole, who shapes, suggests and guides; the actors who – so grateful for any help they receive that a good director will inspire love in his cast – finally interpret the part to which they bring their personality, their ideas and their talent. But when the chips are down it is the actor who is on stage, who is out there in full view, and it is up to him, and him alone, to convince the audience, to carry the author's message.

Many actors, no doubt, will disagree with my experience; it's a personal one and must be seen as such. For me acting has been exciting and disappointing, thrilling and heartbreaking. In the short run I find little to recommend in it, but perhaps the future holds surprises. That's one of the good things about this job, one decent part can change everything. Even so, on reflection, it wouldn't change my opinion that Noel Coward was right – Don't, Mrs Worthington.

RONAN O'CASEY

THE AUTHOR

I was born in Montreal in 1922. When my mother's first husband died, and she married my father, who was her godson, my parents thought it advisable to emigrate from Dublin to Canada. I left Canada in 1939 to return to Ireland. When war broke out I joined the RAF and was invalided out in 1942, when I again went back to Ireland.

As I wanted to widen my acting horizons, I came to England in 1945. Since then I have appeared in some thirty films, including Reach for the Sky, The Mudlark, Bitter Victory, Talk of a Million; *in some fifteen West End plays, among them* Kiss Me Kate, The Kidders, First Fish *and* The Shrike; *and in about seventy TV plays. The latter include* A Town Has Turned to Dust *with Rod Steiger and* Travelling Lady, *in which I played opposite Kim Stanley. I've also compèred* Close-Up, Sing a Song of Sixpence *and* Don't Say a Word *on TV.*

Apart from all the forms of acting I've mentioned, I've also been a circus clown and a comic on ice.

I have written for television and would like to devote a greater part of my time to writing. I am married to Louie Ramsay, the actress, and we have a son aged seven.

I am an active member of the Labour Party and have travelled up and down the country in support of Labour candidates at by-elections. Because the alternative is so unspeakable I shall continue to vote Labour, although with reservations. I would like to send Wilson to Vietnam.

The Stockbroker

When I became a stockbroker in the City of London the man who had tried to teach me philosophy at a Scottish university looked puzzled and said it was the last thing he had expected of me. It was the last thing I had expected of myself and, in part, the result of a series of accidents. I suspect that there is more of accident in most careers than is generally acknowledged.

At a secondary school in the early 1940s I had decided I was good at modern languages. Just why I cannot remember. My father lectured in chemistry and my brother excelled in mathematics. The school had an excellent classics master of communist sympathies, who imbued his pupils with a love of the humanities and also allowed them to read the *Daily Worker* under their desks. Despite these influences I became convinced, with the certainty of revealed truth, that I was on the side of the arts rather than the sciences and that, among the arts, I was for the study of modern languages.

The die being cast, I went up to Glasgow University to 'read' (as I have now learned to say) French and Spanish. The Department of French Studies was like a university in miniature and provided me with much intellectual stimulation. In a seminar run jointly by the French and Logic Departments on the philosophy of literature I discovered an interest in abstract thought which I have never been able to indulge to my satisfaction since.

By the time I graduated one conclusion was inescapable: there was no future for me in modern languages. There are in fact only two careers open to the modern linguist – to teach or to interpret. Interpreting is a highly skilled and well-remunerated craft, but its practitioners are no more than onlookers in business and politics; I wanted to participate. I rejected teaching, rightly or wrongly, for a similar reason. Although scholarship and abstract thought interested me, I felt I would have more chance of 'finding myself' in a world of action and decision-making. I liked, and continue to like, responsibility. Contrary to most of my contemporaries, for whom the civil service was the career *par excellence*, I decided to go 'into business'.

So I went on a round of interviews with big companies. Unilever subjected me to a two-day grilling that included interviews with psychologists, intelligence tests and various business games. This destroyed any self-confidence I then possessed. Unilever paid my expenses and turned me down. I have some reason for believing that they thought I would not be a good committee man, which is right.

I turned down ICI, which offered me a job as assistant to the editor of the works magazine in Billingham. Then one day a letter arrived from the university appointments committee which sounded more promising. A large American company with headquarters in New York wished to recruit Spanish-speaking British graduates for work in Latin America. There was to be one year of management training in New York.

It is hard to remember now that, only a decade ago, the United States was out of bounds for most Britons. Our wartime siege economy had not yet been completely dismantled and dollars were simply not available to tourists. I arrived in New York in mid-morning on the first day of July 1956, in a heat of 90° and a humidity of 100%, feeling rather like a traveller arriving on a distant planet.

At that time it was the fashion for graduate trainees in U.S. companies to go on 'orientation programs', which entailed spending a few weeks in each department of the firm. The first department to which I was sent was the corporate planning division, where I was put straight to work on the analysis of the accounts of companies which my employers might consider acquiring. It was a subject I knew nothing about, but I picked it up quickly enough. It required a smattering of accounting; one then went beyond the accounting to certain basic ratios such as the return on assets, the margin on sales, and the price-earnings multiple. People frequently ask the difference between accounting and financial analysis.

The answer is that the financial analyst begins where the accountant leaves off; he is concerned with the interpretation and use of the data which the accountant prepares.

It so happened that there was a vacancy in the corporate planning department, and this I accepted. It so happened also that the office was virtually on Wall Street. As a trainee analyst working on Wall Street I was more than half-way to being a stockbroker. The threat of Latin America, which had always been vague, disappeared altogether. In time I wrote the company's manual of financial analysis.

Three years after arriving in New York I had had enough of the heat, cold, humidity and pace, and I found myself a place as manager of the London office of a leading US firm of stockbrokers. I was thirty years old and was made responsible for eighteen people. Later, when the office was incorporated as a British company, I became chairman and managing director. I can now look back on six years of stockbroking in London.

Broadly speaking, there are at least three types of stockbroker in the London market. First there are the men who start as clerks or messengers and by dint of hard work and determination achieve membership of the Exchange and partnership in a firm. Then there is what Anthony Sampson in *Anatomy of Britain Today* has unkindly described as the 'public-school proletariat', who may also start in a menial position but can hope to buy a partnership and achieve membership rather more quickly. Finally there are the investment (or financial or security) analysts. Most of these are under forty and many are university graduates. They are a post-war development in Britain. Originally the 'backroom boys' of a firm, investment analysts are tending to come to the fore and assume greater responsibility, as they did some years ago in the United States. They are supposed to be the brains of a firm, deciding whether ICI Ordinary should be bought or Courtaulds Debentures sold. As a trade, investment analysis is unsure of its intellectual foundations but full of vitality. Its practitioners are to be found in banks, investment trusts and insurance companies as well as stockbroking companies, and they therefore enjoy considerable mobility.

The function of financial analysis is to lengthen the odds on the success of any given investment. One method by which it sets out to achieve this object is by forecasting the profits to be obtained from an investment in the future, and in the light of the forecast, deciding if the current price is worth paying.

The forecast of profits may be based on past performance. Companies, like people, are judged to a considerable extent by their record. Most financial analysts proceed on the assumption that there is a kind of law of inertia in business and that existing trends are likely to continue unless special factors exist which create a doubt about it. This works both ways. A company with a poor record may suddenly show a great increase in its sales and earnings because of a new development. Equally, a company with an outstanding record may suddenly go into a sharp decline.

The skill of the investment analyst lies not so much in projecting trends (although that is by no means mechanical) as in detecting the special factors that may spell a change of direction. A common example of a special factor is a change of management, particularly when the new executives have a proven record of excellence in other business. This situation may be described as 'old assets under new management'. A classic example occurred when Stuart Saunders, formerly president of the highly successful Norfolk and Western Railroad, assumed the presidency of that ailing giant, the Pennsylvania Railroad.

If a company has to some extent changed its character (as by the appointment of a new president or the development of a new product) and if the market price of the company's shares has not yet discounted the change, an anomaly exists. It is the job of the investment analyst in a competitive market to spot anomalies before anyone else and to recommend the purchase (or sale) of the shares. He assumes that as the general investing public becomes aware of the change in the company's character, the anomaly will correct itself and he will, by the exercise of his skill, have made a capital profit for himself or his client.

There are many things I enjoy about being a stockbroker. One is the age-old satisfaction of being cleverer than the next man. The stock market is a battlefield in which buyer pits his strength and his skill against seller. They can't both be right. The pleasure of winning is experienced in all professions, but in few is it so well defined as in stockbroking. If a share goes up and does not come down again too quickly, one has a delicious sense of being right. Clients coo over the telephone. It is a golden feeling.

Needless to say, one is not infrequently wrong. This is not pleasurable, but it is inevitable and has to be lived with. In some senses it is an essential part of the education of a stockbroker. Many apprentices to the trade have a run of moderate luck, particularly in rising markets. This makes them incautious and impatient of their plodding elders. Then one day luck turns and a share goes sour. The effect is startling. Suddenly they discover the great universal law that there are losses as well as profits. They have, in financial terms, lost their virginity.

It is always interesting to observe a client's response to news of a serious loss. If he is unsophisticated and believes that the universal law need not apply to him, he may either sink into hurt silence or else subject his adviser to abuse. If he understands the law, he will receive the news with milder disappointment. I well recall an occasion some years ago when I went to call on the investment manager of a leading London merchant bank. My object was to discuss a particularly bad piece of advice I had given. He listened attentively, then politely shifted the subject of conversation to one of my more successful recommendations.

Unless he was right more often than not, an intelligent broker would not stay in the business. If he is right a reasonable number of times he can improve his performance by 'cutting his losses and letting his profits run'. However, following this maxim requires more courage than any other decision that has to be made in stockbroking. There is something deep down in us all that tells us to hold on to shares which stand at a loss (in the hope that they will recover) and to sell shares that stand at a profit (in case the profit disappears). It is necessary to go against human nature.

For me another source of pleasure in stockbroking is the wide perspective that a stockbroker enjoys. Bernard Baruch, the late sage of Wall Street, once remarked that 'the stock-market could be termed the total barometer of our civilization'. Many people would consider this an exaggeration – it all depends on the exact metaphoric value one puts on a barometer. Since I do not rate the barometer highly as a source of information about physical reality, I see no objection to the comparison.

The broker with a lively mind can interest himself in labour troubles in the Chilean copper mines (a hardy perennial) or the building of a hydro-electric station in Norway; in peace rumours from Vietnam (in their effect on defence stocks in New York), or in the management of Maxim's restaurant in Paris (which has a nominal quotation in London); in new styles of contraception (pharmaceutical companies) and in burial customs (Rock of Ages Corporation, a leading maker of tombstones, is quoted in New York). To those who study the market it is a subject of eternal fascination, always in motion like the waves of the sea. It has its own dry, unsentimental humour; when Lord Beaverbrook died the shares of Beaverbrook Newspapers Ltd rose; Walt Disney's death had the same effect on the shares of Walt Disney Products Inc. Perhaps the deaths of company officers should be announced only after market hours, to give all investors an equal chance.

Due to the time differential, the New York Stock Exchange does not open until it is afternoon in London. In practice this has allowed me to devote my mornings to administration – and it is surprising how much of this there can be in one small office with under twenty employees, particularly in its formative years – and the afternoons to selling. Selling is an ambiguous term, since in most cases it amounts to urging someone to buy a share. Of equal ambiguity to some is the question of whom the broker is working for, himself or his client. There is a real possibility of a conflict of interest here. Some brokers do work for themselves. However, good brokers generally take the attitude that they serve themselves by serving their clients. A satisfied client will be a source of more business. The client takes the risk and the broker takes the commission. Each morning I try to read the financial sections of several newspapers and ring clients with any news that could interest them. When the New York market opens I and my staff begin ringing clients with opening prices.

The method by which we receive these prices is one of the wonders of modern communications. Prices of securities and commodities in New York, Chicago and other cities are fed into computers from which they are available, in under a second, by a private wire system, to U S brokerage houses in North America and Western Europe. One has on one's desk an object that looks rather like a calculating machine, with a keyboard and a small screen. By pressing the key corresponding to the share, the price appears on the screen. In this way information about some five thousand shares and commodities are disseminated with remarkable speed. Few things are doing more to create one universal capital market than this invention.

A final source of satisfaction is the feeling that as a stockbroker I am performing a useful public function. This is as important to me as the money I earn. My salary puts me in the surtax bracket and is high enough to relieve me of all financial stress. Yet, though adequately paid by English standards, I consider myself underpaid by American or continental European standards. I know people of similar or lesser attainments outside Britain who are paid twice as much as myself. It is often said that Britain is becoming a low-wage country; she is also a low-salary country, and this is one of the factors that attract professionals to leave.

But most modern managers, I think, are concerned with more than their own salary; it is necessary for them to earn their self-respect in terms of feeling they are serving a useful function. Though in fact a *secondary market*, the stockmarket performs such a function. The primary market is in new issues, whose economic function is to gather in the savings of the public and make them available for productive investment in industry. The stockmarket is its handmaiden, in that the public would hesitate to subscribe for new shares unless there was a prospect of being able to dispose of them easily later on. The stockmarket by its existence confers *liquidity* on new issues.

It is an accommodating place. At the one extreme are the conservative investors who look for reasonable income and some capital growth and usually, taking one year with another, get them. At the other extreme are the speculators who, taking one year with another, usually lose money. In between is the average man whose investment objectives fall somewhere between the two extremes and who contrives to get a good deal of fun out of it all. Most investors are probably quite unaware that they are performing any economic function at all.

One of the differences between the British and American stockmarkets is that in Britain (unlike America) it is difficult for the individual who starts from nothing to accumulate wealth. This is in part a result of the extraordinary British tax system, which appears to be designed to keep the rich rich and the poor poor. The situation is very different in the United States, where any successful businessman can hope to accumulate wealth. Millionaires are no longer thought to be remarkable there; it is the billionaires who are an object of public curiosity. There is really no British counterpart to the wealthy American private investor who telephones his broker four times a day and does not consider the day complete unless he does at least one deal in the stockmarket. In Britain, much more so than in the United States, institutional investors such as insurance companies, investment trusts and pension funds dominate the stockmarket.

In Britain it has been a tradition among conservative companies that the directors should not attempt to influence, and indeed should not even be interested in, the share price of their company. Anything else would smack of manipulation, it is thought. US companies tend to take a different line. The ultimate purpose of any investment is not to make aeroplanes or grow corn but to make a profit for the shareholders, and one of the principal forms that profit takes is capital appreciation in the shares. While British companies have a bias towards withholding information, in case it benefits the competitor, US companies have a bias towards releasing it in the hope that it will make their shares more attractive. Financial public relations is big business in the United States.

A rising share price is directly beneficial to a company because it enables the company to acquire other companies for shares on advantageous terms. In the US, where stock options (under which executives are allowed to buy stock in their company over a period of time at a predetermined price) are not taxed out of existence as they are in this country, there is an important secondary advantage. Through the stock option system, rising share prices play an important role in motivating senior management.

In any given year, the bulk of the shares of any given company will not change hands. Nor is there any particular reason why they should. In the US the percentage of shares outstanding that is actually traded in each year has been rising sharply in recent times, which is good for brokers if for no one else. In Britain there is said to be a reduction in the amount of shares traded because of the introduction of capital gains tax, but it is difficult to be definite about this because of the inadequacy of the available statistics. The broker of course generally looks for shares in which there is a good market.

The stockmarket has its own myths. One that is repeated even by quite experienced stockbrokers and financial journalists is that shares rise because there is more buying than selling or, more briefly, because of heavy buying. The fact is that in any market the amount bought and the amount sold is always exactly equal – otherwise transactions would not take place. One could just as well say that a given share rose on heavy selling as on heavy buying. The market price is simply the point at which supply equals demand. It is possible to *want* to sell but not to be able to do so because there is no buyer, and vice versa. It may be objected to this that the 'jobber' (in Britain) or the specialist (in the US) on the floor of the Stock Exchange may on balance be a buyer or a seller of shares on any day, and that the amount of *buying by the investing public* need not equal the amount of *selling by the investing public*. This is, of course, true. However, net purchases or sales by jobbers and specialists tend to be very small in relation to total turnover. It is a principal of good jobbing to 'balance the book' at the end of the day.

Investment analysis carries its own frustrations. One is that it is, rather more than economics or medicine, an art striving – or perhaps better, straining – to be a science. The paradox is that, if it ever did succeed in becoming a science, it would surely abolish itself. This is because markets depend essentially on differences of opinion. If it became a science, then presumably all investors who used the analytical tools correctly would reach the same conclusions. It would be 'buyers only' or 'sellers only' in any given share at any given price, except at the equilibrium price where no trades would take place since it would be neither a buy nor a sell. (The resolution of the paradox is probably to be found in a better definition of the terms art and science, both of which are imprecise.)

How one selects shares continues to be a matter of controversy. Some people regard it as primarily a question of inside information. One hears from a director of company X that next Thursday his company will announce profits up 40 per cent and its dividend up 30 per cent. One buys the shares in anticipation and lo, when the announcement is made the share rises. It would be ridiculous to deny that profits are made by this method. It is a matter of observation that shares tend to rise before favourable news and to fall before unfavourable news. Someone is taking advantage of inside information. However, it seems to me doubtful that one can base an investment policy on inside information.

The trouble is that most tips that purport to be inside information turn out to be wrong. I would put the ratio at, at least, 5:1. Even when the tip is right, the market may misbehave. I recall the case of a certain US utility company which raised its dividend by a substantial amount. The news was issued to the public in the usual manner but for some obscure reason none of the media carried it. It seemed a classic situation for making a killing, with the additional advantage that one appeared to be morally beyond criticism. I bought for certain clients and waited. Eventually the news was published in the *Wall Street Journal* and the share inexplicably went down.

In my experience most successful investments in the stockmarket are made by intelligently assessing news that is *already* publicly available such as the appointment of new management. It is just that other people have not appreciated its full significance.

One of the most valuable activities a financial analyst can undertake is to visit companies – to make 'field trips', in the American jargon. He works primarily with figures, but no analysis is complete unless it is backed up by interviews with senior managers and visits to factories. If he is to do his job properly, the analyst must get mud on his shoes and oil on his fingers. In the United States a good investment analyst may travel thousands of miles in a year and know almost as much about an industry as anyone working in it. The question, of course, arises as to which of the many thousands of publicly quoted companies one investigates. In my case, this has been largely by reading about them in newspapers or magazines. I look out for certain recurring patterns. As I've already mentioned, a change of management is a common reason for a change in a company's fortunes. Because the stockmarket tends to react slowly to changed circumstances, it is sometimes possible to buy the shares of such companies at relatively low prices even after the new management's policies have begun to 'bite' – sometimes after the profits have begun to rise. A case in point was Twentieth Century Fox Corporation. Fox is the company that was almost destroyed by making the film *Cleopatra*. Its presidency was then taken over by one of the ablest of US film-makers, who has turned it into (in some senses) the leading Hollywood movie company. The point I am making is that the shares could be bought at attractive prices even two years after the profits had begun to turn up. I was so taken by the Fox situation that in 1964 I went out to Hollywood and spent a week visiting the company and other movie-makers. The impressions I gained in this way prompted me to put some of my clients' money into Fox shares. At the same time, but for different reasons, I also decided to recommend the purchase of MGM shares. This was because of the amount of assets – chiefly land and old films – which the company possesses. The MGM lot in the heart of Hollywood is so large that the company sometimes does not bother to take down the sets of films that have been completed. I spent a nostalgic afternoon visiting Tara (the house in *Gone with the Wind*), Mrs Miniver's cottage, the bridge on which D'Artagnan duelled, and even a Garbo set from the 1920s. As a film-goer I revelled in it; as a financial analyst I longed to see it go under the auctioneer's hammer. Real estate in down-town Hollywood is as expensive as anywhere in the US.

From my base in London I have been able to visit the United States several times a year and make field trips not only to Hollywood but to beefpackers in the Middle West and textile manufacturers in New England, to mention only these. Unfortunately, British companies are by no means as receptive to field trips, although this is changing.

What does one look for when visiting a company? There is no one thing. A good analyst will carry a checklist of perhaps twenty points about which he would like information. Above all, he wants to know if the management is alert and well-informed. This can often be discovered by inquiring about competition. In one company the analyst will discover that the senior executives 'know the competition' like the backs of their hands. They know what it makes, where, how and at what price. In another company he finds that the senior executives either do not know about the competition or are possessed of misleading information about it. A second way of discovering management's alertness is to inquire into how much the executives know about their own company. It is quite remarkable to discover the number of executives who cannot tell you what return their company is making on its own invested capital.

The financial analyst may not be able to learn very much from looking at plant and machinery, but he can learn a lot from the men who are in charge of it. Hence the importance of a visit to the factory itself with a knowledgeable employee. I recall visiting a company in Philadelphia some years ago. Not long before it had come under new management. A vast factory building was being partly demolished. It was explained to me that all the processes in the building had been analysed and it had been discovered that they could be efficiently concentrated in one-third of the space. This was being done. The estimated annual savings in maintenance and fabric alone were $300,000. I then lunched with the foremen who answered my questions fully and enthusiastically. I came away with the strong impression that this company's shares should be bought, and events have not proved me altogether wrong.

Another source of frustration is that, although a stockbroker paints on a wide canvas, he is often forced to use a broad brush. He can easily end up knowing a little about most shares and not very much about any. Superficiality is his standing temptation.

In the United States, where much more information is available about quoted companies, there is a ready answer to this problem in specialization. For decades brokers have devoted themselves to particular fields. Broker A would be the well-known railroad analyst, B a utilities analyst, C an automobile analyst and so on. This brought its own inevitable consequence, a narrowing of the mind; there is nothing quite so depressingly monomaniacal as a US railroad analyst. Since 1960 this tendency has been carried a step further. Brokers may now be found who specialize in one share only. For a few brief months I found myself 'the' expert on one obscure share. The gain in depth is offset by a loss in the breadth, which is one of the basic attractions of the business. This is a dilemma that is not unique to stockbroking. In many disciplines breadth is being sacrificed to depth and universality is disappearing. Man cannot understand the world he has created. Perhaps the computer, data processing and new learning techniques will restore the balance.

A final frustration for me as a stockbroker has been the lack of a visible impact from my activities on the economy. Broking is concerned largely with the exchange of existing shares – the companies whose shares are exchanged remain largely unaffected by the transactions. Of course, if enough stockbrokers encouraged their clients to buy (or sell) the shares of a given company, that company's prospects of raising new capital would be bettered (or worsened) and its own investment programme could be affected. However, it is difficult for any one stockbroker to trace the impact of his own actions and beliefs in this way. He lacks the satisfaction of the businessman who builds a company, or the engineer who builds a bridge. The end-product of stockbroking, like the end-product of soldiering, is important but diffuse. It is this factor above all which has made me give up stockbroking in recent months and go to work in a merchant bank on international financing.

WILLIAM HOPPER

THE AUTHOR

I was born in Glasgow in 1929, of parents born in Northern Ireland of 'Scotch-Irish' stock. My father was a senior lecturer in chemistry. I was educated at primary and secondary schools in Glasgow, and obtained an MA in Modern Languages at Glasgow University in 1953.

After two years in the RAF, I became a financial analyst in a US corporation in New York, where I remained from 1955 to 1959. I then became head of a US stockbroking office in London.

I am a Conservative and author of two Bow Group pamphlets: one on the role of the City in the development of the European capital market; the other on British economic policy.

I believe in the free market as the best means of allocating resources and creating wealth, but I am not opposed to properly conceived state intervention to buttress the market (where it is in danger of breaking down); to provide a substitute for it (where it has broken down); or to suppress it (where its workings are considered harmful on social or other grounds).

Despite penal taxation and the Labour government I remain in England, and live in London, because I find it an agreeable and humane place to be in and also because I believe it will have an important role – not just financial – in a United Europe.

Factory Money

A lot of the time, when there's been trouble, it's about the money. On the occasions when a complaint or stoppage of work has been long enough and insistent enough to push the shop steward, the foreman or the rate-fixer into the manager's office, somebody or other hasn't been getting what he considered the rate for the job.

It isn't by any means the only grievance or the only criticism that workers make of the management. We've had stoppages of work because of the cold or the damp, but usually it's the money, perhaps because on these matters one can get the minimal support of the shop stewards and the potential support of the union. This is what the union is supposed to be for, by tradition.

For instance, the decision to provide snack meals only instead of cooked dinners, at the canteen, hit many of us below the belt, as it were, but between rumour and *fait accompli* the drift of talk around the dinner tables had not hardened into any decision to see the manager. Of course we knew, by long experience, what the result would have been. We would have been given 'an explanation'. Under pressure, the manager would often concede that we were entitled to an explanation. A committee of workers could have run the canteen just as a committee runs the social club; but such schemes require a stronger leadership, some altruism and a fluent tongue, qualities in short supply here. We can scarcely be called a militant workshop.

The factory produces domestic laundry appliances, hot-water boilers, chemical toilets and various sheet-metal products. It's a small factory – you can walk from the office round all the departments and back again in ten minutes – employing today about 160 men and women, though in the immediate post-war boom it employed four times as many. I work as a storeman, and I've been with the firm since 1932.

Before the war, there was no 'trouble' about pay; we

received the trade-union rate; work was seasonal with always the possibility of being laid off in the winter; and with plenty of men on the dole to take their place, few cared to risk being marked as a 'trouble-maker.'

After the war, in a period of full employment and full order books, many local firms set up bonus schemes in order to keep and attract workers. Ours didn't. But gradually the stories of bonuses of 30s. or more being earned elsewhere wore down the passivity of the work-staff. Workmen – some of the best the firm had – began to leave. Others came and didn't stay. Worker-management relations sank to an all-time low. It wasn't that the workers could plead poverty (the cost-of-living index had not risen significantly), but they felt they were being exploited.

Even the mildest orders of the foremen were resented, and there occurred what is best described as a 'withdrawal of spontaneous cooperation'. Not planned or organized – indeed there was no collective action to secure better pay or a bonus scheme. I knew one man who put through a whole batch of casings, knowing the foreman had set the jig wrong – 'I'm not paid to use my brains'. But such things were, I think, rare; what slowed down production was the hundreds of small things not done since no one had actually been told to do them.

Faced with a sullen uncooperative work-staff, the management decided on a bonus scheme. The details were explained to representatives from each department by the manager. There was to be a bonus on all production above a certain norm; 10 per cent more production meant 10 per cent more pay, and so on. There was to be a profit bonus payable quarterly. And, as evidence of goodwill, we were to receive a bonus on profit over the past year; for some of us, it meant almost a month's pay.

It was this latter item, which seemed almost an act of repentance, that electrified the workshop. It was generally agreed that the management had been generous. After the representatives had reported back, workmen stood about in groups – discussing what to do about the laggards, how to eliminate the bottlenecks, ways in which production might be speeded up. Resentment, tension, vanished overnight.

The change was evident from the first day. The loading gang, between lorries, would move back into production. Men sent to another department for material and finding none ready, would join in and help to get it ready. If there was a bottleneck in assembly, someone would temporarily transfer himself to the section concerned. If a man was late or absent through sickness, the situation would be 'remedied' often before the foreman could do so himself. The division between sections and between departments began to blur.

More important was the effect on the level of decision-making. Decisions formerly referred to foremen would be taken by chargehands; decisions normally taken by chargehands would be taken by workers, or, more often, taken by workers in consultation with chargehands. Foremen would often be asked, not to say what should be done, but to sanction what had been done.

I don't want to overstress these changes. The workshop didn't become an arena of feverish activity and the workmen didn't start running things themselves; but the habitual pattern of work and of authority had begun to change. Here and there, in the new atmosphere, a man would make a decision and take some action he would not have done before; and it was not simply that they worked harder; they began cutting out unnecessary movement and unnecessary work. The firm had always lacked a good motion-study engineer.

This was the 'honeymoon period' of the bonus scheme; and perhaps it would not have lasted anyway; but soon the edge of this enthusiasm was blunted. For one thing, the foremen began to reassert their authority and this 'interference' was resented. The foremen had some reason; for though production had been increased, the quota for each type of product was not always met. Delivery dates had to be met and so a section would be switched to another product – 'Not later, now' – or men moved to another department – and told to stay there. Which invariably meant delays, dislocation, a man doing an unfamiliar job, too many men on one production line, re-tooling a press after only a short run, and so on. In relation to total production, the loss may not have been significant, but to the section or the men concerned, it meant that much of their effort and ability to increase production had been in vain. They felt doubly frustrated, because, as the men on the spot they could almost always see a better way of meeting the foremen's requirements. A foreman cannot transfer half a man to another section; a good working team can adjust.

There was a growing belief that the foremen were not really interested in increased production.

A more serious matter, however, was that the bonus never seemed to have much relation to what one's particular section or department had produced; there was some suspicion that certain departments, working in separate buildings and thus cut off from the main stream of production, were not pulling their weight. But suspicion finally turned on the production index figure itself. This figure was based on the amount of products dispatched each week, each product counting for so many 'units' according to size and complexity. The loading gang could thus make a rough – but only a rough – assessment of what the bonus would be. And we would sometimes get a low production index figure that neither the loading gang nor the packing section could understand or explain. When this occurred some men would wander through the departments, checking on stocks of unfinished products, looking for an explanation.

Looking for an explanation. This was the point on which the bonus scheme weakened and finally broke – a failure of communication. The explanation of the scheme had been purely verbal; nothing was ever posted on the notice board, except the production index figure, the excess production and the amount of the bonus. Was some department idling? Was there something about the scheme that had not been explained? No one knew – and the gap was filled with rumours. Men no longer felt themselves to be part of a working team. The honeymoon period was over.

One Monday morning some of the men, glancing at the

bonus announcement on the board, noticed a peculiar thing. The production index figure – which ran into thousands and was worked out to four places of decimals – was exactly the same as the previous week, *down to the fourth decimal*!

Not even the foremen could swallow this massive coincidence. Men stood in groups talking, just as they had done when the bonus scheme was announced; they were united once again, this time in the belief that the whole thing was a fiddle. A deputation – shop stewards and one man from each department – went to see the manager.

The manager explained that he had recently taken over the running of the bonus scheme and found that it had been misinterpreted. Figures had been based on products *loaded* for dispatch but which had not actually left the works. He had put this right; as there was always a number of lorries loaded at week-end ready to leave on the Monday, this would have meant a week without bonus for us; so he had spread this loss by fixing the bonus at the previous week's low figure. We asked why this information was not posted on the notice board. He replied that the scheme was an informal one freely granted by the management and he did not wish to 'formalize' it by posting explanatory notices. Some of us, knowing his peculiar reluctance to set anything down on paper, believed this. He asked us to point out to the men that he had simply been trying to prevent a week without bonus. But he said that the scheme could be revised or wound up at any time, without notice.

We told the men. Maybe less articulately and less convincingly than the manager; it didn't sound good when we told it, and the men didn't take it good. 'Was the production figure a true statement or was it not?' 'It was not.' 'The bonus had been fixed by the manager?' 'Yes.' It could be so fixed, or ended, again by the manager. (The profit bonus had been stopped some time before, with no notice or explanation at all.) The whole thing, they judged, was a 'fiddle'.

From that time on, though we still continued to earn extra money, the bonus scheme, as an incentive, was dead. We have a piecework system now. This was what the men had always wanted, something they could calculate for themselves, to the nearest halfpenny, and which was not dependent on fellows at the other end of the shop also working hard. In theory, the system was generous, allowing for 10 per cent above the 'day-rate' working at normal speed, and more, of course, if one worked quicker.

Only, in practice it didn't work out like that. In the first place, the 'task definition' wasn't too good. Arguments arose later as to whether rejects counted, who did the rectification, what allowance was made for faulty or badly fitting material, etc. Pieceworkers were dependent on 'day-rate' workers for the bringing of material and the removing of the finished product; and when, later, the number of these day-rate workers was reduced, some of these tasks fell very gradually on the shoulders of the pieceworkers. Secondly, there were fierce arguments about the accuracy of the timing; but as this was not a union-negotiated system one had to accept the rate given – though sometimes you could get it revised, by a combination of bluff and bluster; sweet reason got you nowhere. So we ended up with some rates that were quite good – one assembly line was known as 'The Golden Mile' – and many that were not so good. On these, not only did the piecework fail to live up to the rosy promises of the management; you sometimes had to cut corners to break even with the day rate. And since few people like to turn out sub-standard work this was a double cause for resentment.

Storemen, the loading gang and others whose work could not be timed for piecerate were given a fixed bonus in lieu of piecework. Fair enough, we thought. But later various pressures were applied to speed up the work – the word would filter down from the management that there were too many 'unproductive' workers. So, resenting the stick, we were not inclined to feel grateful for the carrot.

In the machine-shop making the outer casings for the wash-boilers, the piecerates were notoriously bad, and the labour turnover became terrific. If six new hands started on a Monday, perhaps two might turn up the following Monday. It became a standing joke that the foreman there 'had handled more men than General Montgomery'.

This, I believe, was one of the factors that led to a further change a few years ago. Another thing was that it became not so easy to get new hands. Although cotton, once the main industry in our town, had slumped, the pool of labour this created didn't stretch far enough; we were now competing for labour with radio firms and car accessory firms with more to offer in the way of better conditions and bigger bonuses. Finally – perhaps a more important factor – there was a considerable change in management personnel, new men who were not personally committed to the original piecework rates. And since then many of these rates have been re-timed and revised upwards.

This is still fresh in the minds of the workers; in assessing their pay, comparison is made with the old rate – 'it's better than it used to be'. So there is much less tension between management and men now; the feeling of exploitation isn't so evident. But it doesn't help to read of car-workers in the Midlands earning £30 a week; it doesn't help to find we are well below the national average of £17–18 a weekfor manual workers. And it doesn't help to hear that this man or that girl is making a pound or two more than you with apparently less effort.

For even if piecework 'norms' are accurately timed, the amount one can earn above the norm varies according to the nature of the operation. A riveter or spot-welder handling light, easy material may earn 40–50 per cent above the norm without undue exertion; a worker handling the heavy metal sheets earns his extra money by the sweat of his brow; a power-press operator is handicapped – he can increase his own speed, but not the speed of his machine.

Other changes have led to better relations. The threat of the sack is not so potent now; bad time-keeping is condoned to a surprising extent; and about half the 160 or so employees are women, many of whom are not looking for a permanent job anyway. And the old type of foreman or manager who prowled around looking for idlers is no longer present.

The threat of redundancy through seasonal variations in trade has also receded. We have new products not affected by this. There is a gas-heated 'back boiler unit' that will provide instant hot water for the house and is small enough to fit behind a gas fire – an astute piece of foresight this, that takes advantage of the spread of smokeless zones and cheaper North Sea gas. And we make those gleaming chrome-plated water-boilers that adorn the counters of cafeterias and snack-bars.

The iron hand of authority is less in evidence. The smallness of the factory helps, because the sort of instructions you find in large firms, handed down through manager, section manager, department head, foreman and so on, and difficult to question, modify and have explained, is much less common here. There is more on-the-spot consultation, more spontaneous cooperation between sections.

This is particularly so in the stores where I work. The job is not repetitive; we are not constantly pushing levers or continuously turning screws. Making the best possible use of our limited storage space is a bit like doing the sort of puzzles one gets in the Sunday newspapers at Christmas; and keeping track of a thousand or so different items often involves some interesting detective work.

But I have no illusions that these conditions will last. A rise in unemployment, a rise in the cost of living along with a 'wage pause', a take-over bid for the firm, a return to autocratic management – any of these can upset them. We didn't create the conditions, they 'happened' to us, and we are not able to maintain them. Our shop stewards are not the spearhead of a workers' movement, they are Ombudsmen dealing with individual complaints. There are thus still undercurrents of resentment in the workshop, but no unity of resentment, no sense of sharing in a common problem. For the management, piecework is a policy of divide and rule, and the policy has so far paid off.

Despite the relatively improved conditions, what have we got? We're not 'pushed around'; the time passes. But that's all. We spend a third of our lives in the factory, but there is no overall purpose or meaning to it other than the money. Back from one holiday, we start counting up the weeks to the next; no other dates qualify for significance except the date when we are free. There is no sense of achievement about the work, no feeling that we are creating or building something; producing the umpteenth chemical toilet bucket will give us no more satisfaction than producing the first.

'Meaning' for me begins when I clock out at half past four. 'Purpose' is going down to a CND meeting or getting out a protest letter about Vietnam. And 'freedom' is striding along the slopes of Scafell on a fine week-end.

So, if better conditions make work for some of us a bit easier, they don't change anything basic. We are still two nations, at least in our corner of industry, and between the two there is a gulf, a gap which nothing can adequately fill.

Most of the workers, I am sure, are not driven by an urge to get as much for their labour as possible. In part they are seeking those things that make them human – a certain dignity, a measure of equality, and above all their self-respect. In our culture, a man's pay is a status symbol as well as a means of existence; so 'not getting the rate for the job' is a blow to a man's pride as well as his pocket.

I am equally sure that the management are not out to get something for next to nothing either. But this is not the point. They are not simply running a factory, they are helping to maintain a social structure in which the worker comes to them already deprived and under-privileged, dispossessed of the means of production, obliged to sell his labour and take orders from others. Someone once said that he can always 'vote with his feet' if he dislikes the conditions. But this is simply exchanging Manager Tweedledum for Manager Tweedledee.

There is an answer. The term 'democracy' has been so much perverted, nationally and internationally, that it is now almost a dirty word. But somewhere among the mish-mash of ideas about democracy, there are worthwhile experiments that might re-create and sustain the atmosphere we had in those first weeks of the bonus system.

We have had plenty of legislation which has *limited* the power of employers. But what legislation is there which *transfers* any power from the employers to the workers?

'Economic democracy', 'workers' control', call it what you will, is the right of workers to vary certain things according to their own requirements, the power to choose between alternatives. And the right of factory inspectors, trade unions or Ombudsmen is to see that employers do not usurp these rights. Until there are experiments in this direction, then for those of us here, and perhaps for many of the non-voters and the sometimes voters whose support the Labour Party seeks, the more things change the more they will stay the same.

EDWARD SUTCLIFFE

THE AUTHOR

I was born in 1915 in Burnley, Lancashire. After leaving elementary school at fourteen, I joined my brother and two cousins, who were weavers, my father and two uncles who were loom overlookers, at the near-by cotton mill. Two years of bad trade ended in a strike and a lock-out, and it was then I joined my present firm – 'Gas Engineers, Makers of Domestic Laundry Appliances, Sheet Metal Workers'.

Politically I'm a 'late developer'; I didn't begin to question the world around me until 1939. Among the books I read about 'why we were at war' was one by a Mr H. G. Wells. For years afterwards I read everything by Wells I could lay my hands on. Quite certainly no one else has had such a profound effect on my life.

During the Second World War I spent part of my service in the intelligence section of an infantry battalion. After the war I joined anything which seemed to be going in the direction Wells had pointed: towards a world state of free peoples living in peace. For fifteen years I was secretary of our United Nations Association branch.

At present, disillusioned with the Christian church but not with Christianity, disillusioned with the Labour Party but not with socialism, I'm in that political wilderness, the 'peace and new left movement'.

My own future? I never find time to think about that. I'm not married and so have no family dependent on me. What worries me today is Vietnamese kids being roasted alive by napalm, and a world which, twenty-one years after the Second World War, is hell-bent towards the third.

The Forelady

I'm a forelady in a garment factory employing 400 people, and I've worked there twenty-seven years. The department I oversee has about sixty women, divided between section work and 'make-through', as it's called, in which a woman makes an entire garment. In section work different parts of the garment are made by different women. My job is to chase the work right the way through every stage of the garment and make sure production is kept up.

We make mainly men's and women's coats. Unlike section work in some factories, where the garment moves along the bench from one girl to the next, we don't use this conveyor-belt system. I don't know why. Perhaps we haven't the room, or perhaps it's because it would need more supervisors and wouldn't be as profitable as our system, which seems to pay off. In place of a line, with a supervisor at the end, I distribute the work to the girls on the various benches when the bundles come down from the cutting room upstairs. This means that different sections of the garment are on different benches, and a major part of my job is to see that the girls have work.

At the start every morning I have to check up on the production to be got through that day, and also to see which girls haven't come in and without whom the work can't get done. This is especially important for the specialist machinists on felling and button-holing, for example. If any are missing, I go to the foreman or forelady in the other room, where they are doing the same sort of work, and see if I can borrow. We lend girls in this way from one room to another. I also have to make sure there's work for the final passers who inspect and clean the garments, which often get soiled or stained during machining. The one thing I don't have to bother much about is the speed of the girls' work, since they are all on piecework.

In the making of a coat, one with a detachable hood for

example, there may be as many as a dozen different sections, with a woman working on each. There's a girl machining the hood, another button-holing and sewing the buttons on (she also does the 'shanking' – the thread wound round the back of the button – on a different machine, swivelling on her stool), another the sleeves. There's a girl making the straps, another the points on the straps, and a third marking where the straps are to be sewn. The fronts have to be made, and then the fronts and backs joined by a girl who does the closing and runs the sleeves in; another girl runs the hoods on and turns back the facings, while still another does the linings right through. Then there's the 'bagging out', pulling the lining through and lock-stitching it, pressing and final passing. . . . To keep an eye on all this, as well as making sure there aren't any snags in the flow of work, can keep you pretty busy.

The more the girls do the more they earn. You only get slowing down when you've got youngsters who are trying out and they aren't on piecework. It makes a big difference. Even so, there's often trouble about the piecework rates.

When we start a new coat, I always make it my business to machine a sample. This way I know what I'm talking about when it comes to the rates as well as to production problems. Not so long ago, for instance, the designers designed a coat which had an edge without stitching – what we call a 'bluffed' edge. I know that when you've got a separate facing like this that has to be button-holed, it takes a long time to press. I said straightaway that it was no good for production. I went to see the designer and told him it was no good. I've got to see the garments through production, and if the job is going to get done efficiently it's necessary for me to be able to influence the design in this sort of way. Of course, I could get by without bothering, but it seems important to me. I can always go to see any of the people who matter – the owner himself, or the two managing directors who are his son and his son-in-law, or the general manager who comes from outside.

When I've machined a sample I have a fair idea of the

price the general manager is likely to allow in comparison with a simple one. There's a more or less standard price for straight sleeves, straight pockets and that sort of thing. I weigh up the extras; a bit of decorative stitching may be worth another copper or two, a flap on a pocket threepence perhaps. So I tot it all up. Of course, the general manager may take no notice of me. I might say 10s., for example, and he'd say, 'Not bloody likely, I'm not paying that.' He'll offer maybe 9s., and we put that price on and watch the reaction. I give the price when I bring the sample down and give it to the girl who puts the work on the table where the other girls come to fetch it. But as soon as they see my face they all shout from the benches, 'How much then? Eight, nine, ten shillings?' The language gets pretty choice. Often they don't agree. 'How the hell does he think we're going to do it for that price?'

If a girl disagrees, she gets her mates on her side and tells me to tell the general manager they're not starting. Sometimes I'll say, 'You've done none, try it,' and then my name is mud because they say I'm on management's side. But I tell them no, they'll get their own way in the end. If the general manager wants a garment doing, he'll give in. I'm on both sides really, though I usually go a bit below in the price because I know the girls will always fight for more. At other times I get on the phone or go up to see the general manager, and he says, 'Right oh! Send up some of the girls.'

Usually, I try to send one from each bench. I ask who is going to speak for the rest. Often the girls say no, they went up last time and to ask somebody else. I more or less make my way and pick because I know who was up the previous time.

You've got to be a bit crafty, because you've got to ask some of them who aren't eager at all. But why should the same ones always go up and fight for everybody every time? There are some who just sit there and natter all day long, why shouldn't they have to go up? Otherwise those who go every time will get a bad name.

There's no union in the factory; the owner has always been against it. He reckons we have always been paid above union rates, though I don't know for sure what the rates are. Piece-rates in other local factories are similar though, as we know when girls come to us from them. We've had the men outside trying to organize the place, but it has never taken on. Not many of the garment factories in the town are unionized. I'm not against the union, but you never know how the boss could turn it if we wanted to join.

We've had stoppages, but we've always fought it out in the family, so to speak. If we haven't seen the owner we've seen his son or his son-in-law. The trouble has always been over the piecework rates. When they've seen the old man – he comes round the floor every day – the girls have turned their machines off and sat with their arms crossed. 'You're not getting anything else,' he shouts; he doesn't mind shouting. 'You can try it or go home.' He knows very well they won't go home; he might not let them in again – not that it's ever come down to that yet. He's often told them, and they've often said they would, but the furthest they've gone is outside in the street. Listening to what the girls have been saying, dashing to the boss, I've been like a hen on hot bricks. When I tell him they've gone outside, he says, 'Go on, go after them quick, tell them I'll see them in the canteen.' And then he'll usually persuade them to try it, give them another 3d. perhaps. We've never had a total stoppage because the sections working on other garments don't come out in sympathy; each one has to fight its own battles. But another reason is that the factory has always had good runs. We can go all season on one coat, for instance, since most of our production is for a group of good-quality department stores. We've never been on short time in the twenty-seven years I've been in the factory, and that must be something of a record in this business.

Where money is concerned, all the girls in a factory like ours can speak up for themselves. For that reason it doesn't matter who I send up to see the general manager, although some aren't so keen because they think they might be victimized. But I persuade them to go, and in the end they can't refuse, since if one said she wasn't going that might cause a row amongst themselves. This forces them in a way. Sometimes you get a girl who becomes a leader but in the end when it comes down to money, they are all leaders, I think. They are all out for money, nothing else, and the way they grab sickens me sometimes. Years ago, when I started, if a girl was sick or had to have a lie down or got a finger under the needle, she'd come back and find one or two of her mates had done a bit of her work for her to help her. You'd never find that now. They're all out for themselves, they can't get enough.

There are a lot of girls on section work who can't put a coat together who come out with more than I do, a damn sight more. I'm on a flat £14 a week before deductions – after ten years as a forelady. This is why I call it a Cinderella job. Some of the girls may make £16 a week, and without any of my responsibilities. But the management doesn't want to pay for responsibility. A few weeks ago I asked for a rise, and the owner's son said, 'If you have more money you'll have more to worry about.' 'Well, I'll chance it,' I said. Then he said, 'Well, you know there's a wage freeze on.' 'I think you've been freezing me long enough,' I replied. But all he said was, 'I'll have a talk with my father,' and that was that. I'll have to go again. I've never had an individual rise, they've never given me anything out of the goodness of their hearts, so to speak. The only increases have come from cost-of-living rises or when some of us on standing wage have been dissatisfied and gone to see the old man ('My father', as some of us older ones call him) and he's given us five or ten bob a week more. Small rises, but never anything substantial.

Some years back, when the son-in-law more or less had control of the factory, he engaged new foremen on good fixed salaries, £20 to £25 a week. But I and one or two others who have been there a long time have never been well done by at all. And my flat rate isn't even guaranteed: if I'm off a day I can't be sure I'll get the money, it all depends on what they think. I often wonder why I don't leave. But it's not that easy at fifty, you get used to a place, and if I went anywhere else it would take me a long time to know all I know at this place. I often think that it's wrong to stay so long at a place, because they just take you for granted. And as time goes on you get more and more responsibility pushed on to you, or you take it on. Like the samples. I don't have to machine these, but if I didn't I'd feel I might not know the problems involved, either from the girls' angle or the general production. But it means I have to drop everything, and when I go back I have to chase like mad. Like some of the others, when I've had these small rises I've said to myself, 'Well, little and regular.' It's the only way you get used to it . . .

When I started work at fourteen, you got a month to learn the trade. As it was all make-through in those days you had to make the whole garment from written instructions or a diagram. You had to make your own measurements for things like pleats and depth of pockets, and you had to come to work with your own tape measure, pencil, pair of scissors, etc. After a month's training at 7s. 6d. a week you were put on your own time. In the first week on my own I earned 15s. On the Saturday the forelady told me that she didn't think I deserved the money because I had spoken twice during that week. I was heart-broken, I'd told my mother I was bringing back 15s. and she was expecting it. I got the money, but in those days a girl on the bench was frightened to talk, they expected you just to sit there and do your work.

Today, with the introduction of section work, things are different. Everything is marked, notched, so the girls on section work don't need the sort of skills we learnt. As soon as a girl can machine she'll be put on a section. If we're 'bang up', as we say, and have got no more sleeves or fronts to put together, she's not capable of doing anything else, and the forelady has to go up to the cutting room and beg for something else for her to carry on. I think it's a pity the girls don't get more training.

At school-leaving time we get a batch of fifteen-year-olds

who come in as trainees. Sometimes they're put on a bench of their own to learn, but not always. We put them in front of a power machine to let them get the feel of it. It's a terrible feeling the first time you put your foot on the machine, you think it's gone mad. You draw it back and break the needle as like as not. Once they've got the feel, I show them how to thread up and let them run on odd pieces of material. There was a time when we had paper linen squares with a black line and the trainees used to learn by running on the line. As soon as they could run straight they could start. Some could learn in a day; others could take a month and some could never learn. Those who couldn't we put on special machines like buttoners, which are pre-set and where the button is put into a clamp and the machine does the rest. But any that could learn would go on to a section, though they wouldn't know how to do more than one of the jobs: sleeves or fronts, perhaps.

When I first came to this factory at the start of the Second World War I used to try to teach trainees a bit more. I'd get a lot of remnants and show them how to make linings and pockets, which I'd cut out. If I thought they were capable, I'd teach them everything so they could go on to make-through. But today there's no chance of a section worker going on to make-through, even if she wanted to, which one or two do because the earnings are higher there. There ought to be some sort of training school for girls who want to go into the trade and learn it properly. Section work was introduced after the war, when the owner's son came out of the forces. It's more profitable. We've often reckoned it up – they can get the same coat through at a half to two-thirds cheaper in section work than in make-through. And this is allowing for the fact that on section work you need more passers and more alterations which most of the girls aren't capable of doing, whereas in make-through you can throw the garment right back at the girl and she can make the alterations. If it hadn't been for the old man, the son would have got rid of the make-through department after the war. I told him to his face that if he did he'd be losing all his best workers and he realized it was true. You get a better garment from the make-through women as the old man knows, and he's always stuck up for them. Most of the women in make-through are about my age, and one or two have been there longer than I have. They're the old man's 'babies', as we used to say at one time, and he has a loyalty to them and they to him. Not that they don't twist him over prices, because they know they can get their own way with him as they always have – which is one of the reasons why his son is against the department. Now he tries to have as little to do with it as possible. 'Ask my father,' he says to me if I go to him with any problems about the make-through. The old man's a bit soft-hearted and he's the boss: if he wants a thing he'll have it and that's all there is to it. But mainly I think it's because he knows they do a better job than in section work. Often the two departments, section and make-through, are producing the same coat, which is how I can compare the two. The make-through is also on piecework, though the rate is for the whole garment instead of for a section. The women make more than in section work and some of them may clear anything up to £20 a week without working the full hours, going home at 4 or 4.30, or with a day a week short. It's not all earned in work-time though, and this is the point. A girl will take flaps up to the canteen at dinner-time to turn them out, or she'll take flaps and collars home at night. Or at dinner-time she may not go up when the bell goes because she may have a dozen coats that want turning out which would take her a lot of her work-time otherwise. This is what we call 'sweating'; the management knows it goes on and allows it. If the union came into it they might stop all this.

There's a much better attitude in make-through than in section work. The women take a pride in their work because they can make a garment right the way through. Knowing this, and because they're older women with family responsibilities, they're tougher about piecerates. They've always been used to decent money, though sometimes I think they're greedy.

On section work I don't think a lot of the rates are fair. Very often girls on the simpler sections are better paid than on the others. Many of the sections don't get paid enough, in my opinion. The girls often complain about it, but what can they do? When I can I try to knock a bit off a simple section and put it on another one. Or I let a week go and show the girls' pay-sheets to the general manager. But either way, you've got to take it off one if you want to give it to another.

Now and then, if the girls complain, the general manager will come and do timings. In the old days the son-in-law would do this, but he's given over most of this side of his work to the new general manager. He'll come and sit by the girls with a stopwatch to arrive at a price. A lot of the girls get nervous about this, and when they're nervous they usually work faster. In that way, even the timings aren't really fair.

The speeds of the girls on the bench vary very much. Some of them look all the time as though they're 'sweating', while others look as though they're not working at all hard, and yet they're earning the same or more. It all depends on how a girl handles a garment. One girl will make three movements, another only two. There's a rhythm to the work and only a girl who can find the rhythm can do the job easily.

Except about money, the attitude of the girls on section work is 'couldn't-care-less'. They know the majority of factories round here run section work, and there's always a shortage of girls. On the other hand they know we don't get a laying-off of work, and you've got to do something special to get sacked, so most of them grouse about the prices, but settle down. The majority of them are young, and they haven't the responsibilities of married women; as long as they earn enough to take them out at night they don't seem to care. They're cheeky in comparison to girls when I started, and a lot of them will give you fifty words for one. And even though they want to earn, there's never a day passes when I haven't got to root them out of the lavatories where they go in groups to natter and smoke. A lot of them get moody, too, and do bad work, and then I have to take them up to the general manager. Whatever I have to say I say in front of the girl, so that she knows exactly what I've told him. Most of them respond, realizing they've got to do something about their work. It's very rare that anyone gets sacked, though we do get a run of girls leaving, particularly those who have never worked anywhere else, who go off to see if it's better somewhere else.

At present we've got a lot of Greek and West Indian girls. We've always had a fair share of foreigners in the factory – French, Czechoslovaks, Poles. If they can speak English they are all right, but some of them can't speak a word. All you can do is show them. It creates a lot of difficulties. They ought to be given a slight language test before being taking on but, as there's always a shortage of women, they aren't. If they can't speak English they usually come with a friend who can and who speaks for them. Once they are on the bench you have to try to make them understand, and it isn't always easy. The other day, for instance, I had a girl who took the sheet of pink tissue paper which is put in to divide the shades in the bundles of work and went to the cotton room to get matching cotton to machine it. Generally, these girls can only do linings and seams, but as time goes on and they get their speed up they can earn good money.

The old man started the firm from nothing in the 1930s. He only had a small house at the time, with one or two machines in a back bedroom, and he has built it up to its present size. It's a remarkable achievement to me, because he had to work hard against odds to make it.

I respect him because I get my bread and butter out of him, so to speak. He's a pusher, he's pushing all the time for production. He screams at you for it. I used to ask him to speak a bit more civilly to me, not that it did much good. He'll shout at anyone when he comes round every morning. If a girl on the bench backchats him a bit, he'll say 'Cheeky little swine', or something, and go off muttering. These days you often hear him muttering, 'I'm still the boss.'

A lot of the older women, including me, call him 'my father'. Years ago when his son used to come round he'd often ask me if I'd seen 'my father'. After a time he seemed to expect us to say 'father' when talking to him about his father. It has happened that I've called the old man father to his face; he gave me a funny look but he didn't say anything.

When he retires, or rather when he dies because he'll probably never retire, I doubt whether the factory will be the same place. As far as the work is concerned there won't be much change – though the make-through will probably be squashed; it's the human side that will be different. In some ways the old man is like a father to us. You can go to him with all sorts of problems, even personal ones, and he'll help you. Quite often when the girls see him coming round they'll go and get a 'sub' – an advance – on their wages off him. Sometimes he puts it through the office himself or else he tells me to go to the accounts department and get it passed.

Not so long ago I was overseeing another section during the holiday period. There was a girl on section work who had been off three weeks, on holiday, I thought. I turned round suddenly and saw she was pushing her work under the bench and her head was twisted on one side. Someone said she had been off with fibrositis. I asked the general manager to come down and when he saw her he went to speak to the old man, while I found out who her doctor was. The old man contacted her doctor and got her an appointment with a specialist, which he paid for. These are the sort of things he will do, and everyone knows about them. I don't know whether, when he's gone, we won't be just so many workers to the others. We've never had the experience.

When the job is going right I get pleasure out of it. I know we're making good stuff and we've got a standard to set, producing for this particular group. When the old man comes round and says a coat is selling, it gives us an incentive to work, particularly in the make-through, where the girls feel this sort of pride. Since there's no profit-sharing, I don't get any benefit, but I feel pleased. But at other times, when they're screaming at you for production, I get pretty steamed up. I feel they're asking too much, expecting too much responsibility for £14 a week to get that production out every day. The old man comes down and checks the daily totals and screams: 'I want figures, figures, it's no bloody use what you did yesterday.' And the only thing to do is to shout back at him. At least I never say, yessir, yessir, three bags full.

I'm glad my daughter hasn't had to work in a factory, you miss such a lot of life. And it's worse in this factory because it's half underground and you can't even see the outside. It's a world on its own. I suppose I'll go on working there as long as I can, but I can't help thinking it's a mistake to stay in one place so long that they can take you for granted.

ALICE BROWN

THE AUTHOR

I was born twelve days after my father was killed in the First World War. My mother was left with four of us to look after, and it was a struggle for her. I left elementary school at fourteen and went straight into a garment factory. Everything I earned was for my mother. It has always been my one regret that I didn't have a good education, but my mother couldn't afford it.

I've never changed my type of work, though I've done every sort of machining. At the start of the Second World War, when everyone was going into munitions factories, I applied at the Labour Exchange, but was told they were keeping machinists in their jobs. I was directed to my present firm, which was then on government work making battle-dresses. But as I had been a machinist on fine work previously I was directed to the dress section, which was still allowed a small production. Every time I got a card to go on munitions work, the boss phoned up to get me an exemption. So, as time went on, I just stayed there.

I married in 1940, a few months before going to the firm. I only had a fortnight's married life before my husband went into the forces. He was away six years, a prisoner of war for two of them. I didn't know whether he was dead or alive. He came back in 1945 and I had a break for eighteen months – the only one since I began work – when my daughter was born. About that time I was more or less made in charge of my department and put on standing wage, but I've only had the figurehead title of forelady for about ten years.

I'm happy that I've been able to put my daughter through grammar school and college. I wouldn't have wanted her to work as hard as I have had to.

Member of Parliament

When I was declared the member of parliament for Epping in October 1964, I had been engaged in active political work for over fifteen years. As a convinced socialist, I believed profoundly – and still do – in the need for fundamental political and social change, and regarded my election as a step towards the achievement of this objective.

This is not to say that I had any illusions about parliament as a dynamic instrument of social revolution. Having been on friendly terms with a number of members of parliament who shared my outlook in broad terms, I was well aware of some of the difficulties which they had encountered. Furthermore, I had often argued with people who rejected the possibility of working for socialism through parliament, and I had read books like *The Labour Government and British Industry 1945–51*, by Rogow and Shore, which highlighted the failures of the past.

My attitude, therefore, was not wildly optimistic about the chances of dramatic political change. In this respect I differed from many of my supporters who, carried away by the exhilaration of our victory, seemed to imagine that the knell of the old order had at last been tolled. For them parliament was the fount of all authority, and they were convinced that henceforward I should be able to exercise a real influence on government decisions. I had now only to go down to the House and expound my cause. With a torrent of oratory I should overwhelm my opponents and watch the walls of Jericho collapse.

My first impressions of the House of Commons as a member were very ordinary. It reminded me of being a pupil at a new school. I needed to visit a number of officials – at the Lees Office about income tax and National Insurance contributions, at the Serjeant-at-Arms' store to obtain House of Commons stationery – and I was continually asking for directions and losing my way. Everything seemed strange and unfamiliar, and there seemed to be little guidance for the new member.

Once I had adjusted myself, I was able to take stock of my new surroundings. Aneurin Bevan said that the House reminded him of a church. To me, however, it was a kind of living museum: the Speaker dressed as he would have been in the eighteenth century; the Serjeant-at-Arms and his deputies also in antique dress; and in the members' cloakroom, beneath each hook, a loop of pink ribbon religiously renewed whenever it faded, for each member to hang up his sword!

The outward picturesque survivals, as I increasingly realized once business began in earnest, are manifestations of an attitude which permeates almost every part of the House and its procedures. Almost everything is liable to be hallowed by time-honoured usage and it is to the past that one tends to look for guidance and inspiration.

The chamber was not rebuilt after its destruction in the Second World War to provide seats for all members, but virtually as a replica of the former chamber. Rulings from the Chair are meticulously based on earlier rulings. Nearly everything is connected with tradition, and there is a strong tendency to make decisions according to precedent without reference to the needs of the present. This makes the House of Commons an ideal arena for evasion, procrastination and delay. The very essence is inimical to radical change, and like other backbench members I rapidly came up against the parliamentary facts of life.

For a start, the established conventions are inhibiting. I was nervous about making a mistake in referring to another member, particularly after the House nearly went into convulsions when Dame Irene Ward called someone on the government front bench her 'Honourable Friend'. I learnt that while it is correct to refer to members of the same party as 'Honourable Friends', those on the other side are normally 'Honourable Gentlemen' or 'Honourable Members'. However, Privy Councillors are 'Right Honourable Friends', 'Gentlemen' or 'Members', according to whether they sit on the same or opposite sides of the House. Retired officers of the armed services are 'Honourable' or 'Right Honourable and Gallant'. Lawyers are 'Honourable' or 'Right Honourable and Learned'. Peers are 'Noble Lords'. And one is also supposed to distinguish individual members by referring to their constituencies.

The conventions are not limited to the use of what is to begin with an unfamiliar terminology, but cover the way in which debates are conducted throughout. They also cover behaviour in the chamber.

I remember during the course of the 1964 general election Sir Alec Douglas-Home, the prime minister at the time, ran into some stiff heckling and attempts were made to shout him down by hostile sections of his audiences. This was denounced on all sides, and rightly so, in my opinion. In the House of Commons, however, I discovered that this practice is generally accepted. On one occasion shortly after Edward Heath had succeeded Sir Alec, one of Harold Wilson's speeches was rendered almost completely inaudible by noise almost the whole way through.

Seeing a piece of paper being passed from hand to hand on the other side of the House, I inquired amid the hubbub of an old and experienced colleague what was going on. He explained that the paper probably had instructions to talk written on it, and this explained the noise from the Conservative benches . . .

'Disgraceful,' I commented in anger. 'If only the public could see this!'

At this my colleague informed me not to get so excited. 'After all,' he said, 'we did it when they were in.'

My retort was that we ought to be ashamed that this was so, but it is difficult not to accept these conventions after a time. I have seen the most down-to-earth men and women adopt the full repertoire of hackneyed exclamations and phrases which are generally in use in the chamber: 'Oh!' to indicate an admission by the other side; 'Answer!' when a member attempts to evade the point of an intervention'; 'Sit down!' if somebody with whom one disagrees attempts to intervene when a front bench spokesman is on his feet; 'Reading! Reading!' if a member appears to be using a note to help him formulate a supplementary question.

Individual variations and bogus points of order abound when the object is to give a speaker a rough passage, and I was disgusted at the uproarious behaviour of the House when the cancellation of the TSR2 was discussed – behaviour which largely prevented serious consideration of the arguments on the floor of the House.

In some ways the debates are reminiscent of university debating societies. I recall a debate during my own period as a student on a motion to make Lilian the Ludpole a life member of the society while the main business was held up. The atmosphere in the House of Commons is rather like this. Opportunities for filibustering and wasting time are enormous, and there are many skilled exponents of the art of delay.

It soon dawned upon me, however, that this situation reflects the general realization that the real power of making decisions has been almost entirely withdrawn from the Houses of Parliament. In fact debates often bear more resemblance to a formalized display of opinions – even a charade – than to a genuine consideration of facts and arguments.

On the very day that I took my seat I found myself next to a member of many years' experience, who said to me: 'You don't want to think that you can get anything in here,' indicating the floor of the House.

I did not fully appreciate the point of his remark at the time, but I have since then had it demonstrated time and again. Any change of front, any alteration in the form of legislation, must be secured, if it is to be secured at all, by lobbying and consultation before it reaches the floor. Interested parties – whether groups of employers, trade unions, trade associations or others – do all the crucial work behind the scenes.

Members of parliament are not usually consulted on the most critical issues, but are expected to fall into line according to the guidance of the whip. It is not for them to reason why on the floor of the House, or to expect their arguments to produce a fundamental change of direction which has not been previously accepted.

I remember some months after my election being deeply concerned about the position of that small and declining section of the population which is not entitled to a retirement pension. A Conservative member, Mr Airey Neave, introduced a private member's bill to grant a pension to such persons, but the government was determined that the measure should not go through, and it became clear that Labour MPs would be required to oppose it. Along with a number of other Labour backbenchers who felt as I did, I went along to the chief whip and indicated how strongly I objected to opposing the bill. We were most courteously received but were left in no possible doubt that for us to withhold our votes in any circumstances in which the government had a majority of only three would be a most serious act. In the event a procedural device was conjured up to prevent the bill being debated which probably represented a gesture to our feelings.

On another occasion I was strongly opposed to certain provisions of the Slum Clearance Compensation Bill and spoke against them in the House. When, however, the official Opposition forced a division, I voted with a heavy heart against amendments with which I entirely agreed. The reason I did this on this occasion, and most members do it at times, is the realization that one is not really voting on the merits of a particular question. One is actually voting on whether or not one still has confidence in the government. Although defeat on a minor issue would not be regarded as loss of confidence, the modern British system of government in effect involves members in the acceptance of a package deal. One cannot take what one approves of and reject the rest. It is all or nothing. If I decide to vote against my government on a wide range of issues and others do likewise, the government can no longer rely on our support and its majority is accordingly reduced. If the majority disappears, according to the rules of the game, the government must resign.

In its origins, this system owes much to the first prime minister of Britain, Sir Robert Walpole, probably the greatest exponent of the art of bribery and corruption who ever held high office in this country. By means of this system he kept himself in power from 1721 to 1742, a period not yet equalled by any other prime minister.

It is apt that his picture – that of a benevolent, and bewigged eighteenth-century gentleman – should still adorn the Cabinet Room to this day. The threat of government resignation and the consequent need to defend one's seat at a general election – possibly with the withdrawal of official party support, and perhaps against an official party candidate – is a factor which every MP who considers voting against his party whip must take into account.

Even ministers, including Cabinet ministers, must accept decisions. They are not permitted to speak in the House on matters which do not come within the purview of their own departments, and even in this sphere they are subject to the over-riding authority of the Cabinet. Thus, in the last resort, all they can do is resign, as Christopher Mayhew and Frank Cousins did. It is no easy step and certainly not one to be taken lightly.

With such enormous pressures on members, whatever the arguments deployed, it is unlikely in the extreme that a member will be influenced by what is said during a debate to cast his vote in a way that he was not prepared for previously. Accordingly, debates are not occasions to win over members' votes, but to get publicity outside the House, for the national press may, and the local press almost certainly will, report what a member says.

Indirectly, of course, what is said may influence a minister by its impact on the public. Apprehension about possible public response may be an important factor in the minds of ministers. As a direct means of influencing policy, however, a speech in the House is of limited worth.

This fact became clear to me early on, and like most MPs

therefore I now regard press reports of what is said as one of the foremost purposes of any contributions which are made in debate.

The same is true of parliamentary questions. A very wily parliamentarian pointed out to me that a question is often worth more in terms of publicity than a speech. The majority of answers are given according to precedent or prescribed rules. One is usually aware of the answer beforehand, but puts down a question to publicize an issue or embarrass a minister.

A minister may of course make use of a question to make an important announcement, but decisions are not normally made, nor could one expect them to be, on the floor of the House. In any case, the civil servant who prepares the answer for a minister is often the same man who prepared it for his predecessor of the opposite party. Many issues in fact are decided by people in an advisory capacity who never fight an election.

At first I expected much more than this, but I have now come to terms with the fact that parliament is not so much a place for taking decisions as for obtaining publicity and bringing pressure to bear. Even this, however, is not easy.

On numerous occasions I have determined that I would like to speak on a particular subject. In accordance with normal procedure, I have written to the Speaker hoping that I might 'catch his eye' in the debate. For a whole day from 3.30 p.m. I have been in my place with my notes in my hand; these may have taken me the morning to prepare. Each time a member has sat down at the conclusion of his speech, I have risen in hope: but to no avail. I have been called in very few important debates.

In the autumn of 1966 I took great trouble to prepare a speech on economic affairs for a two-day debate and sat through the best part of the full course. Unfortunately, front bench speakers on the second day took so long that along with a number of my colleagues I was disappointed and at 7.30 p.m. gave up.

There are, of course, other methods of gaining publicity

and exercising pressure. If these are effective, they may enhance a member's chance of being called to speak.

One such method is to put down so-called Early Day motions, which will never be debated but to which other members may add their names as an indication of their support. The more signatures, the greater the press attention, and therefore it is normal to canvass members to sign.

The first six who do so are known as sponsors and receive extra publicity, and there is therefore some competition for the honour. I have acted as a sponsor on various occasions, but only once as the number one sponsor.

This was on the occasion when American bombers attacked the oil installations on the outskirts of Hanoi in June 1966. I was one of those who felt very strongly about this and suggested an Early Day motion calling on the government to dissociate Britain from US policy. This was in due course tabled and received 113 signatures – the highest number on a motion opposing US policy in Vietnam to that date. This caused considerable ferment along with demands in the chamber for a debate on the subject, and on the strength of official Opposition support – largely given in order to embarrass the Government, whose policy for the most part they approved – a debate was fixed.

At this a number of my colleagues and I who had sponsored the Early Day motion tabled an amendment to the government motion in similar terms and sought to persuade the Speaker to call it. Although our motion went down before that of the official Opposition, in concert with precedent it was not called, and at one time it appeared doubtful if any of its sponsors would be given the opportunity to speak in the debate at all.

Eventually, after a lot of running hither and thither, I was called to speak – the only occasion in the two years which I have sat in the House that I have managed to make a contribution in a foreign affairs debate. When the House divided at the end of the debate, without our amendment having been called, it was difficult to decide how we could make our views clear, even if we determined to defy the whips, without identifying ourselves either with the government position or with that of the Conservative Opposition, which was critical only on the grounds that British support of the Americans had wavered over the bombing of Hanoi. Furthermore, it was feared by some of my colleagues that failure to support the government in the division lobbies would be represented as a refusal to support Wilson's proposed trip to Moscow, which was announced on the eve of the debate.

All sorts of consultations, discussions and exchanges took place, and when the division was called thirty-two members, of whom I was one, refused to vote – most of us sitting in the chamber while the division was taken – to publicize our position.

Some of those who agreed with me entirely on the principle involved voted, while others who were not naturally vocal on the issue abstained. Although many of us regarded the issue as one of consi ence, we were not agreed on the way in which we should exercise our dissent.

This was the only occasion on which the war in Vietnam came before the House of Commons for a division in 1964, 1965 or 1966. When I spoke from the plinth in Trafalgar Square some months previously on the subject, however, I was booed by a section of the audience on the grounds that I had not voted against the war. The truth is that, for better or worse, as I tried in vain to explain, the issue had not been presented at that time in a form in which a vote was possible.

For people outside the House it is difficult to grasp how little power a backbench member has to determine what issues will be discussed, and the dearth of opportunities to put his views forward.

A year after my election, when I was scheduled to address a local Labour Party meeting in my constituency, a reporter on one of my local newspapers wrote, in anticipation of my speech, which was to take the form of a report back: 'What does it feel like to make a maiden speech before a House full of hardened and critical politicians?' Unfortunately, most critical and hardened politicians are not likely to flock into the chamber to listen to me or any other backbench member

– with the exception of Michael Foot. If they are in the chamber at all, it is probable that they are hoping to speak themselves and are anxious that I should not go on too long and perhaps deny them this opportunity.

All this inevitably has made me even more cynical than I was about the role of parliament in modern Britain. However, I had my doubts before I was elected. In the case of the Parliamentary Labour Party I originally had more hopes.

As a rank-and-file constituency Labour Party worker until 1960, I had always accepted that the annual conference of the party at national level determined policy. After the 1960 Scarborough conference passed a resolution in favour of unilateral nuclear disarmament in the face of strong opposition from the party leadership, I became familiar with the doctrine that power lay not with annual conference after all, but with the Parliamentary Labour Party. Once I arrived in the Parliamentary Labour Party, I found that power had again apparently taken flight and now resided in the Cabinet.

Meetings of the Parliamentary Party were held at irregular intervals and normally lasted only two hours, a sizeable proportion of time being taken up by government spokesmen. Only a very small proportion of members was able to speak within the period available, and resolutions were not normally taken. When they were, discussion was not usually provided for in the way that it would be in a meeting of a Labour Group on a local authority, although the situation has now changed somewhat. Ministers etc., are not expected to speak unless their departments are involved, whatever their views, and it would be unheard of for a minister to oppose government policies in any sphere. So these meetings are in fact not as much an arena in which decisions are made and policy formulated, as one where anxieties are voiced, pressure exerted, and where measurement is taken of the state of opinion among Labour MPs.

In addition to the Parliamentary Party, there is a wide range of subject groups corresponding to the most important departments of government. Eminent speakers, including the minister in charge of the department concerned, are invited, and much information can be obtained. But once again, policy-making is not really a function of their activities, and these groups have no power at their disposal.

After a period, particularly as I was hard-pressed for time, my attendance at those subject group meetings which I had asked to be included on – foreign affairs, economics, housing, education and agriculture – fell off, and at present I only go on a selective basis. As a former teacher I decided to take a particular interest in the education group, and largely because I was one of the few to turn up to a particular meeting, I was chosen chairman of a sub-committee to prepare a report on public schools.

At first we envisaged an ambitious programme of visits to public schools and meetings. But the attendance fell off rapidly, and much of the work was not carried out. Ultimately a paper was produced which was presented to the Secretary of State for Education and Science. Doubtless more of this type of work is possible, but it could well be done equally effectively, if not more so, by groups of interested people who are not MPs. The fact that the deliberations of these groups are merely expressions of opinion robs them of any real importance.

In addition to the official subject groups, I have also attended various unofficial groups of an *ad hoc* variety: meetings under John Mendelson's chairmanship on Vietnam, and meetings of another group of colleagues on the left which came under fire from some supporters of an incomes policy when, along with a number of colleagues, I abstained from supporting the government in the division lobbies on its economic policy in the autumn of 1966.

The pressure of activities in the House is very heavy indeed for anyone with wide interests, and a large proportion of my time is spent outside the chamber at other meetings of one sort or another. This does not mean one is neglecting one's duty. Like most other backbench members, I spend long hours at the House – sometimes lasting into the early hours of the morning, or all night through – waiting for a division which sometimes does not take place. As a government member one is there to support the government in getting its business through, and this involves waiting and not speaking.

The same thing is true if one is appointed to standing committees, which go through bills clause by clause before they are brought back to the floor of the House for the report stage and third reading, and subsequent transmission to the House of Lords. I have been on a number of these committees and have normally had something to say. However, the ideal backbench member of a committee on the government side is one who is always present with his vote to support the government spokesman, but does not hold up the business by his intervention in debate.

The fact that so many things are 'cut and dried', the fact that it is so difficult to influence affairs, the fact that very considerable pressures exist to make the individual member conform, produces a sense of ineffectiveness and frustration that at times makes me feel I am entirely wasting my time. If I realize beforehand that the die is cast and that all my efforts may not even enable me to gain a hearing for my views, I sometimes feel that I must attend to other aspects of my work. When, for example, I remained in the chamber two days during the economic affairs debate without being called, for several weeks afterwards I was too frustrated to risk wasting any more time in the same way.

The sense of ineffectiveness is, however, in complete contrast to the outward signs of importance bestowed on a member. As an ex-miner and schoolteacher, I am still very conscious of being addressed as 'Sir' by every policeman in the House – particularly by men old enough to be my father. I was completely taken aback when I first drove my car out of New Palace Yard and an officer on duty stepped smartly out into Parliament Square to hold up the traffic on my behalf. I am invited to a never-ending list of meetings and special occasions, where I am normally treated with great deference. I am always afraid that if ever it is fully realized how little power I have as an MP my only function will be as a tourist attraction for the entertainment of the vast crowds of visitors who flock to Westminster each year. The trouble is that, in competition with the Guards at Buckingham Palace and the Beefeaters at the Tower of London, who have colourful uniforms, my colleagues and I will be at a great disadvantage!

A very large part of my work is not done at the House at all but in my constituency. Before I was elected I knew that members received letters, conducted advice bureaux and generally took up constituency problems. But I had no idea how enormous the volume of this work was or would become. In fact the major part of my time is occupied with calls on my service from my constituents. I am a kind of local Ombudsman, to whom all and sundry come when they are in difficulties with government offices, local authorities, the police, the Inland Revenue, their own relatives or anyone else.

If a constituent is unable to obtain a house, if he has been refused a pension, if his neighbour's teenage son is taking potshots at the washing on the line in his garden with an air-gun, he comes to me. I am deluged the whole year through with a range of problems which concern almost every aspect of life and activity from the most public to the most intimate issues.

My constituency has the second largest electorate in Britain – nearly 100,000 – who live in five different local-government areas ranging from middle-class London suburb to country villages. I am expected to be an expert in everything from cucumbers to computers. Both are extremely important in my area.

On the first Saturday of every month I hold an advice bureau at four different centres and am normally assisted by councillors in this work. A steady stream of constituents keeps me occupied from 9 a.m. to about 7 p.m. Every day I receive about twenty letters. I am telephoned at home at all hours of the day and throughout the week-end. I am never without some work waiting to be done.

Many of the problems are hardly those one would expect an MP to tackle. I have been asked to pursue a missing letter, to deal with the problem of burst pipes, to take action about the wallpaper being used by council decorators, and even to take up the case of a man who considered his brain was being controlled by a transmitter in outer space. The case of a lady who lost her false teeth while vomiting involved me in a correspondence with the Executive Council for the National Health Service on whether she was entitled to free replacement dentures. The crux of the argument was whether it constituted negligence not to remove one's false teeth before vomiting.

The most serious problems of all concern housing. Not a week passes without a new load of difficulties arriving on my desk. Young married couples who have lived for years with several children in one room; husbands unable to live with their wives; old people who mistakenly give up their own houses to live with married children and who, finding they have made a mistake, are condemned to live their last years in misery; families evicted from tied cottages with nowhere to go. Although I have no direct powers over housing, I always try to assist and to persuade one local authority or another to help. But the insistence of the different housing authorities in my area on residential qualification and differences in their points systems according to which they allocate houses leave some people without any real hope of being housed by anyone.

I recall the case of a respectable working man who came to my advice bureau and told me he had been married for twenty years without getting a house. He showed me his bank book in which he had been saving up to get a deposit to buy, but he could not obtain a mortgage. Consequently he had been living in a caravan and at that time had two sons aged seventeen and twelve. Suddenly he broke down in tears and told me his younger son had been taken off with rheumatic fever and was on no account to return to the caravan, which was damp. No one would let him have a house. In this case the local authority did rehouse the family, but this is not invariably so.

I recognize that I am often only arguing the case for one

applicant for rehousing at the expense of another, but I can see no alternative until more houses are built and the drift to the south-east is reversed. I have tried to get the local authorities in part of my area to cooperate in tackling their housing problems, but as in so many other spheres I have only the power to suggest and the idea has not taken on.

The individual housing cases illustrate – as do so many other individual cases – ghastly national problems. Disputes over pensions, national assistance (or, as it has recently been renamed, supplementary benefit) in the case of the sick, the disabled, the unemployed and the old, the burden of rates (which in one part of my constituency have increased by over £15 a year). . . . These are all part of the crisis in our social services.

However, the problems I have had to deal with have not been limited to those which fall within the sphere of a government department or some other established authority. Human problems which could only be effectively dealt with by social case workers frequently arise. Many of these stem from divorce and separation, and I have had many people clearly in dire need of psychological help approach me. I have come into contact with the plight of the mentally ill and maladjusted to an extent which I never imagined likely before becoming an MP.

Such cases drive home to me how hopeless it is to seek to solve our social problems without a radical overhaul of our social services and our society as a whole.

After all, I am not trained to deal with all the social problems which come my way, neither have I the time to do this. As it is, I am conscious of the fact that I am often compelled to neglect some step which I would very much like to take in the national arena in order to deal with an individual constituent's problem.

Even to write the letters and file the correspondence which I receive is more than I am properly equipped for. In reality I require a full-time secretary and an office. In fact, I make do with a room in my own house, a filing cabinet in my bedroom, the services of a number of casual typists who take down my letters in their own homes, and my wife's services as a filing clerk and telephonist.

Of course, I also have a desk and a filing cabinet at the House of Commons, but as this is in a room with fifteen other members' desks and no secretary can use it, I am not normally able to do the bulk of my work there. This lack of proper facilities for MPs is a great handicap, particularly when there are so many calls on one's time.

The work then is hard and never-ending. The pressure is such that I do not have sufficient time to read books, study the news or to see TV programmes as I did in the past. Moreover, I am always conscious that I must not lose sight of the fundamental reasons which originally led me to devote my leisure time to political work and eventually to parliament. This would be easy to do without realizing it, since the environment in which I now move is so very different from that in which I began.

As a rank-and-file socialist I did not encounter my political opponents at close quarters and I did not know them as persons. Not only am I acquainted with many of them nowadays, but I often find them to be likeable, humane and men of the highest principle.

Furthermore, I am often seeking to achieve short-term objectives – perhaps in connexion with a constituency problem – and often need the help of people who would certainly not support me in my longer-term political aims. At these times the immediate goal is liable to loom much larger than the one which lies on the further horizon. Before becoming an MP I was never subject to the same compulsion to weigh the disadvantages of losing vital support for a particular project against the need to stand firm on principle perhaps for what seems a triviality.

On the issues of socialism and opposition to war, on capital punishment and abortion law reform, on racial prejudice (on which I have certainly lost votes), the issues are much too great to be sacrificed for any gains. But I would not attempt to deny that on some issues of lesser importance in my eyes I have yielded to what appears to be the overwhelming volume of immediate advantage.

On the vital issue of supporting the Labour government, I am constantly aware that, in the establishment of the principle of comprehensive schools, in the ending of evictions from normal rented property, in the advances it has made in social security and in many other spheres, it is doing a job that I regard as vital, despite all the shortcomings.

Yet at the same time I believe that I should be wrong to vote for government support for American policy in Vietnam, or an economic policy which I felt to be fundamentally mistaken, whatever the pressures.

All the same, common endeavours and experiences in the face of archaic procedures and close personal contacts take the edge off political antagonism. The atmosphere of the bars which do not keep normal licensing hours, of dinners and social functions which cut across party allegiances, blur differences of principle and overlay them with genuine ties of personal friendship and respect.

At the same time one is more and more cut off from one's roots. Evenings are often spent in the House or at constituency engagements of a non-partisan character. Less and less time is available for meeting and discussing with ordinary people who are not connected with some organization or another. The increase in MPs' pay, moreover – though a very large slice goes in carrying out one's duties – removed the real financial hardship which was the lot of members without private means before the 1964 general election.

As a member therefore one is subjected to a very strong though subtle influence away from the working-class background which one may previously have been accustomed to. Compromise, the toning down of extreme points of view, pragmatism, appear much more reasonable than ever before – even if one is not fully conscious of the change of emphasis.

Men whom a member of parliament before election never met and whom he regarded as implacably opposed to all he stood for, accept him as an equal and as a feature of the

Establishment. It is easy to conclude that class barriers are a figment of the imagination of the immature and of those with a grievance, and to fit cosily into one's environment, unconscious of the fact that all that has happened in reality is that one has penetrated those barriers which are, despite this, as real as ever, particularly for those who have not been elected Labour MPs.

All this, with the party whips in the background for example, make it much easier to argue the case against wage increases for lower-paid workers at a time of grave economic crisis, while accepting that the incomes of those in positions of great importance in society, like the judges, should be dramatically increased.

Thus in viewing my work as an MP I have mixed emotions. I am frustrated and sceptical at my inability to influence events or policy making, but anxious to keep a Labour government in power. I derive satisfaction from my constituency work, but begrudge the enormous inroads into my time which it makes.

At times I am subjected to a stream of hostile, even abusive letters, and I feel downhearted at the obvious dissatisfaction with what I am doing. Yet at other times I receive encouraging letters, expressions of gratitude and even offers of help.

My work as an MP has left me more convinced than ever of the need for drastic social change, even though I often despair of achieving it as long as we are obliged to work through ancient procedures designed to meet or frustrate the needs of a different age. It has left me convinced of the existence of a whole range of problems at the individual level which will never even be tackled unless far more of our national resources are devoted to housing, health services, education and social welfare. In this respect my socialist convictions are deeper than ever, for if such vast problems exist in a highly developed country like Britain, how much more must they exist in the world at large.

And therefore, frustrated as I am, I still believe that my work as an MP is worthwhile. Whenever I am asked, I am reluctant to concede that I enjoy it, but at least at the present I am glad to be there and intend in the future to do what I can to remain.

STAN NEWENS

THE AUTHOR

My early life was spent in Bethnal Green in the East End of London, where I was born in 1930 and where I attended an LCC primary school. In 1939, at the outbreak of war, my family moved out into west Essex, where I went to a village school and later a County grammar school until going to London University to take a degree in History, and to Westminster Training College for a post-graduate Certificate in Education.

By this time I had become very active in the Labour Party, but was strongly opposed to the Korean War. Though not a pacifist, I refused therefore to go into the armed forces, and spent the next three and a half years as a coal-face worker in the North Staffordshire coal-field. Here I continued my education, but in the new field of manual work and practical trade unionism.

In 1956 I returned to Essex and taught in a secondary school in East London, where I still have strong ties, until I was elected Labour member for Epping in 1964.

I am married with two children by my first wife, who died in 1962, and apart from my political and trade-union work, which includes being chairman of the Movement for Colonial Freedom, a CND supporter, and a member of the National Union of Teachers, as well as numerous other activities, I spend any remaining time studying local history, gardening, visiting places of interest and with my family.

Negotiating at the Top

We came from nearly every part of the country and represented every grade on our railways: shunters, drivers, guards, firemen, signalmen, technicians, salaried grades and every kind of goods, workshops, docks and waterways staff. On the NUR executive we talked for all railwaymen. Few of us liked London, apart perhaps from the four who lived and worked there.

London is a hard city; selfish, soul-destroying, full of deceit and inhibitions where nothing seems to matter more than property, position, possessions. It is a city with a very low sense of human values, invariably bringing the worst out of most people. It is a lonely place. On most evenings, as we made our way back to our digs, we in the executive were lonely men looking forward to Fridays and the week-end with our wives and families. The finest view of London to me was always Alexandra Palace, from the carriage window of an express train travelling north at eighty miles an hour.

When a working bloke suddenly finds himself serving his union on a full-time basis, living in London, he inevitably becomes vulnerable to change. Life at the top in the trade union movement, even for three years – the period for which, as laid down by rule, we serve on our executive – can bring out the real strength of character in a man. It can also feel out his weaknesses. For some it has done much. For others it has meant complete ruin: a broken home, scorn from those who once held them in such high regard.

I knew my course. I had been on the executive for more than two years. In less than a year I would be back on the footplate again. Mine was a small depot. We did not work any of the crack, named trains that thunder along at eighty, ninety and a hundred miles an hour. We worked the heavy, dirty coal trains from the Fife pits to the yards, docks and power stations where coal was needed. We signed on and off duty at all hours of the day and night. The work was very unromantic, but it called for a very high degree of skill; that kind of skill and knowledge that could not be picked up from textbooks or learned in colleges, but could only be acquired by years of experience on the job. When working these heavy loose-coupled trains, in a district with so many mining subsidences, curves and steep gradients, one wrong move on the part of the driver and a solid iron coupling would snap like a piece of thread.

Much had changed at my depot since I had been elected to the executive. Steam engines were now on their way out. Diesels were beginning to take their place. Worst of all, mine was essentially a coal-moving depot, right in the heart of the Fife coalfield, and with so many pits closing down there was now some doubt as to whether the depot would still be there when my time arrived to go back on the job. This was not unusual. Others on the Executive knew they would not be going back to the jobs they had left. They were no longer there to go back to.

I had been a railwayman twenty-five years: checker, porter, engine cleaner, and for twenty-three years a fireman. From an early age I had taken an active interest in trade unionism. As a boy, while others were running wild around the surrounding hills and pit bings, I could often be found standing, unnoticed, at the gable ends in the small village where I was born, listening to the miners, most of them out of work at that time, talking about the miners' unions.

I've always remembered the advice given me by an old miner, long since dead. A lifetime's just a wee while, he used to say, so live it straight and clean and honest. More recently I had had much advice from old Arthur, the engine driver from Warrington who had done more than one stint on the executive. Fearless, without tact, without guile, you could almost see the rough corners on him. He spoke just as he thought, and wrote just as he spoke. I liked him. He rarely wrote me a letter without at least one postscript. Take it easy for a start. Above all, work collectively. You will be amazed to find such bastards there are down there. P.S. If it wasn't for the interference of the government on the wages question, I'd say the forty-hour week was the most important issue. P.S. Try not to quarrel with the general secretary and watch the assistant from your country. P.S. See that personal correspondence is addressed to you at your private address in London, for correspondence is sometimes opened 'by accident' at Head Office. You are better with digs away from the rest.

Old Arthur had said that I would find out I still had a lot to learn. I knew I had. One of the first things I learned in London was how innocent I was.

Like most of us, I had felt confident that the new Labour government would do something to ease the plight of our railways. No union had worked harder to return Labour to power. It was there, we felt, our salvation lay. So far nothing had been done. And nothing, it appeared, was *being* done. Beeching was gone. His 'plan' was still with us.

For many months, quietly, patiently, we had been talking with the Railways Board. We were all working railwaymen with a high sense of responsibility. We also had a rather touchy, inbred pride and a strong sense of loyalty. To none of us was that bond of loyalty stronger than to our mates, the lads who had sent us to London to look after their interests.

Our members were among the lowest paid with the worst conditions in the country. In the past few years we had watched the complement of staff in the industry slump by over 150,000 through technical changes and wholesale closures, and our members had little to show for all this, except for some improvements in their redundancy agreements.

A trade union must legislate for those remaining in an industry as well as for those who are being driven out. Most people agreed that it was a disgrace that an engine driver should be forced to retire, after fifty years' service, on a pension of 13s. a week; or a porter, after the same length of service, on 9s. a week. And most people agreed that it was wrong that so many thousands of railwaymen should have to go home, after a full week's work, with less than £10 in their pockets. We also felt that because of their shift work railwaymen, like most other workers, should be given a forty-hour week and three weeks' annual holidays.

These were the things we had been talking about for so long. It was conceded that we had a strong case. But – ah, there was one snag, the railways were not paying their way. We were rather tired of hearing this. Were our dockyards, schools, hospitals, police force, army, navy, air force all paying their way? Were our sewers paying their way? The service we were providing was also vitally necessary. Our people, too, were entitled to decent wages, holidays, pensions and conditions.

We carried on talking. Our members were getting impatient. At last an offer was made by the chairman of the Railways Board. It fell a bit short of our modest claims. We were bound to take action. Convinced of the strength of our case, we could think of nothing better than to go to the Railway Staff National Tribunal. Then came the pawky move which resulted in our decision to bring all our members out on strike.

A Prices and Incomes Board had been set up. We were first of all approached *on the quiet* and asked to take our case to the new Board, then, after we had agreed privately to 'acquiesce' in going there, we were publicly approached on the question. We were sure that the Board was bound to find in our favour. No body of workers in the country could have gone there with a stronger case. Surely it would now be simply a matter of waiting. Justice would be done.

How wrong we were. Perhaps we deserved all we got. Having so many of the country's lower-paid workers in our own union, we had supported the government's prices and incomes policy, immorally wanting it to work for workers in other industries but not for those in our own. Although we had been tricked into going to the Prices and Incomes Board, we went there in good faith, and under Clause 15 of a White Paper which made special provision for the lower-paid workers.

The report from the PIB recommended worse, much worse, than what had already been offered by the Railways

Board. Something had to be done about it. We simply could not sit back passively. Our pride had been sorely hurt. Worse, we had all been cheated.

We talked about the report when we went for our tea that night. We talked about it as we smoked over a pint, thought about it as we sat and watched a show. We were still pondering over it as we went home to our bed-sitters. Some of us felt we had been kicked in the teeth. Most of us felt we had been getting kicked in the teeth far too often and for far too long.

We were lonely men as we went to bed that night.

A special meeting of the executive committee was called. We were twenty-three angry men around the massive table inside the oak-panelled boardroom at Unity House. In the vernaculars from every part of the country anger was expressed. The resolution calling for strike action was moved and seconded. There were no amendments. Three voted against.

We knew the implications of a national rail strike. Our decision had not been taken lightly. What other decision could we have taken? We could not take our case to the Railway Staff National Tribunal. Not now. Not after having just been to the highest tribunal in the country.

Until we took that decision, the impression seemed to prevail that railways did not matter very much any longer. The attitude began to show signs of change now, slowly at first, then in a very profound way as the hour of decision drew nearer. We did not want a strike. We wanted justice.

Some people in high places tried to make us lonely men feel more lonely than ever. They declared that they would not talk to us until we withdrew our decision to strike. We did not withdraw our decision. People did talk to us. At times we could not get our tea at night, could hardly get to our beds, for people wanting to talk to us. It was pleasing to see that railwaymen still mattered.

The chairman of the Railways Board was the first to ask us to talk to him. He begged us on the negotiating team to call off the strike decision so that he could have a proper talk with us. He certainly was not going to talk to us *under duress*. So he said, anyway; then he went on to do nearly all the talking.

I felt sorry for him that morning. He was a man with tremendous responsibility, but very little power. He said that all he did was eat, drink and sleep railways. Could we help him to help us? For nearly an hour he talked, talked desperately. Yes, he did have something to offer. It might not be as much as wholly to satisfy us. But it might ease the situation.

What do you have to offer?

I am not going to negotiate *under duress*.

Fair enough. We went into another room, had a quiet chat among ourselves, decided that we could not recommend to the full executive that the strike decision be withdrawn without any positive offer having been made, then went back to tell the chairman of the Railways Board just exactly where we stood.

He seemed a very lonely man as we picked up our papers and made our way back to the boardroom in Unity House.

It was the next morning before we reported back to the full executive. Not only was our strike decision reaffirmed, we were more resolute than ever, with only two voting against. Then, around five that evening, things began to get more eventful. Just as we were getting ready to go for tea a whisper went round the building that a special government messenger had called at the office. The First Secretary of State wanted to meet us in *our* boardroom. Could he come along in an hour's time? Of course he could. We knew the strength of our case.

Meeting ministers of the government in times like these was not unusual. But for one of them to want to come and meet us was a bit away from the ordinary. And was not this the man who had persuaded us to take our claim to the PIB in the first place?

We went into session at six o'clock. It was shortly after that that our guest arrived. He had with him a male secretary and a female note-taker. He looked fatigued. The usual bounce was out of his step, a key chain dangled down the side of his trouser leg, a handkerchief hung untidily half out of his pocket and his normally high-pitched voice came through a bit flat at times.

Straight away he told us he was first and foremost a trade unionist, one of us. He couldn't understand why the hell we were being so obstructive.

He had been given a chair beside the huge oval table, quite near to the president. For a while he talked, then sank back in the chair, silent. He threw back his head again and told us that there was quite a lot he could do to help us, but we must first of all take away the strike threat. Had the situation not been one of such gravity, it would all have been very entertaining.

Keep the strike threat on and it's over the bloody brink we go. If you want to go over the brink, it's over the bloody brink we go. I know where I stand. I'm a trade unionist first, second, third and fourth. That's me. If we lose the next election I'll go back to the T & GW. But I want to help you. I can help you. So let's sit and talk. But get your strike called off. While it's on I can't do a thing.

Our strike decision stayed. Then he went on – under duress – to tell us all about the improvements he had to offer. There were four issues on which we were seeking improvements. Wages. Pensions. Hours. Holidays. He was anxious to help us. Just tell me what you want. We did. Oh – no, we could not have that. But I'll bring forward your forty-hour week by four weeks. Or instead of an extra three days' holidays for staff with more than ten years' service, I'll give you an extra two days for everybody with more than five years' service. Just tell me what you want.

We want the $3\frac{1}{2}$ per cent increase brought forward from October to February. And we want to hear more about the better pensions we've been promised.

No. I've absolutely no reason to say I can give you anything on pensions. But if you pushed me really hard, possibly I could help you on money. Possibly. Perhaps I could have the $3\frac{1}{2}$ per cent brought forward four weeks. That would cost a million pounds. But don't push me hard on that one. I want you to settle on those two other things I've offered.

He sank back into the chair again.

A sense of humour is a grand thing at times like these. We sat quiet for a bit, watching, waiting. One of the lads quietly suggested that we should take our guest downstairs and give him a drink.

But he had been silent for somewhat longer this time. Slowly, looking very tired, he raised his head. He looked about the circle of faces around him. Then he glowered across the table at the blacksmith's striker from Cowlairs who was seated directly opposite. You. Yes – you! Look at me when I'm talking!

He was lucky that time. The blacksmith's striker from Cowlairs Works did not like people talking to him in an offensive way. We waited for the clash. It did not come. There could be but one answer. The blacksmith's striker, being rather deaf, used a hearing aid. He could not have been tuned in when the remark was fired at him. He must have switched off some time ago.

It was the wagon examiner from Glasgow who began to insist that our guest leave the boardroom so that we could seriously debate all that had been put before us. As soon as he was outside we began the debate.

Some were really worried. Some had begun to weaken all right. But our guest was with us again. He had another proposition to make. You've heard my offer. Well you can have any of the two things I've offered. Any two things. I don't want to go over the bloody brink with you. I'm a trade unionist. I *will* go over the bloody brink if I have to. But I don't want to. I want to help you. So you can have any two things from the four things I've offered. We're tired. And I've other work to do. Call your bloody strike off. Do that tonight. Then, first thing in the morning, my good friend Sidney and another four of you – more if you like – can come along to my flat and we can sort the whole thing out over breakfast.

Again we asked him to leave the boardroom. We did a lot of talking. Time limits were lifted. Standing orders were pushed aside. Several times our guest wanted to return.

At 9.30 a note was handed in. It read: It will be a terrible tragedy if things go wrong. Some of us began to wonder who was really *under duress* now. Shortly after that note was handed in, our feelings were tested. A vote was taken. By eleven votes to eleven our strike was still on.

Our guest must have been a lonely man as he motored back to Whitehall that night.

But still we went on talking, still *under duress*.

Again we met the Railways Board. Again I felt sorry for the chairman. He was trying his utmost, within his very limited powers, to resolve the position, but nobody had bothered to tell him anything about all that had been offered by others with greater authority. In his innocence he offered us less, and with a whole number of strings attached. Never could he have felt more lonely than when that debacle of a meeting ended.

The clocks kept ticking away. The hour of decision was drawing near. As we climbed the stone staircase to that room at Storeys Gate where, with representatives from the other rail unions, we had been once more invited to meet members of the government, we knew that in just more than sixty hours time the signals on our railways would all be switched to danger and wheels would come grinding to a halt. If the strike took place, no one would ever be able to count the cost. To have it called off, something like £5,000,000 was needed.

The government had a formidable platform at Storeys Gate that morning. There was the First Secretary of State, the Minister of Labour and the Minister of Transport. They looked well sitting there. They must have found it comforting to know that the other rail unions were against strike action. There was some talk about winks being as good as nods to blind horses. We were not interested in nods and winks and blind horses. We wanted straight talk and some concrete improvements in what had been offered. No progress was made.

When I went home to my bed-sitter that night a note had been handed in asking me to be at Storeys Gate at ten o'clock the next morning again. The setting was much the same as it had been the morning before, except that we were gathered in a smaller room and the other rail unions had not been invited. The strain had been considerable over the past ten days, meeting all those people *under duress* who kept saying that they would not meet us *under duress*. Just before the eleven–eleven vote was cast in our boardroom, one of the lads had been called away to the funeral of a close relative. There was much speculation as to how he would have voted. Only he knew. Now we would all know.

Some of the chinks in our armour, scarcely perceivable at first, were now gaping cracks. Could a majority hold out? We were wielding the only weapon we possessed. It was still a powerful weapon. Our real strength lay in the strength of our case.

Nothing new was put to us. It was all the mixture as before, although there were some new *promises* about new concepts of our railways and their true role, and about the tin can being kicked from the tail of public transport, and about big changes being introduced as quickly as possible. After a lot of talking the three members of the government and their scribes left the room and we went into private session. Feelings ran rather high. The strain had been too much for one of us. He didn't talk, he shouted, as desperately, unashamedly, he tried everything to get the strike called off. There were less than forty hours left. A vote was taken. We reaffirmed our decision by twelve votes to eleven. The First Secretary of State came back into the room, alone, heard of our decision, made the sign of a cross on his breast, then said something about hoping we would still all be friends when the whole thing was over.

He looked a lonely man as he sat there with a whole side of that huge table all to himself.

We were very hungry. We had been in that room for

hours. It seemed that they might have been trying to starve us into submission. We had asked for sandwiches. Some had been brought in, but not enough to go round. As it was now long past lunchtime, we moved off in groups in search of something to eat.

This was Friday. I felt like a wash. This was the day we normally went home for the week-end. Not this week-end. It was around five when I got back to Unity House, so I decided to give my wife a ring. It was she who told me I had to go to 10 Downing Street at six o'clock. That was in less than an hour's time. That was the first of me hearing anything about that invitation. Was this the Prime Minister wanting to talk to us now, still *under duress*? Yes, it was. A special announcement had been made on TV. Official word had now reached the office.

On guard against another hungry session, instead of having a shower and a shave, I chose to have something to eat. A few of us went down to our usual little café, just off Euston Road. We must have looked a bit scruffy as we squeezed into a taxi, for when the cabby asked us where we were going and we told him 10 Downing Street he thought we were trying to be funny. We had a job convincing him that that was where we really wanted to go.

The final curtain was raised now, the last act about to begin. Our reception was warm, could not have been more friendly. The Prime Minister was there to shake each of our hands in turn. Here was the professional politician; the successful, professional politician, right in form, pretending to be quite unperturbed by the trend of events. Yes, just show them all into the Cabinet room. We can talk in there. We'll all be able to squeeze in. And in we went. Took our seats. We were all made to feel very much at home.

Our host looked fresh and youthful, had a nice tan. Where did he get that at this time of the year? Or was it a tan. Perhaps he had just had his make-up on in readiness for appearing before the cameras later in the evening. He certainly looked well. And so did Sister Barbara on his left, although Brother Ray, on his right, was not looking too good, already beginning to show beads of sweat on his brow. Someone said he had been ill. We all noticed that one of the leading performers was missing.

There was very little pomp and a lot less ceremony here. Of course, we now had only thirty hours left in which to sort out our differences. Now then, are we all here? And you've all got a seat? Fine. The whisky was there too. So was the brandy, the cigars, the cigarettes. Drinks were poured. The beer, sausages, pies and sandwiches were to be brought in later.

He got down to the job straight away. Now you've all got a drink? Fine. We are meeting here completely informally. I've chased all the civil servants out of the place. Although we are not all members of the same party, we are all members of the same movement. And we want to look at a much broader canvas than the PIB Report. I was once employed by your union, you know, to work out problems of finance. And I'm the only prime minister who has had a railwayman for a grandfather – and he wasn't a director.

He had much to tell us. He had a high regard for Fraser, but *he* was not getting on with the job fast enough. That's why I've appointed Barbara to the job. She's been given *her* mandate. She's getting on with it. I am very concerned about the future of our transport industry, including railways. But I have also the responsibility of fixing the date for the next general election. I must not make the wrong decision on that.

He'd better not make the wrong decision on this either. We must make that clear to him. We did. Railwaymen are beginning to lose faith in this government. We are not asking for much. Unless you help us out of our difficulties you are going to lose a lot of seats at the next general election, no matter who fixes the date. We could reach agreement straight away if you agree to have our $3\frac{1}{2}$ per cent increase brought forward from October to the end of February. That's all there is between us.

He had expected us to make that point. Of course he had. There was a faint trace of a smile in his eyes as he took the pipe from his mouth and had a small sip of brandy. He spoke very quietly. I'm talking politically now. Many people want a showdown between us. If there is a showdown, while we may lose a few 'railway' seats, we can win the next election by a landslide. Make no mistake about that. We lose lots of votes every time the fares go up. That is one of the reasons why Barbara is on the job. There will still be closures. Of course there will. But I am trying hard to get rid of the old outlook. I would like this to be the start of a happier era for all of us.

A cockney voice spoke next, in even lower tones than those we had just heard from the other side of the table. This is the second time we've been caught up in a situation of this kind. The last time was with Selwyn Lloyd. All we seek is to have the 3½ per cent brought forward to the date of operation of the forty-hour week. That would help to restore the Guillebaud comparability.

He laid down his pipe, smoothed his hair. You railwaymen are caught between the wind and the water. And not for the first time. You can't make a wage claim on the basis of profitability. We cannot relate many railwaymen to productivity in the same way as we cannot relate a hospital nurse to productivity. I can understand you wanting to fight to improve the conditions of your members. It's your job to do that. I would be doing the same. But in the present situation we are in a jam. Your union is like my constituency. It has more than its share of the country's lower-paid workers. I want to do something for you. I regret you've been pushed into a corner. But every penny you get goes on to the taxpayer. My job is to govern. If there is going to be a strike everything is in the melting pot.

There is no need for a strike. All we want is to have the 3½ per cent brought forward.

If I said I could bring forward the 3½ per cent I would be deluding you. I wish it was as easy as you suggest.

Anyway, you say you can't bring forward the 3½ per cent.

To say I could would be deluding you. I appreciate you have a very strong case, a very compelling case. And, as I've said, you carry more than your share of the country's lower-paid workers. I would like to talk to you about the whole structure of wages in your industry, I would like to examine the whole structure of wages within your industry. I want to get these talks started straight away. We can have our first meeting a month tonight. I can take the chair at that first meeting. It will fall on my birthday, but that's all right. Ray can possibly take over the chair after the first meeting. I am not asking you to give up Guillebaud. I feel that decent wages must be tied up with productivity, but I am not pressing you on that just now either. What we need now is to be able to sit down and talk in a better atmosphere. So I'm at your disposal the whole of tonight and tomorrow as well, if you like.

That quiet calm voice from Glasgow again. If you can't move to get us out of our present troubles, I don't see much sense in us having an all-night sitting. We've had a hectic day. So I suggest that we break up here and now, go home for a meal, have a good night's sleep, and we can, if you like, meet again tomorrow when we all feel fresh and rested.

Oh, no, we mustn't do that. All eyes are on us. We must stay here and do all we can within our power to clear things up. There is a battery of lights and cameras on that door out there. Just have another drink. I'm having some beer and some food brought in. Have another drink while we're waiting. And have a cigar. Just pass the box round. I'm not sure where these came from. A present from somewhere, I suppose. . . . The stakes were running high now. Bluffs were being called. It was like a siege. The clock kept ticking away.

Sandwiches. Pies. Sausages. Whisky. Beer. More cigars. Yawns. The clock ticking. From where was the compromise to come?

It was nearly nine o'clock when we adjourned, our whole executive, along with the officers, going into another room. Tension was high. We had been offered nothing new, apart from a few more promises. Passionate pleas were made for the strike decision to be withdrawn. Others stood firm, calling for an adjournment so that we could resume talks in a healthier atmosphere after a good night's rest. Good night's rest, said a small voice, where can I get a good night's rest. I haven't slept for nights on end. More talking. In my own mind I was absolutely convinced that it was now simply a case of holding out. The money was there all right. The £5 million, a once and for all payment to bring the $3\frac{1}{2}$ per cent forward a few months, to avert the national catastrophe which, we had been told, a rail strike would bring in its wake. We had been told we had a *compelling* case. All that was needed was to get a decision which would enable us to return to the Cabinet room and make it known that we had decided on an adjournment.

That was not to be. Now some were speaking in a quiet, broken tone of voice, unable to conceal their worry about the situation. They begged those who still stood firm to call off the decision to strike. See how much the members stand to lose if the strike takes place? See how little they stand to gain? Was it not the government we were about to take on? *Our* government. The government we had worked so hard to put in office. Could we beat the government? Of course we couldn't. We have already won concessions, big concessions. Most important of all were the assurances we had been given on the future of the industry itself. What could mean more to us than to have these mass redundancies checked at last? The whole of the Beeching-Marples concept of our railways was to be destroyed. Had we not just been promised so? Of course we had. But go ahead with the strike and everything is lost.

All of us did not share these views. None of us knew what was going on outside that room as we debated inside. Those outside held the trump cards inasmuch as they knew they could force us to sweat it out right up until the very last hour. Theirs was to be a very shallow victory. Had we taken a decision for an adjournment, those outside would have had to do the sweating. They were fully prepared for their sweat not to last too long.

Unknown to us, as we each argued for what we felt was in the best interests of our members, urgent calls were being sent out to bring more people on to the stage before the final curtain was rung down. On to the side wings had been brought officials from the other rail unions, along with the Chancellor of the Exchequer, the man with the purse.

Why had those others been brought in? Had we not decided by thirteen votes to ten to call off our decision to strike, we would all have known. But we never knew those others were in the building until we began to gather in the hallway around one o'clock in the morning to wait for the transport that was being laid on to take us home to our bed-sitters.

ROBERT BONNAR

THE AUTHOR

I was born in the small Fife mining village of Hill of Beath. My father was a miner, and I was the second oldest in a family of ten: four brothers and five sisters. Aged forty-four, I'm married with two sons of seventeen and nineteen.

I worked at anything and everything until I found steady employment on the railway at the age of sixteen when war was declared in 1939. I had an early interest in trade unionism, and became secretary of the shed committee when I was twenty-two. I must have stood the test of time as I have again been made secretary of the same committee.

I hated school, it was like a prison to me. I would much rather have been working, earning, to make things easier for the large family to which I belonged.

I went to secondary school when I was twelve. This was even more like prison. Masters seemed to enjoy thinking that miners' sons were incapable of being educated. I applied for exemption from school when I was thirteen, but the application was turned down.

I am very fond of poetry. I have written a novel with a strong railway background called Stewartie, *which was published three years ago. I hope to publish another on which I have been working for some time.*

I served on the executive committee of the NUR for a three-year period, 1964–6.

The Unemployed Self

BY ALVIN W. GOULDER

The quality of work in industrial society, like several other realms there, is not quite what it seems. (Or perhaps the trouble is that it is exactly what it seems.) The world of work is, on the one side, a familiar world of mundane meanings and routine encounters, a hammer and saw, a button and switch, a mix together and assemble world, a pound and shilling and a buy and sell world, a Monday through Friday world – a perfectly ordinary, everyday world. That, on the one side; but there is also another.

Cached within the self-contained shell of industrial affluence of power, and of seemingly settled meaning, there is another, inner world – a not-enough world. We may glimpse it in some of the comments made: this not-enough world, says the toolmaker, is 'the fundamentally alien world of machines . . .'. It is, remarks the town planner, a world of 'interest and energy evaporated'; it is also, asserts the storeman, a place where there is a lack of 'those things that make men human – a certain dignity, a measure of equality and above all . . . self-respect'. For many in modern industrial society, for the member of parliament no less than the coal-miner, the world of work then is one of human insufficiency or of downright failure in the midst of technological triumph, of personal confusion in the midst of detailed organizational blueprints. Men's resistance to work is ingenious and ancient and the complaints about it are familiar and traditional. Yet in reading these reports I also thought I detected the emergence of a somewhat new sound, the still muffled sound of a slow and steady leak in the well-engineered world of work; an emerging awareness that work, as many know it, is nothing less than the wasting of life.

In what follows, I shall try to outline my understanding of some of the sources and significances of this sense of a life wasted: I shall try to do so in a manner that sees work as part of a larger system and from a standpoint which, if it does not explicitly exhibit a systematic perspective may, at least, suggest some of its lineaments.

In industrial society, with its complex division of labour and its confining occupational specializations, no man is responsible for any object, but only for a function of it. We buy things from persons who know (or care) little about how they work, have them maintained by servicemen who know only a bit more, and these objects were made in the first place not by any one man who could see and understand them as a whole. In the passage from the largely agricultural and craft economy, in which the maker of things commonly sold them, to an industrial and commercial one, we have created a mountain of objects that no one has made, that few can maintain, that fewer still know much if anything about, even though surrounded by them daily in homes and work places. The 'alien world of machines' is only a special case of the alien world of objects in industrial society. We commonly know little or nothing about how these objects work, and content ourselves with knowing what they are supposed to do, that is with their supposed usefulness.

Our orientation toward most objects then is, in the first place, concerned with their usefulness and, in the second, when there is a plethora of objects to choose from, with their design, appearance or decoration. In referring to this ordering or priority of standards, it is not my intention to denigrate aesthetic criteria, but only to suggest the place they have in contemporary society. For most of us, decorative considerations are secondary to, and are made within a framework of, utilitarian concerns. Indeed, this is why they are deemed decoration rather than art. So pervasive and powerful are standards of utility that even conceptions of true or fine art – as distinct from decoration – are commonly formulated with reference to them, often entailing a polemical emphasis on pure form. Art, that is, is negatively defined; it is that which does *not* serve a practical use or does not have an instrumental significance.

In large reaches of our society, but particularly in its industrial sector, it is not the man that is wanted. It is, rather, the function he performs and it is the skill with which he performs it for which he is paid. If a man's skill is not needed, the man is not needed. If a man's function can be performed more economically by a machine, the man is replaced. This has at least two obvious implications. First, that opportunities for social participation in the industrial sector are contingent upon a man's imputed usefulness, so that in order to gain admission to it – and the rewards it brings – people must submit to an education and to a socialization that early validates and cultivates only selected parts of themselves, that is, those that are expected to have subsequent utility. Secondly, once admitted to participation in the industrial sector, men are appraised and rewarded in terms of their utility and are advanced or removed in accordance with their utility as compared with that of other men.

Both processes have, of course, one common consequence, namely, they operate as selective mechanisms, admitting some persons and some individual talents or faculties, while at the same time excluding still others, thereby roughly dividing men and their talents into two pools, those useful and those not useful to industrial society. So far as men are concerned, the not useful may constitute the unemployed or the unemployables, the aged, unskilled, unreliable or intractable. Much the same selective inclusion and exclusion occurs so far as the attributes of individual persons are concerned. The useless qualities of persons are, at first, either unrewarded or actively punished should they intrude upon the employment of a useful skill. In other words, the system rewards and fosters those skills deemed useful and suppresses the expression of talents and faculties deemed useless, and thereby structures and imprints itself upon the individual personality and self.

Correspondingly, the individual learns what the system requires; he learns which parts of himself are unwanted and unworthy; he comes to organize his self and personality in conformity with the operating standards of utility, and thereby minimizes his costs of participating in such a system. In short, vast parts of any personality must be suppressed or repressed in the course of playing a role in industrial society. All that a man is that is not useful will somehow be excluded, or at least not be allowed to intrude, and he thereby becomes alienated or estranged from a large sector of his own interests, needs and capacities. Thus, just as there are unemployed men, there is also the unemployed self. Here, then, in the exclusions of self fostered by an industrial system oriented towards utility, is a fundamental source of the sense of a life wasted which is so pervasive, even if muffled, in an industrial society. For the excluded self, while muffled, is not voiceless and makes its protest heard. That it also takes its revenge upon its betrayer is illustrated, with sad but poetic justice, in the personal life of the ascetic prophet of time and motion studies, F. W. Taylor, who spent his days creating a hellish efficiency and who spent his nights propped up, perpetually stricken with insomnia and nightmares.

A central problem confronting a society organized around utilitarian values is the disposal and control of 'useless' men and of their useless traits. So far as useless men are concerned, various strategies of disposal may be noted. They may, for example, be ecologically separated out and extruded into spatially distant locales where they are not painfully visible to the useful. They may be placed, as American Indians were, on reservations; they may come to live in ethnic ghettos, as American Negroes do; or, if they have the means to do so, they may choose to live in benign environments as in communities for the aged in Florida; they may be placed in special training or retraining camps, as with certain unskilled and unemployed American youth, often Negro; or again, they may be placed in prisons or in insane asylums following routine certification by juridical or medical authorities.

A transition to a welfare state implies a greater involvement of the state in the planning for and in the management of disposal strategies. In some part, the growth of the welfare state means that the disposal problem is becoming so great and complex that it can no longer be left to the informal control of market or traditional institutions. Increasingly, the welfare state's disposal strategies seek to transform the sick, the deviant, and the unskilled into 'useful citizens', and to return them to 'society' after periods of hospitalization, treatment, counselling, training or retraining. It is this emphasis upon the reshaping of persons which differentiates the welfare state's disposal strategies from those earlier employed, which tended to cope with the useless primarily by custody, exclusion and insulation from society. The newer strategies differ from the old in that they are, in the long run, self-financing, for the aim is to increase the supply of the useful and to diminish that of the useless.

One problem with this strategy, however, is that it is a treadmill operation: it is continually striving to keep abreast of continuing increases in mechanization and automation, with their tendency to generate at least temporary unemployment of men and continual obsolescence of skills. In one part, the welfare state constitutes an effort to use the state to dispose of the uselessness created by the private sector's own familiar disposal strategies which are, fundamentally, mechanization and automation. That is, in the private sector the useless traits of persons are eliminated, so far as they can be, by creating machines which perform functions once performed by men without, however, being linked to useless traits.

Within the private sector, the central disposal strategies developed are programmes for 'human relations in industry'. These constitute an effort to cope with the problems of the unemployed self, to teach management how to utilize the useless parts of self, by redefining these as not being useless. That is, the excluded self is now seen as impinging on the effective employment of skills, and non-pecuniary motives are seen as affecting productivity. Thus larger and larger reaches of self and social structure are fitted into utilitarian appraisal. Here the system has not changed its values, but simply extended the range of things it seeks to manage from the same utilitarian standpoint. Modern sophisticated management thus seeks to subject the 'informal' group structures of factory life, which had hitherto provided opportunities for the compensatory expression of human qualities excluded or neglected by utilitarian culture, and to bring these under deliberate and rational management. It sees a new usefulness in these once neglected social structures, and it extends the sway of utilitarian standards over them, thereby cutting off the sociological hinterland into which the personality could formerly retreat and from which it could once wage a kind of guerrilla resistance.

In other words, one of the main disposal strategies of a utilitarian culture is continuously to transform useless things into useful 'by-products'; personality components and social structures hitherto regarded as areas of privacy, and once ignored or junked, now become viewed as potentially useful. The escape routes become increasingly closed. With such enclosures, the unemployed self is required increasingly to cease resistance altogether, or to come out in open rebellion against the system's utilitarian values.

The welfare state will in good time discover that this, a very new breed of problem, confronts it, and will bestir itself once again. It is in the nature of the welfare state to be a counter-puncher, acting only after and in response to the acute emergence of a 'problem'. Yet, insofar as it seeks to mobilize itself against these new problems it will, I suspect, be even more ineffectual than usual. For one thing, the welfare apparatus that will be used against the middle-class deserters of utilitarian culture will be staffed by those who have already caught, or who are vulnerable to, the malaise that they will be asked to stamp out. The administrative classes of the modern state have not even been able to safeguard themselves from foreign subversion and espionage! How much more receptive, then, will they be to a domestic subversion of a utilitarian social order that can be defined as a new form of Enlightenment? Still, their vested interest will require that they do something. Whatever their private adaptations, I think it likely that they will increasingly define the various forms of resistance to utilitarian culture as a 'sickness' or illness that requires humane and expert treatment by competent authorities – psychiatrists, social workers, counsellors, etc.

The problem-solving style of the welfare state is, I have suggested, a reactive and *post factum* one. Since its operations are costly, the middle class is loath to submit to taxes except for problems already fully manifest. Rather than taking a lead on the target, therefore, the welfare state commonly shoots directly at or behind it. The ineffectuality of the welfare state, however, derives fundamentally from the fact that it must seek solutions within the framework of the master institutions that cause the problem. It tends, therefore, to search for better remedial arrangements – for example, for better prisons and reformatories – rather than for the causes and prevention of crime. Accommodate as it must to the private sector, the welfare state will commonly prefer to attack problems whose 'solutions' yield gratifications to those supplying them, quite apart from their effectiveness in relieving the suffering of those who experience the problem. Nations thus pile up armaments without any relation to the degree that these enhance national security. Similarly, the level of activity of the welfare state, or of investment in it, bears little demonstrable connexion with the effectiveness of its programme. Often, what finally clinches the adoption of a welfare programme – i.e., the selection of a specific solution – is not merely the visibility of a critical problem, not only a humane concern for human suffering, and not only a prudent political preparation for the next election. What is also of particular importance is that the solution adopted requires public expenditures for goods and services to be disbursed among those who are *not* on welfare. It is this that enables the welfare state to attract and retain a middle-class constituency.

It is in the nature of a one-dimensional society, where each specialized role and organization has its own narrow span of attention, to produce a host of unanticipated and often troublesome consequences. The task of the welfare state is to pick these up, one by one, as they surface to public visibility. It is the great number and enormous variety of these problems that underlies the massive sprawl of the welfare state, which leads it to seek and acquire responsibility for all manner of new problems, to develop a sensitivity to their interaction, and a conception that its task is not simply the management of an economy but rather of a society composed of diverse and interdependent elements. The welfare state, in short, has an interest in and a need to think in terms of 'social systems', and it correspondingly develops an ideology that counterposes a concern for broader social utilities to the narrower and more traditional economic utility. Correspondingly, the welfare state has a need to use and to mobilize all forms of intellectual expertise, and particularly those whose interests reflect the multi-dimensional character of the state's concerns.

It is in large measure because this is the nature of sociology that it becomes, *par excellence*, the social science of the welfare state, at least in that period after Keynesian economics permitted intervention with respect to more traditional economic variables. The distinctive organizing focus of contemporary sociology, particularly of its dominating school of 'functional theory', is on society as a system of interacting variables, upon the manner in which their complex interaction commonly yields unanticipated consequences, and, also, a tendency to neglect or to take as given the role of economic variables.

The principal ideological thrust of mature functional theory in sociology was aimed at overcoming the narrowly economic conception of utility common to the early middle class and its political economy. It sought to show that every social phenomenon – not merely those deliberately planned – persisted only because it had some 'social function', even if unintended and unrecognized. Functional theory served to defend traditional, non-economic, social arrangements from a parochial criticism based on a narrowly conceived standard of economic utility; it sought to show that if things were not economically useful they were, nonetheless, socially 'functional'. In these respects, modern sociology could not more fully reflect and coordinate with the aims of the welfare state if it had been expressly designed to do so.

The welfare state is thus the repository of problems generated by a one-dimensional society; it is an accommodation to associational egoism. It is a public sector that attacks problems produced by the organization of the private sector, but which must do so in ways that are limited by the capacity of its solutions to yield gratifications to those who are not suffering from the problems with which it attempts to cope. But the development of the welfare state does not oppose the basic principle of utility on which industrial society is organized; instead, it constitutes an accommodation to it which allows the private sector to maintain its narrow commitment to utility. The welfare society becomes the agency through which the useless are resocialized into an 'adjustment' to a useful life. Welfare and the welfare state are the socialized expressions of the commitment to utility.

That workers in modern industrial societies express a sense and a fear of a life wasted testifies in some part, I would suggest, to the gradual attenuation of the problem of exploitation – at least in these societies – and to the fact that the increased provision of elemental needs may have now permitted the surfacing of a problem at the root of our industrial system, that of human uselessness; a human uselessness generated not only by hard times but during work and by employment itself. Increasingly, the problem of exploitation is giving way to the problem of uselessness. The bitter truth seems to be that the current militancy of

American Negroes is less a product of their exploitation than of their growing uselessness in an increasingly automated economy. One can bargain and negotiate and thus affect the terms and conditions of exploitation; but one can only grow desperate and overtly rebellious in the face of a sense of growing uselessness. For when men are not wanted at all, when they have little or nothing that they can give which is deemed useful, then they can only turn to the generation of *dis*utilities – in short, the production of cost-increasing protest – to have their needs met.

In earlier stages of industrialization the central problem of the working class was the achievement of the basic requisites for both individual survival and, also, of family maintenance and thus of the stable incomes necessary for these. Among those sections of the working classes in the advanced industrial nations whose real incomes have historically improved, what abides in working-class discontent with work seems to be nothing less than the most fundamental of discontents, the unemployed self's sense of life wasted. To this degree, the discontents of the working class merge increasingly with those of an increasingly bureaucratized middle-class and white-collar group. From this standpoint, then, it would be expected that the character and the intensity of modern class-conflicts or alliances will be changing radically.

The malaise of modern industrial society, then, derives from the fact that it relates to men and incorporates them primarily as utilities useful for performing functions, that it has no commitment toward the talents or needs of men except as they are useful in the production of marketable objects or services. It pays for a man's skills but everything else he is, or has, or wants, is – within the context of producing objects or services – subordinated to their efficient employment.

Disturbing though it is, the sense of a life wasted is commonly expressed, at least by workers who have participated in the growing affluence or who have experienced steady employment, with cloudy pathos rather than sharp polemic.

When verbalizable at all, it is voiced with an almost shy diffidence. One reason for this is that many are afraid to see the full dimensions of the problem clearly. They may glimpse it, but are not sure that they can believe what they see. Moreover, there is no institutional or organizational framework within which men can openly communicate this view of the industrial world to one another, and might thereby validate their sense of its reality. For unions, after all, limit and confine the range of the freely discussable, even among their own members, to that which is contractually relevant. To this extent they are participants in the repressive process.

And most politically powerful socialist parties have largely accepted the premises of a repressive utilitarianism, particularly as they come to power and equate national productivity with national power and security. The unemployed self, then, still largely tends to be a latent rather than a manifest social problem, a festering but suppressed problem, and a not yet well focalized and publicly voiced grievance. The wasted life is the big secret that everyone suspects but that all are embarrassed to discuss and may, therefore, remain thankfully uncertain about. Central to the repression of this problem is that, first, men often feel it was ever thus, that not very much can be done about it now or in the future, that it is best not to dwell on the insoluble and, secondly, the further sense that the utilitarian arrangements that stunt their lives are somehow fundamentally legitimate. Men today can often no more imagine that it is possible that things might be otherwise than could the greatest philosophers of antiquity imagine a world without slaves. In other words, most workers believe in the validity of the very arrangements that waste their lives.

Having suggested that the problem of work cannot be understood apart from the constraints of the utilitarian, one-dimensional culture, what are the prospects of transforming this culture in directions that would permit the remedy of work and its dissatisfactions? One of the more popular and beguiling conceptions of the future conceives of the present as essentially transitional and self-correcting. With the fuller development of automation, it is expected that the amount of time required by work will in the future be so reduced that work will no longer be so significant a centre of human dissatisfactions. It is assumed that, even if the utilitarian character of work remains unchanged, its net impact on persons' lives will be altered fundamentally. Work will then still be unpleasant but, like sitting in a dentist's chair, relief will be but a few minutes away.

From this perspective, life will then devolve around freely chosen leisure pursuits to which the central part of the day will be devoted, and the sacrifice of self in work will become marginal. The assumptions involved are essentially those of evolutionary positivism with the traditional messianic expectations attached to technology and science. In the contemporary, as in the classical version of the theory, the future is already here. That is, the future is conceived of as being only quantitatively different from the present; it will just be more of the same – more and more technological development. And this, it is implied, is in any event irresistible, so why fight it? Why not simply ride the wave of the future, allowing it to take us to shore. In this happy beach-boy philosophy the anticipated future contains the remedy of the present. The technology that once confined and enslaved us will be transformed into its opposite, now liberating us into a fulfilling life of leisure. In this view, there is no need to struggle for a better existence, for the development of technology – on which all this is said to depend – is deemed absolutely certain. It is paradoxical that this position is often held by men who otherwise take a dim view of deterministic philosophies. They have simply graciously decided to make an exception of technology.

Yet they are not alone, for so far as the development of technology is concerned, it seems that almost everyone is a determinist. And determinists must be optimists in this matter. Those who regard the development of modern technology as irresistible are under considerable pressure to see a virtue in this necessity, and to focus selectively upon its benign outcomes. Otherwise they would be in much the same position as devout believers who have become convinced that their all powerful God meant them no good, or was indifferent to their fate. Many men could simply not accept such a prospect. It is certainly more comforting to believe that either God – or the God-in-the-machine – means to save us in the end.

Such a prospect of a purely technological salvation implies that the present is in essence benign; that it already contains the seeds of its own salvation; that no basic changes need to be sought or made in the master institutions or the deeper structures of our culture.

Yet one may accept the postulated extrapolation of technological development, but still doubt that the resultant increase in leisure will benignly resolve the problems of a utilitarian culture. For one thing, it very much depends upon how men will use – or be allowed to use – their expanded non-work time, and whether they will regard themselves well for having used it in this manner. One possibility is that all – men and women alike – will now find themselves in the no-man's-land of the housewife who, even when comfortably supported, may still have the deepest doubts about her worth, since she lacks clear-cut validations of her utility. In short, the development of automation may simply mean that the prospect before us is one of the blanketing spread of a 'housewife culture', in which we live surrounded by still more objects that we own but do not possess, use but do not know. This prospect is not a chilling chamber of horrors; it is merely depressing. It envisages a society of piddlers, of men searching out projects to keep them busy, but lacking in the powerful gratifications that women may still find in giving birth to and raising children or lacking, for that matter, in the time-consuming exigencies of housework that can distract attention from self-doubts. In this prospect, then, the leisured society would be one in which men—like suburban middle-class housewives today – seek out good causes or new projects that they may convince themselves that what they are doing is of some use to the world. It envisages a society in which such efforts would be warmly regarded by the state – so long as they did not lead to disturbing alternatives – and with the prideful pleasure of the middle-class husband beaming upon his wife's latest showcase project or charitable cause and seeing in it evidence of the decency that has made him love her and which, he also knows, keeps her happy at home.

But perhaps the culture of the future leisured society will be different. Perhaps it will be more like the lives led by the aged and retired around us now, who often enough conform to stereotype and live out their lives listlessly. In short, it may be a culture in which everyone will be born with grey hair. It may be objected that this may be true only for those who have been first geared to a utilitarian society, and that those who are born to the new leisured society, having no expectations of days of sustained involvements or personal achievement, would not be frustrated. Perhaps, then, a better model of the future than the housewife or the aged would be the lives and cultures created and lived by those who were born rich. Yet, if one is to judge from present indications of contentment with their lives, such a prospect is far from reassuring. The prospects of extended leisure through technological triumph, then, do not seem to lead irresistibly to the conclusion that the new leisure will produce a contentment superior to the work we now know.

Since the end of the Second World War we have, I believe, seen the beginnings of a new resistance on an international scale against a society organized around utilitarian values – a resistance, in short, against industrial, not merely capitalist, societies. The emergence of new, deviant social types – the cool cats, the beats, the swingers, the hippies or the drop-outs – is among the various symptoms of resistance to utilitarian values. The emergence of 'hippie' culture – if I may summarize the various forms with this single term – differs profoundly from previous protest movements and 'causes', however politically radical, in that it rejects the central values to which all variants of industrial society are committed. Not only does it reject the commercial form of industrialization, holding money or money-making and status-striving in disdain, but – and I think more fundamentally – it also rejects achievement-striving, routine economic roles whether high or low, expressive discipline or impulse repression, and all the characterological requisites of a society organized around the optimization of utility. Hippie culture rejects the standard of a conforming usefulness, and counterposes to it the value that each must 'do his own thing'.

In short, many – particularly among the young – are now orienting themselves increasingly to expressive rather than utilitarian standards, achieved through the aid of drugs and sex, and sometimes expressed in new communitarian social forms. To many among them, this is just a last fling before they become the conforming cadres of a utilitarian culture. To some, this is a compensation for their already costly experience of participating in that culture. But to others, however, it is a full-time commitment often coloured by genuine religious overtones. Despite the blatant vulgarities of some in this resistance movement against utilitarianism, their preference for atrocious art nouveau styles, their youthfully obnoxious self-certainty, and, not infrequently, their defiance of the olfactory senses, this is, I believe, a very serious movement indeed.

To assert that it is a new species of a long familiar romanticism is, I think, essentially true; but to imply that it is 'merely' such is to miss the point about both 'classical' romanticism and its modern offspring. Classical or nineteenth-century romanticism was, from the word go, a revolt against utilitarian culture. What, after all, was the 'Philistine' whom the romanticists held in contempt except a species of utilitarian? Recognizing the earlier romantic antecedents of the contemporary resistance movement should not, however, blind us to the importance of either version as a reaction against utilitarianism; if nothing else, the long history of romanticism should testify to the fact that it has not concerned itself with a transient or peripheral problem of the culture. Recognizing this continuity, moreover, should also not blind us to the differences between earlier and contemporary versions of romanticism. When Southey remarked that '... the principle of our social system ... is awfully opposed to the spirit of Christianity', he was quite typical of earlier romanticists in his employment of Christian values as a standpoint for social criticism; but our modern versions of romanticism do not at all commonly adopt Christianity as a standard, however strongly religious their impulses may be. Sometimes this is because they reject the ascetic strain in Christianity and sometimes it is because, living in the God-is-Dead epoch, they simply never took Christianity seriously in the first place. Moreover, modern hippie romanticism, unlike the earlier version, emerges in an economy of affluence, and at a stage when the industrial economy has reached high maturation. In other words, early romanticism rejected what were then the merely promised fruits of industrial society; contemporary hippie romanticism rejects the actually achieved fruits of industrialism. Hippie culture therefore represents the rejection of success, or at least of a system that has succeeded by its own standards, and that being so, it signifies that the system has reached a new and deeper level of crisis. For if a system cannot win loyalties when it accomplishes what it sets out to do, when can it?

Western socialists today live a divided existence: they are divided between their solidarity with the people of imperialistically dominated areas, on the one hand, and their daily involvement in the most technologically advanced societies, on the other; between their identification with the life and death struggles of the distant guerilla *foco* and everyday parliamentary routines and trade-union politics. Theirs is a schismed, guilt-edged existence, in which their solidarity with the battles of the world's exploited may come unwittingly to serve as a vicarious militancy, compensatory for their sense of stalemate or impotence in their own societies.

The times thus often seem singularly ill-suited for a search for greater intellectual clarity about the nature of work, about advanced industrial societies, about the character of the socialist alternative, or, for that matter, about the deepest questions of socialist theory. It is not that the character of an industrial socialism is a question that can be tabled because socialists already know its nature, but, rather, that the struggle for power in the developing world, as well as the mobilization of support for the struggle, constantly threatens to absorb all energies and creative intelligence.

I therefore agree with Debray when he frankly acknowledges:

> It is easy to concede that inequalities of world development, especially demographic growth, suppose uneven forms and rhythms of revolutionary action. But – why not state it clearly? – it is equally evident that the different sectors of world revolutionary activity may enter into secondary contradiction with each other, to the extent that the questions between them are not acknowledged.*

And I would add that this is an optimistic appraisal, supposing as it does that acknowledgment of the 'secondary contradiction' will suffice to avoid it.

From Debray's work alone (and it is not alone), it is clear that socialists have been much more intellectually and programmatically ingenious and much less controlled by hidebound formulae when they address themselves to the tactics of winning power, than when they deal with the detailed questions of the socialist reformation of industrial society. These tactical innovations have demonstrated their effectiveness on a world-wide scale. And they have made evident a fundamental lesson about the character of (at least certain) contemporary societies; they have taught us how fragile and precarious many of these societies are, or at least how vulnerable they are to determined struggle.

In the midst of the bitter conflicts raging in the world today, it would be easy to forget that three major revolutions have taken place and that power has changed hands in

* *New Left Review*, September–October 1967, No. 45.

half the world in half a century. This Olympian historical perspective is small comfort to those who are now bleeding to death; yet those who forget them, do so at their peril. Those now leading the struggle against imperialism in the developing sectors have not forgotten them. On the contrary. It is this fundamental and world-wide discovery of the fragility of established societies that is the deepest root of the emerging strategies of revolution today. Revolutionary strategy today rests upon this one great hedgehog truth: the tigers in the world today are neither paper nor magical – they may be hunted successfully.

I suspect that it is not revolutionaries in the developing sectors but, rather, Western socialists who have sometimes lost sight of the implications of the last fifty years. Yet this history should not be read merely as a bland counsel of courage or militancy. It should also be taken as a reminder. The demonstrated fragility of established societies may well remind socialists in advanced industrial countries that there may be more of a possibility of winning power than they have guessed and, also, that there is more of a need to know, clearly and distinctly, what to do with it after it has been won.

Clarity about means and ends are very much interconnected. For the vision of a better future, a concrete conception of a meaningful socialist alternative, can spur men to struggle against even an affluent present. It is not simply the failures of present industrial society that by themselves generate resistance to it, nor is it the gratifications that they provide that by themselves bind men to it. What men count as 'failure' or 'success' – what they will tolerate or reject in the present – depends greatly upon the alternatives that they have. If the alternatives presented are vague, or are seen as only doubtfully and marginally better than the social world they already know, men will surely not devote themselves to the pursuit of these alternatives, let alone sacrifice their lives on their behalf.

For many in the West, socialism has lost its pull as a true alternative. The more that sober attitudes prevail toward the Soviet Union and do not paranoiacally distort its true reality, and the more that it is commonly accepted as a form of socialism, then the more will socialism lose its appeal as a viable alternative to the masses in the West. Socialism comes to be seen as simply one variant of utilitarian industrialism. The growing affluence of the industrially advanced nations does not allow a utilitarian socialism, one that comes increasingly to be regarded simply as a question of the stomach and of material comforts, to be seen as an inspiring alternative. One no longer offers a radical alternative in presenting a nationalized industrialized society as the fundamental lineaments of a decent life. Neither the vague slogan of 'socialization of the means of production' nor that of 'industrial democracy' any longer constitute a devotion-enthusing alternative. Men may vote for it, but they will not die for it.

The guerrillas in the sierra or the rice paddies can be sustained by their hatred of an old order they know only too well. They need only look at the diseased bodies of their children or at the skin colour of the enemy soldiery to know why they are fighting. They need deliverance from the present rather than a vision of a better future. It suffices for them to know that, whatever the character of the future, if they win it will be their own future – that it will be made by them. More than that, it may well be that to focus upon the issues and choices of the industrial future may serve more to disunite the guerrilla column than to inspire it. When the enemy is engaged close up, the moment is not propitious for debates about industrial democracy or the dangers of bureaucratic socialism. The more militant and violent the struggle for power, the more do the issues tend to reduce themselves to survival and victory.

Here, I believe, is one basic aspect of the 'secondary contradiction' of which Debray spoke. For the intellectual requirements – as distinct from the material and moral needs – of those engaged in open warfare are for a manual of arms, the painstakingly detailed discussion of the technics of the guerrilla column. But Western socialists, wherever their hearts may be, live in a very different condition, a very different economy, demography, ecology and culture. The existence of massive Socialist, Communist, and Labour Parties in Europe cannot conceal the fact that they have been steadily losing the intellectual and ideological initiative. In large measure this reflects the fact that they have not yet moved creatively beyond a utilitarian conception of socialism, that they are commonly still wedded either to merely exegetical discussion of Marxism or 'reinterpretations' that fall far short of fundamental appraisal. Western socialists have much to learn from others about the tactics and strategies of winning power; they also have an obligation to develop and deepen our understanding of what this power is for. Without such clarity there is no alternative that will once again stir Europe.

More About Penguins and Pelicans

Penguin Book News, which appears every month, contains details of all the new books issued by Penguins as they are published. From time to time it is supplemented by *Penguins in Print*, which is a complete list of all books published by Penguins which are in print. (There are over three thousand of these.)

A specimen copy of *Penguin Book News* will be sent to you free on request, and you can become a subscriber for the price of the postage – 4s. for a year's issues (including the complete lists). Just write to Dept EP, Penguin Books Ltd, Harmondsworth, Middlesex, enclosing a cheque or postal order, and your name will be added to the mailing list.

Work · Volume 1 is described overleaf.

Note: *Penguin Book News* and *Penguins in Print* are not available in the U.S.A. or Canada

Also edited by Ronald Fraser - the companion to this book

Work – Twenty Personal Accounts

We all find it convenient to place people by the work they do – but we can seldom fully enter into the world of other people's occupations. *Work*, a collection of essays originally published in *New Left Review*, is an imaginative attempt to show what it means in human terms to be doing a particular job, its satisfactions and frustrations, how it shapes lives. Twenty men and women in a wide variety of occupations write with feeling about the personal meaning of their work. They range from nightwatchman to policeman; bus driver to housewife; accountant to journalist; clerk to croupière; signalwoman to programmer; research scientist to man on the dole. From these intensely human vignettes there emerges a clear picture of the workings of our society. The wider implications – beyond that of an individual in an individual situation – are commented on by Raymond Williams in a concluding essay.